Adoption Unfiltered

"Sara Easterly, Kelsey Vander Vliet Ranyard, and Lori Holden model beautifully the complexities of the Both/And of adoption. As someone who has worked in the adoption industry since 1990, I know firsthand the dedication it takes to sit in community with other members of the adoption constellation (in this case an adoptee, a birth/first parent, and an adoptive parent) with the common goal of creating a body of work that is respectful and empathetic, while also critical and innovative. In *Adoption Unfiltered*, the authors show us how it's done!"
—**ASTRID CASTRO**, adoptee and CEO/Founder of Adoption Mosaic

"*Adoption Unfiltered* is a dream come true. As an adoptee and the leader of an organization that values inclusiveness, collaboration, courage, and trust, this book resonated with me deeply. I found myself cheering the authors on as I read. We grow in our understanding through listening to others, hearing them, feeling with them, and honoring their lived experiences. *Adoption Unfiltered* provides a unique opportunity to do just this. The authors structured their work and successfully collaborated to elevate authentic voices, with the adoptee at the center. They expose many of the raw issues, the ones that are hardest for many to acknowledge. The hard truths. They also provide sound suggestions for individual, and institutional, healing. Nuanced and thought-provoking, this book should be required reading for everyone, from adoptees and their families to adoption professionals and policymakers. This book is a true gem that offers a unique perspective on adoption and illuminates the way forward for understanding, healing, and growth." —**BETSIE NORRIS**, adoptee; founder and executive director of Adoption Network Cleveland

"As both scholarly examination and deeply personal narrative, this is a carefully crafted, highly respectful, broadly readable examination of adoption. This is a meeting of minds, hearts, advocacy, and empathy. There's just so much here!"
—**GLENN MOREY**, adoptee and creator of the *Side by Side* project and the *New York Times* Op Doc and Audible Original *Given Away*

"As a person adopted in the 1960s, this is the kind of ground-breaking book I wish my adoptive parents had read. It does not shy away from the harsh realities of what adoption truly means to everyone. The pages are full of honest accounts of the emotional impact to all parties. I identified with it all and read each word with relief that this factual book is now informing our culture. This is the truth of our experience, which so many choose to not want to understand. But understand we must for the sake of all families affected by adoption. I highly recommend this book to anyone considering adoption, or who is associated with adoption in any way. Adoption will continue to take place, but honest books like this will help make sure that this next generation of adoptees do not have to suffer in the way so many of us have and still do." —**ZARA PHILLIPS**, adoptee, singer, songwriter, playwright, and author of *Somebody's Daughter*

"*Adoption Unfiltered* is a powerful book that is based entirely on lived-experience expertise from each triad member, yet centers the adoptee. So much wisdom learned over decades by those who have made mistakes and now know better, covering all the complexities I wish everyone knew—the real truths about adoption. I highly recommend *Adoption Unfiltered* for anyone but especially for the adoptee and their parents, biological and adoptive—and it should be mandatory reading in adoption education and for anyone considering adoption, as it will help prevent the ongoing trauma we adoptees typically experience in most adoptions to date." —**LYNELLE LONG**, adoptee and founding director of InterCountry Adoptee Voices (ICAV)

"*Adoption Unfiltered* is a brilliant blend of diverse perspectives, clinical findings, and lived experience. The authors offer thoughtful, beautifully written insight synthesized through not only three positions in the adoption constellation, but from three distinct generations as well: Gen X adoptee, millennial birth mother, and boomer adoptive parent. Our three united authors deliver both breadth and depth as they weave a diversity of voices and experience in the adoption community through their thoughtful, powerful narratives. At times painful, at times healing, and consistently candid and triumphant, this trio of exceptional and caring authors guide us to a passionate mandate for not only change in the way of adoption reform, but a practical road map to get there. *Adoption Unfiltered* is what happens when people really speak up and listen to each other in community and invites us to embrace its lessons of enlightenment and the possibility of personal and systemic change. This authentic, dynamic, and unique work is an important contribution to the adoption canon." —**SUZANNE BACHNER**, adoptee; author and director of the award-winning play T*he Good Adoptee*

"*Adoption Unfiltered* is required reading for anyone who is part of the adoption constellation, including the central core triad. Using voices and perspectives from adoptees, birth parents, and adopting parents, this book reveals the inner thoughts, challenges, and possibilities each have experienced within themselves and the American culture, providing a map to navigate these complicated and complex roles. Kudos for creating a space for this much-needed conversation."
—**SUSAN DEVAN HARNESS**, adoptee and author of *Bitterroot: A Salish Memoir of Transracial Adoption*

"*Adoption Unfiltered* is a blazing, insightful, expansive, and informative triumph centering the lives of those touched by the complexities of adoption. The trio of authors present a masterwork that blends the perspectives and challenges faced by adoptees, birth parents, and adoptive parents in a way that holds their shared humanity while challenging existing systems in adoption. A must-read."
—**TONY HYNES**, adoptee, author of *The Son With Two Moms*, and training specialist at Center for Adoption Support and Education (C.A.S.E.)

"*Adoption Unfiltered* is a well-researched tapestry of adoptee, birth/first family, and adoptive parent voices, experiences, and resources expertly woven into a pathway of hope for future generations. The trio of authors have created a space for compassionate truism while dispelling myths with the hard facts about the complexities of adoption. A compelling read for anyone seeking to understand the multi-faceted world of adoption." —**MARCIE J KEITHLEY**, first mom, co-founder/executive leader of National Association of Adoptees and Parents (NAAP), and author of *The ShoeboxEffect: Transforming Pain Into Fortitude and Purpose*

"The chapter titles alone should pull people into NEEDING to read this book. *Adoption Unfiltered* is a book we must gather around in the adoption community so we can share among the general public. Adoption is still largely misunderstood and the system of adoption in the U.S. is in need of an overhaul. It is clear from the first pages of *Adoption Unfiltered* that the voices within it are raising ALL the issues that should be considered as we move forward in evolving adoption in America and elsewhere." —**REBECCA RICARDO**, LCSW, adoptee, birth parent, and executive director of C2Adopt

"*Adoption Unfiltered* belongs in the hands of all adoptive parents and those considering becoming one, natural parents who have endured adoption's loss, adult adoptees who are on the journey of putting themselves together—and everyone working in the field of adoption. Expect to be surprised." —**LORRAINE DUSKY**, birth parent and author of *Hole in My Heart* and *Birthmark*

"Finally a truth-telling book that validates the lived trauma of adoption and shows a way out of the suffering through truth, courage, grieving, and change. The stories are moving, the analysis is sound, the compassion is comforting, and the call for change is clear. We must not and cannot remain unmoved. *Adoption Unfiltered* is a must-read for all who care, whether personally involved in a story of adoption or not. It is not only adoption unfiltered; it calls us to be adoption wise." —**GORDON NEUFELD, PH.D.**, clinical psychologist, founder of the Neufeld Institute, and bestselling author of *Hold On to Your Kids*

"*Adoption Unfiltered* fills an immense gap in adoption-related course curriculum and resources for individuals immediately impacted by adoption, their allies, and policy makers. Importantly, the authors understand adoptive families as a profound public and private social institution, born out of separation, subject to societal issues of classism, racism, and inequity. Writing across their own divergent standpoints as adoptee, birth parent, and adoptive parent, the authors create a unique space for honing skills in listening and communicating across difference—essential for today's often polarizing family communicative environment. In *Adoption Unfiltered*, the authors illuminate paradoxes of adoption—voicing the constraints and losses of adoption as they interanimate with the generative potential of adoptive identities, family relatedness, and communication." — **ELIZABETH A. SUTER, PH.D.**, adoptive parent, professor of Communication Studies at University of Denver, adoption researcher, and adoption educator

"What a welcome addition to our adoption libraries! *Adoption Unfiltered* provides a clear-eyed look at adoption from those most impacted—adoptees, birth parents, and adoptive parents. I appreciated that they neither overly praise nor condemn the institution of adoption. Rather, they allow space for both the beauty and pain, aiming to make life better for this current generation of adoptees, birth parents, and adoptive parents." —**DAWN DAVENPORT**, adoptive parent and executive director of Creating a Family

"Brilliantly written, *Adoption Unfiltered* may not be an easy read (because of the way it challenges old ideas), but it skillfully and thoroughly probes the societal narrative about adoption, leaving the reader to deeply re-examine their own beliefs. *Adoption Unfiltered* should be mandatory reading for anyone contemplating entry into adoption, as well as for their friends, co-workers, and family members." —**KATIE BIRON**, foster/adoptive parent; creator of the Family Connections Program™ and author of *The Love Tree*

"It's never been more important for all parties of the adoption constellation to come to the table to craft essential reform. Change can't happen, however, until we all have a better understanding of each other's perspectives. *Adoption Unfiltered* has the ability to do just that—break down the walls to start candid conversations. This book amplifies the seldom-heard adoptee voice, expresses the journey of loss for birth parents, and includes the often dominant voice of adoptive parents. All parties agree change has to happen, but not until we pull back the veil and share rarely heard, raw first-hand experiences from those who have lived it." —**REBECCA VAHLE, M.Ed.**, adoptive parent; founder and executive director of Family to Family Support Network

"*Adoption Unfiltered* is not only an excellent resource, it is a needed, invaluable resource for every conversation and consideration of adoption—past, present, and future. As an adoptive parent who has felt the lack of substance and overemphasis on adoptive parent voices and perspectives for far too long, this book deserves to lead and take up wide space. I learned so much from every page and I know that I will go back to it again and again. It is a book of hope for the future." —**TASHA JUN**, adoptive parent and author of *Tell Me the Dream Again: Reflections on Family, Ethnicity, and the Sacred Work of Belonging*

"*Adoption Unfiltered* casts a clear, unflinching eye on the complexities, inequities, and failures of the adoption system, pointing to the need for a more ethical practice that centers the well-being of adoptees while considering all members of the adoption constellation." —**B.K. JACKSON**, editor, *Severance* magazine

Adoption Unfiltered

Revelations from Adoptees, Birth Parents, Adoptive Parents, and Allies

Sara Easterly
Kelsey Vander Vliet Ranyard
Lori Holden

Foreword by Joyce Maguire Pavao, EdD, LCSW, LMFT
Lecturer in Psychiatry at Harvard Medical School

ROWMAN & LITTLEFIELD
Lanham • Boulder • New York • London

Rowman & Littlefield
Bloomsbury Publishing Inc, 1385 Broadway, New York, NY 10018, USA
Bloomsbury Publishing Plc, 50 Bedford Square, London, WC1B 3DP, UK
Bloomsbury Publishing Ireland, 29 Earlsfort Terrace, Dublin 2, D02 AY28, Ireland
www.bloomsbury.com

First published in the United States of America 2024
Paperback edition published 2025

Copyright © 2025 by Sara Easterly, Kelsey Vander Vliet Ranyard, and Lori Holden

All rights reserved. No part of this publication may be: i) reproduced or transmitted in any form, electronic or mechanical, including photocopying, recording or by means of any information storage or retrieval system without prior permission in writing from the publishers; or ii) used or reproduced in any way for the training, development or operation of artificial intelligence (AI) technologies, including generative AI technologies. The rights holders expressly reserve this publication from the text and data mining exception as per Article 4(3) of the Digital Single Market Directive (EU) 2019/790.

British Library Cataloguing in Publication Information available

Library of Congress Cataloging-in-Publication Data available

978-1-5381-7469-2 (cloth)
979-8-2163-6815-1 (paperback)
978-1-5381-7470-8 (electronic)

For product safety related questions contact productsafety@bloomsbury.com.

∞™ The paper used in this publication meets the minimum requirements of American National Standard for Information Sciences—Permanence of Paper for Printed Library Materials, ANSI/NISO Z39.48-1992.

Authors' Note

THE AUTHORS ARE NOT TRAINED PSYCHOLOGISTS AND THIS BOOK is not intended to serve as therapeutic advice or to treat or diagnose any condition or illness. Some of the adoption-related content encountered in this book could be upsetting. If you are new to looking up-close at adoption, you may wish to first, or concurrently, consider working with an adoption-fluent therapist and/or seeking an adoption support group. Hosting or attending a book club? Find our book club kit at AdoptionUnfiltered.com.

To Adoptee Voices writers. Your stories matter.
—*Sara*

To my children in heart and home: near or far, I love you dearly. To my husband, Louis: thank you for always being a safe and loving place to land.
—*Kelsey*

For my roots, branches, and leaves: Fred, Dottie, Roger, Sheri, Tami, Tom, Gino, Tessa, Reed, Jake, Ben, Ross, Dominic (2005-2022), and Eleana. You ground me, help me fly, and keep me the appropriate degree of unfiltered.
—*Lori*

Contents

Foreword by Joyce Maguire Pavao, EdD, LCSW, LMFT . . . xv
Introduction 1

Part I: Adoptees Unfiltered 17
Chapter 1 Meet the Adoptee Contributors 25

Emotional Responses to Separation:
Chapter 2 Adoptees' Heartache and Pain 35
Chapter 3 In Pursuit of Love . . . Or, Pushing It Away . . . 43
Chapter 4 Living Anxious and Alarmed 54
Chapter 5 Full of Frustration, Light on Feeling 66

Systemic Problems in Adoption:
Chapter 6 The Tentacles of Classism and Racism
in Adoption 77
Chapter 7 Religion's Pain Points for Adoptees 90

Part II: Birth Parents Unfiltered 103
Chapter 8 Scarcity: Unbiased Information and
Post-Placement Support 106
Chapter 9 Making the "Right" Choice: Religion's Role
in Relinquishment 115
Chapter 10 Emotional Health: The Residue of
Trauma and Grief 120
Chapter 11 Power Dynamics: Race, Class, and
the Hierarchy of Adoption 130

Chapter 12 Birth Parent Challenges in Open Adoption. . 137
Chapter 13 Downstream Effects of Our Decision 146

Part III: Adoptive Parents Unfiltered 155
Chapter 14 Getting to True Openness in Adoption 157
Chapter 15 Unacknowledged Grief 165
Chapter 16 Insecurity 172
Chapter 17 Parenting Through the Complexities
of Adoption 181
Chapter 18 When Religion Hurts: Reexamining
Religious Adoption Narratives 195
Chapter 19 NOT Adopting Amid the Cultural
Backdrop of Pronatalism 203
Chapter 20 Adoptive Parents and the Dance
of Attachment 211

Part IV: Healing and Hope 219
Chapter 21 Supporting Adoptee Maturation:
Advice for Parents and Other Caregivers 221
Chapter 22 Journeying Home: Words of
Encouragement for Adult Adoptees. 239
Chapter 23 What Now? How Adoption Must Evolve. . . 249

Acknowledgments 259
Resources. 263
Notes 267
Bibliography 287
Index 299
About the Authors 311

Foreword

Dr. Joyce Maguire Pavao

WHEN FIRST APPROACHED ABOUT WRITING THE FOREWORD TO *Adoption Unfiltered*, I was interested in just how "unfiltered" adoption was going to be. I recalled the summer-intensive adoption conferences I did in Cape Cod for thirty years, called "Adoption on the Edge," where we would break up into like-groups. It was freeing to be able to speak from the heart and not to "edit" or "filter" how one felt as an adoptee or a birth/first parent or an adoptive parent. This book has taken on that same perspective. We have the chance to listen in on the inner conversations of each group, as they make sense of this complex world of adoption.

I've been living in the world of adoption for seventy-six years and working in adoption for fifty years. Over the decades, I've seen and heard a lot. I made Adoption my political and professional work as well as my personal life story. I started various clinics such as PACT (Pre/Post Adoption Consulting and Training), Adoption Resource Center, and the Center for Family Connections—mental health and training centers that were the only ones in the country at the time that provided mental-health services without being connected to placement agencies. To me, that was very important. It seems to be a conflict of interest to "do" adoptions while providing services and guidance to those involved. I also worked with Dr. Gary Mallon to create a post-graduate course at Hunter Graduate School of Social Work that would give therapists and professionals a much-needed overview and competency in adoption—something that did not really exist. I was also proud and pleased to be a Lecturer in Psychiatry at Harvard Medical School after my graduate professors at Harvard had constantly told me that there was "no psychology of adoption"—something that having lived as an adoptee, I knew was not true.

While I've led change and witnessed change, we need more. Our model for adoption and foster care is still wrong. It is based on the belief that we can possess human beings and that they are better off in adoption. It is a business model, even though adoptees should not be a business. It suggests that agencies know what families and children need and "deserve"—even if they (the agencies and their staff) have little or no experience in this world of adoption.

I have always stated that if you are an adoptive parent, a birth parent, or even an adoptee—yours is a "case study of one" and you must learn about the myriad of situations that exist in the world of adoption. In Family Systems Therapy, we talk about multiple realities. For example, there may be four family members who experienced one trauma together, but each of them has their own view and their own story about what happened. Even though their interpretations differ, each of them is right. This is what Sara, Kelsey, and Lori offer in *Adoption Unfiltered*, through the various perspectives and viewpoints of so many people in the adoption constellation.

As the authors have lain out, adoption must be reimagined, and the reimagining must rise out of lived-experience perspectives. It is most important that we honor the view of the adopted people. It is also necessary to hear what the birth/first parents, adoptive and foster parents, and professionals are doing, thinking, and creating in the midst of adoption. Honoring each other's truths leads to mutual understanding—the precursor to reimagining adoption and the starting point for change, on individual and systemic levels. This is what *Adoption Unfiltered* calls us toward and what the authors have modeled through their collaboration of writing this book.

I hope this book will be a text and trade book. I recommend it for graduate schools, professionals, and educators, as well as family members. *Adoption Unfiltered* should give us all an unfiltered view of the good, the bad, and the ugly of current adoption and how we should commit to understand the people who are in the middle of it, first and foremost, in order to know how to effect change.

Read this book and give it to someone. Pass this knowledge on!

Joyce Maguire Pavao, EdD, LCSW, LMFT
Adoptee and Lecturer in Psychiatry at Harvard Medical School

Introduction

WELCOME TO *ADOPTION UNFILTERED: REVELATIONS FROM ADOPtees, Birth Parents, Adoptive Parents, and Allies.* This book is for anyone immediately impacted by adoption as well as the people who stand by them, support them, and are loved by them. We invite you to join the three of us—and many others—as we examine the nuances and lived experiences of adoption from insiders' perspectives with a primary goal of better supporting adoptees and their families. Our desire is to lead the way toward stronger and more authentic relationships, as well as inspire better practices and policies that truly have adoptees' best interests in mind.

As you may have already surmised, we get pretty candid in this book. We don't shy away from hard conversations, challenging topics, heated emotions, or complex politics. We look them square in the eye and bring them out into the open. In so doing, our aim is to lift the secrecy and shame that can so often be tied up in adoption, much to the detriment of adoptees' emotional and physical health, along with birth parents' and adoptive parents' well-being.

As you'll notice, we make space for both the good and the hard in adoption—and we hope you will too. Without pathologizing, we talk openly about many of the common struggles adoptees can live with due to the deep and lasting pain of separation trauma. Without sugarcoating, we share about birth parents' difficult experiences and deepest heartaches. Without blame or shame, we discuss hard-won lessons adoptive parents have come by through their own pain, unawareness, or mistakes.

This Book is for You!

Well, hopefully it is. This is neither a book to praise adoption nor is it a book to skewer it; though you might, at times, think it is one or the other. If you are someone who needs adoption to be all one thing, this book may *not* be for you. If you are someone who is curious about and open to the complexities of adoption, who can enter into the messy space between "Adoption is love! Adoption is beautiful!" and "Adoption is evil and should be abolished!"—you will find much to ponder in these pages.

In the past, the "adoption triad" was a term coined for those most directly impacted by adoption: the adoptee, the birth parent, and the adoptive parent. While the three of us are members of the adoption triad, we have written this book for the "adoption constellation," a term which has become more widely accepted because it makes room for all who are affected by adoption and who influence its policies and practices. According to the National Council for Adoption's 2017 report, *Adoption: By the Numbers*, "Some experts estimate that 100 million Americans have either been personally touched by adoption within their families or know someone who is or has adopted."[1]

Our sense is that this number is even greater. Adoption is a journey that affects adoptees, and thus those around them, for life—and for generations. As illustrated in Figure 1: Adoption Constellation, there are many people impacted by adoption. While this image couldn't possibly capture everyone, we hope it will give you a sense of the breadth and complexity of the constellation.

Adoption's reach is extensive, affecting all who are close to us at different points in our lives. Adoptees encounter relationships and circumstances that expand the constellation more and more as they grow. In the beginning, a number of these people may be behind the scenes, influencing and orchestrating the fate

INTRODUCTION

ADOPTION CONSTELLATION

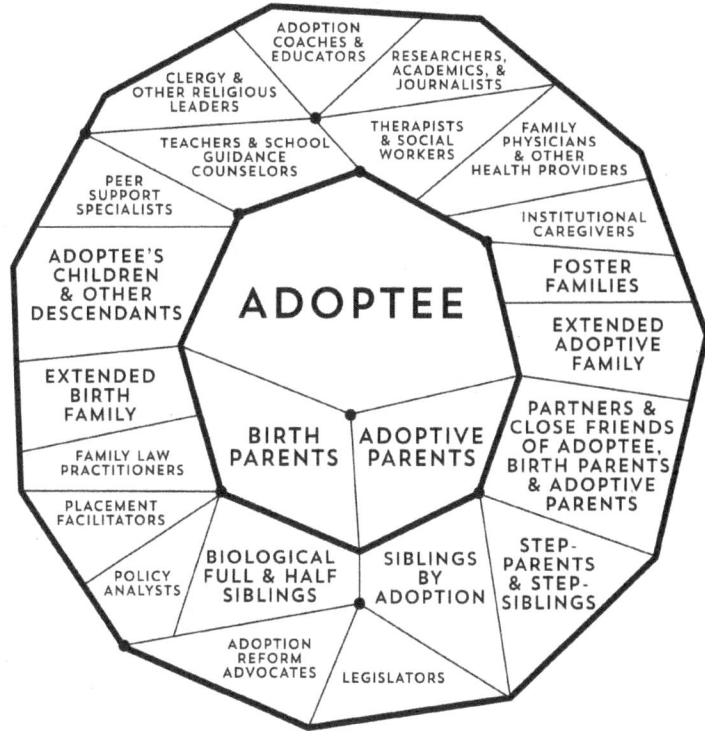

Figure 1

of adoptees' lives before they're old enough to verbalize any emotions or say over the matter. Others will widen the constellation, as adoptees age and attend school, form relationships outside their birth and adoptive families, raise their own families or find chosen ones, and seek support from helping professionals, healthcare professionals, or peer support groups. Birth parents may go on to partner with someone new, who they will rely upon for emotional support, or raise children later in life who will be related to the child they placed for adoption. Adoptive parents may rely on family members, friends, and a host of healthcare and educational providers on the path to adoption and as key supports in their village of attachment. This book is for each and every one of you—and then some. If you know an adoptee, birth parent, or adoptive parent, we hope you'll read this book to better and more fully understand their experience.

Adoption Unfiltered is not only for people looking for ways to better interact with those in their own adoption constellations but also for anyone who wants to effect change on a larger scale, whether that's through helping to educate others about what adoption is really like for its insiders, or supporting a reforming of adoption laws, policies, and practices in ways that better serve adoptees. Not every reader will want to flex an activist muscle, but some will. While this is not a book outlining needed reforms or policies, our hope is that the insights offered will guide you in seeing what's needed and inspire you to support the many advocacy groups out there doing some incredible work in this regard. (We point you to several of them in the Resources section.)

Goals

Adoption Unfiltered is arranged in four main sections. Flipping the typical script, in which adoptive parents take the lion's share of the narrative, this book leads with adoptee stories. Next is a section with stories of challenges and perspectives of birth parents—so often marginalized and silent. The third section offers narratives from adoptive parents who are working through their unique challenges. The final section offers ideas for how to move forward in our homes and in society.

We hope you'll find reading the stories and perspectives in this book to be validating and normalizing. Listening to honest conversations or heavy emotional subjects may also be challenging at times, but we can't address problems without knowing what we're dealing with. As Dr. Gabor Maté says, "In order to heal, it is essential to gather the strength to think negatively. Negative thinking is not a doleful, pessimistic view that masquerades as 'realism.' Rather, it is a willingness to consider what is not working."[2]

Introduction

Yet our aim is not just to lay out problems. We also hope you'll discover ways to move toward healing and wholeness. While it's impossible to provide you with scripts and definitive answers—given that each adoptee and adoption situation is unique—our desire is to support a perspective shift that helps get you through the inevitable challenges that come with adoption. It may take some time to integrate it all. You may need to go through this book in small doses, or flip through it, depending on what's most alive for you right now.

About Us

Sara Easterly is an adoptee, Kelsey Vander Vliet Ranyard is a birth parent, and Lori Holden is an adoptive parent. Collectively, we bring seventy-five years of lived experience relating to adoption, and we span the Millenial, Gen X, and Baby Boomer generations. Incidentally, while writing this book, we each celebrated a milestone birthday: Kelsey turning thirty; Sara turning fifty; and Lori turning sixty. The three of us live, work, advocate, and lead in the adoption space in different ways, and together we understand much of the history, challenges, and trends experienced by people living in adoption.

Sara is an award-winning author of books and essays. Her spiritual memoir, *Searching for Mom*, won a 2020 Illumination Book Award gold medal, among many others, and her adoption-focused articles and essays have been widely published. She is founder of Adoptee Voices writing groups where she's had the privilege of supporting other adoptee-writers and hearing over a thousand adoptee stories. She's studied attachment and child development as a trained facilitator with the Neufeld Institute.

Kelsey is a birth mother who is passionate about raising the standards in adoption to better serve children, mothers, and families. Adoption has been a monumental part of her entire life: Kelsey is also the daughter and granddaughter of adoptees. She is the Director of Advocacy and Policy at Ethical Family Building,

INTRODUCTION

supporting public-policy issues related to adoption, and has worked at agencies and law firms in the adoption field. She is also a co-host of the first-ever birth mom podcast, *Twisted Sisterhood*.

Lori is a veteran adoptive parent of two newly minted young adults. She writes at LavenderLuz.com and hosts the podcast *Adoption: The Long View*. She's the author of the acclaimed book, *The Open-Hearted Way to Open Adoption: Helping Your Child Grow Up Whole*—written with her daughter's birth mom—recommended by *People* magazine in 2021 and included on national adoption agency required-reading lists. She has keynoted and presented at adoption conferences around the United States and Canada and was honored as an Angel in Adoption® by the Congressional Coalition on Adoption Institute (CCAI).

REPRESENTING A RANGE IN ADOPTION EXPERIENCES

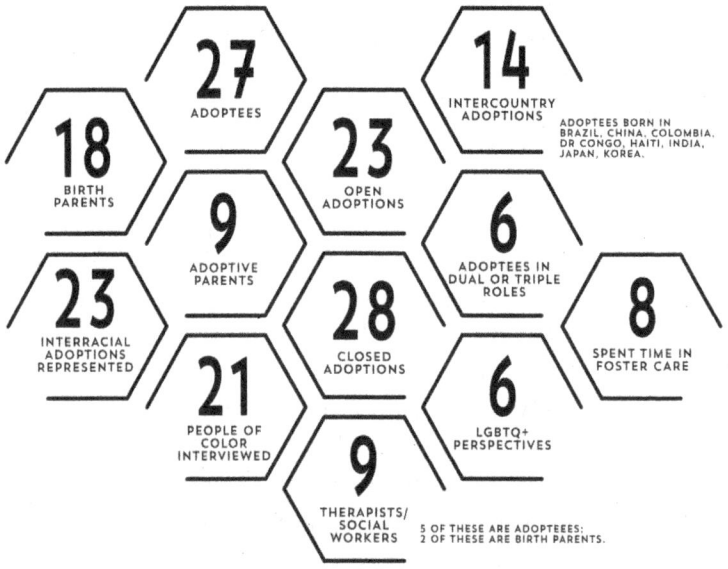

Figure 2

Of course, there are many more perspectives than the three of us can offer. To help tell a broader and more inclusive story of adoption, we interviewed more than four dozen others from within the adoption constellation. Recognizing that we are cisgendered White women, we intentionally sought and included a range of other experiences and perspectives for this book (Figure 2). We have portrayed a mix of open and closed adoptions; intercountry and domestic adoptions; interracial and same-race adoptions. We strived for diversity in race, age, gender, sexual orientation, and more. We also included a balance in views on adoption, because we believe there is value in hearing from voices along the spectrum, and that readers are enriched by even the most difficult-to-hear viewpoints—maybe even especially so.

It's Not Always Rosy

If you've spent time in adoption spaces online, you may have noticed there's a lot of heartache—especially for adoptees. Paul Sunderland, addictions psychotherapist, consultant, and trainer, says, "Relinquishment is an abandonment trauma that's experienced as life-threatening at the beginning of life. It's hard to imagine a bigger trauma than loss-of-mother at the beginning of life."[3] This should make intuitive sense, and yet the cultural narrative of adoption has often overlooked this—adoption often painted, instead, as overly simplistic and rosy.

Interestingly, in providing space for people to vulnerably share their stories, we discovered that adoptees aren't the only ones in the adoption constellation who are hurting. Birth parents regularly shut down after being shut out by adoptive parents or by not having the support they so desperately need after relinquishment. Adoptive parents often struggle with unique parenting challenges and hidden insecurity, feeling the need to hide the fact that they are not the Super Parents they led the agency to believe they would be. It's time for a reconsideration of the narratives and a recalibration on the ways we support adoptees, birth parents, and adoptive parents.

INTRODUCTION

True change is more likely to happen when we all come together in the spirit of transparency and listening—to learn and do better for future generations of adoptees and their first and adoptive families, but that doesn't mean it's going to be easy. For valid reasons based on a history of great pain, many constellation members are unable to reach across the aisles to work together. Wounding from the past can easily rise to the present, and those who've been silenced or spoken over for so long—typically by adoptive parents—may be understandably hesitant or unable to hear from people in groups that have traditionally held dominant and misinformed perspectives.

Even though it can be hard, we believe in the power of collaboration. In order to write this book, we had to work together. We had to walk the walk, not just talk the talk. Have we agreed on everything? No. Have we had interesting discussions on our points of disagreement? Yes. Have these new insights made it into this book? Yes!

To write together, we had to be vulnerable. We had to create a safe place to get things wrong in order to land on new insights, to eventually get things right. With a spirit of partnership, we came together as our whole selves, bringing humility, ferocity, and everything in between. Paramount was a willingness to move past our blind spots and flaws toward a better understanding of each other and ourselves; an effective model for adulting in adoption!

THE FOG

Sometimes we, and many of our contributors, refer to the fog. "Coming out of the fog" is a phrase often used to describe becoming more aware of adoption's effects on one's life. While we may start with a noncritical eye, a thorough understanding of adoption requires us to also develop a critical eye. The metaphor of the fog has been used to primarily describe an adoptee experience, though it is not unique to adoptees. Birth parents and adoptive parents may also be prompted to engage in critical examination of adoption. It happens anytime a person transitions from the simplicity of seeing a thing in black and white, good and bad, awesome and awful into the complexity of understanding a thing in gradients.

To come out of the fog is not a destination—it's a lifelong journey. Adoptees and parents will have new realizations all the time as we age, accrue new experiences, and mature. "Coming out of the fog" is a term that can be weaponized and used in a condescending way. Nobody can tell another person whether they are in or out of the fog. It's too personal. And obviously, we discourage any sentiment that discounts or demeans a person's own journey, narrative, and story unfolding at its own pace.

Ethical Storytelling

Astrid Castro, Founder and CEO of Adoption Mosaic, makes ethical storytelling a foundational piece of her *We the Experts* series, and we have modeled her policy in the way we include the stories of our contributors. Because adoptees don't often have opportunities to unload their uncensored stories, when finally given a chance to share, they sometimes overshare. Or, if they are worried about their parents' reactions, with or without awareness, their responses may be tainted. While the point of the book is to remove the filters, we recognize that filters are always in place to some degree—and may need to be. To honor our contributors, we were careful to select only those who have been reflecting on adoption for some time. While there are layers to "coming out of the fog" or coming to consciousness, and it's an ongoing, perhaps endless journey, we tried to ensure that truths told in the pages of this book won't eventually hurt those involved. In addition, we offered our contributors opportunities for review and approval.

How to Read *Adoption Unfiltered*

You may find some of the stories told here easy to read, especially the ones that fit your existing view of adoption. We caution that

INTRODUCTION

you will also find some of the stories here difficult, even painful to read. They may bring on feelings of disbelief, anger, guilt, or sorrow, and you may find yourself triggered. Here is a handy chart for what TO do and what NOT to do if and when this happens.

When triggered, DON'T:	When triggered, DO:
Throw the book at a person or in the garbage.	Breathe. Walk away. Get curious about why you got triggered. Come back to book when ready.

Growth happens at the boundary between comfort and discomfort. Our book would be pointless if zero pages made you squirm and reconsider what you "know" about adoption and those involved. To give more specific instructions for the four primary participants in adoption, we have the following custom advice:

For adoptive parents, from Lori:

Sore spots are sore when there is something under the surface to irritate them. What could be going on under your surface when you find a viewpoint that bothers you? What would it take to neutralize that emotional charge within yourself?

For me, after the initial stab and much introspection, I usually end up considering these distressing moments as gifts (sometimes painful ones) that help me grow and do better as an adoptive mom. Do I need to agree with every viewpoint? Nope. But considering a foreign-to-me viewpoint, and diving into why this is true for the teller is valuable even if, in trying the story on for myself, I find it doesn't fit me.

If I feel anger, I try to figure out why. If I feel sadness, I offer compassion. If I feel guilt, I give myself grace for doing the best I could at the time and vow to continually grow and do better. I've found that the way I react to my adoption triggers corresponds to the way I relate as an adoptive parent to my daughter and son. I urge adoptive parents to continually increase their capacity to hear adoptees and birth parents, and to aim to respond mindfully rather than react mindlessly.

For birth parents, from Kelsey:
It's hard to imagine *that one choice we made* would have this much effect in more lives than just our own. One thing I have struggled with in my post-placement life is the concept of "forever" and my naïveté of what forever truly feels like. Reading the accounts of adult adoptees who have lived through challenges that have been a result of our one choice can be difficult. We may carry guilt, sadness, or shut down to hearing more. Please keep going. While we are not to blame for every event that happened after we placed our children for adoption, we do carry responsibility and it's crucial that we shoulder some of that.

More than anything, I want you to feel belonging and understanding in this book. I want you to understand your children as well as *be* understood. Birth parents should no longer remain a mystery to the other members of the constellation. If you're reading this book at a time when your adoptee is young, don't let fear of the future consume you. Use these words and stories as tools so that one day, if any of this begins to feel familiar to your own adoption, you can reach back to feel less alone, less crazy, and more equipped to handle whatever adoption throws at you.

For adoptees, from Sara:
I wholeheartedly believe in this collaboration, but I'm not here to tell you that you have to listen to the

INTRODUCTION

nonadopted voices in this book. My heart is for adoptees, first and foremost, and I join you in feeling frustrated by the ways that others, especially adoptive parents, have led adoption narratives for so long. We've only just started to get comfortable sharing our versions of these narratives, which don't always tell the same story. Many of us have been silenced, discounted, misunderstood, called ungrateful, forever treated like children, had our records falsified, been made responsible for our parents' feelings, and more. I see your pain and validate it.

Others of us may not want to look at adoption up close. We might have a nagging feeling that adoption could be related to certain troubling dynamics in our lives but "going there" isn't something we feel ready for just yet. I spent forty years of that mindset and respect the defenses in place to protect us. For this reason, I encourage you to take breaks and seek professional support if at any time reading this book feels like too much.

I hope that you're able to find comfort and camaraderie in Part I, finding some words and attachment insights to help make sense of your experiences through hearing about others' and reminded that you're absolutely not alone.

If things are going well for you, and it's where your interest lies, reading birth parents' perspectives in Part II and adoptive parents' honest sharing in Part III may offer you new layers of understanding. I have personally found that being one-step removed from my personal history, and hearing vulnerable stories from people not connected to my own adoption—especially people like Kelsey and Lori who've been listening to adoptees for a while and try hard to sensitively respond to the adoptees in their care—gives me added opportunities to learn and grow and heal. Even if the details are different from mine, I often come away with new ways to understand and grieve my adoptive and birth parents' blind spots or decisions. I gently encourage you to be open to this, too, and suggest that you read with benevolence—but again, at a pace that works for you. Have compassion and grace for yourself. This can be challenging emotional work.

For adoption professionals, from Kelsey:

I am putting on my adoption professional hat to write you this tough love letter, though I will not remove my birth mother hat, simply because I cannot (even if I could, I wouldn't). However, when I speak to you, I also include myself. I am not superior, nor have I worked in this space without making costly mistakes, just like you. I have worked in the adoption field for six years now. I have worked in agencies in the Midwest, East Coast, as well as a children's law firm on the West Coast. Currently, I have the privilege and honor of working on domestic adoption policy issues for a nonprofit in the Los Angeles area. I started working in adoption far too early after the relinquishment of my child. In my six years of professional work, I have learned a lot about how adoption procedures and practices work, and maybe more so, how they do not. If there's one thing I love, it's to criticize adoption practices. But don't worry, I lose sleep just like you do.

As you read this book, acknowledge the great honor of reading the multitude of perspectives and experiences from the people we work with and ultimately impact. Although I want you to also recognize that if we are doing our jobs wholly and thoroughly, none of the information contained in this book should come as a shock. I often hear professionals say "I've heard it all, I've seen it all," but when someone suggests that we do something differently, they act as though they've just heard the most diabolical, broken suggestion to ever have been uttered. We must come to a conclusion that *we are not our best*. We must reach higher in pursuit of the betterment of the people in this book. If no client has told us that they deserved better, I truly believe we just weren't listening. Use this book as the point of no return. We have no more excuses. Read these words, and then let's keep listening and changing. Let's do this better.

IS THIS BOOK FOR THOSE IN OPEN ADOPTIONS OR CLOSED ADOPTIONS?

Yes! As for so many situations in this book, the answer is both. This book is relevant for those involved in closed adoptions and open adoptions and everything in between.

Adoption Unfiltered is for you whether your experience includes contact with birth parents or not. In fact, we've devoted an entire chapter to explaining why the line between closed and open adoption is meaningless in what truly matters, and why contact as the measure of an open adoption, while pervasive, is inadequate. We propose a better and more inclusive way to bridge the dichotomy of open versus closed adoption, which is rapidly going the way of the dinosaur. Rather than from an asteroid, closed adoption is in its death rattle due to the twin technological developments of the Internet and DNA testing. Adoption secrets that could once be kept forever are a thing of the past. Due to these advancements, familial connections previously hidden are manifesting in ways unforeseen. Even if adopted from another country, even if a birth father was listed as unknown, even if birth records were "burned in a fire" or "lost in a flood"[4]— if just one biological relative swabs a cheek and begins building a family tree with an online registry, connections will be made, secrets will be revealed, stories will be told.

Anonymity no longer exists. Any professional who offers anonymity and any person who seeks a completely closed adoption proceeds at significant peril. We must, instead, prepare for openness in adoption and begin paving the way for only truth and transparency, whether that is within our homes or at a policy level.

A Word about Words

Some of the terms used around adoption have no consensus around them. One of those is the use of *expectant parent* and *birth parent* or *first parent*. In keeping with current industry language, we use the term "expectant parent" to describe a pregnant parent prior to giving birth. Once a parent has signed consent forms for placement, they are considered a birth or first parent. We have opted to primarily use "birth parent" for its widespread understanding, though we acknowledge that "birth" is inaccurate for a father and conveys only a sliver of the importance and contributions of biological parents.

Another word choice we looked at is *transracial* versus *interracial*. Though transracial adoption is currently better understood, we agree with adoptee Tony Hynes when he points out, "If we are being literal, *trans* is to transition. As transracial adoptees, we're not trying to transition to any different race within our households."[5] We primarily use the word *interracial*, but you'll see some use of *transracial*, depending on the preferences of those we are quoting.

Lastly, we debated among ourselves about the words *relinquished* versus *placed* for adoption. Many adoptees describe adoption as an experience of being relinquished, but this word can feel loaded for birth parents, especially if they've made difficult adoption decisions with thought and care, or if their "decisions" leading to adoption involved pressure, force, or coercion. We use the two words interchangeably but make space for the complexity of a variety of situations and the limitations of our English language to fully convey all of the emotional experiences around adoption.

INTRODUCTION

LET THE UNFILTERING BEGIN

Through our work interviewing adoptees, birth parents, adoptive parents, and allies, we realize what a privilege it is to have a front row seat to the storytelling from people who trusted us enough to let their guard down. We hope this is not lost on you as you read this book. We are so excited to offer you these real and raw stories of people who have valuable things to say about adoption. We invite you to let your guard down, too. Come as you are, and find the wisdom within.

PART I

ADOPTEES UNFILTERED

Welcome to the first section of *Adoption Unfiltered*, written by me, Sara Easterly, an adoptee.

Right off, I'll share that it's been daunting to write this adoptee-focused section of the book—not from lack of words—but because it is so important to me to properly honor the contributors who helped inform this project as well as support you, the reader—whether you are also an adoptee, or whether you've come to this book because you care about an adoptee. What's more, as I've been writing about some of adoptees' common struggles of adoption, I've had to wrestle with my own residue of separation trauma.

I've battled perfectionism to get the words you're reading now onto the page. The wish for perfection isn't about me, but it's because it matters so much to me to represent adoptees with care, compassion, understanding, and accuracy. Since there are as many different adoption stories as there are adoptees, we are not a monolith. No matter how many adoptees' voices I include in this book, I won't be able to capture or represent every experience of every adoptee and not all adoptees will agree with all that is shared here. That futility has been hard to swallow as has the fact that sharing mine and other adoptees' perspectives in print puts a time-stamp on them, when the reality is that understanding adoption is a continual evolution for each adoptee. As

Part I

we grow through different life stages, we're typically discovering new ways that separation impacts us and healing our wounds a little more every day. At the time you're reading this, I, and other adoptees I've interviewed, likely already have more to add to the dialogue.

In spite of these and my human limitations, I sincerely hope that what I *am* able to offer ultimately serves adoptees well and that this book as a whole centers adoptees' experiences when it comes to understanding adoption, its impact on us, and the dire need for reform.

As you read, please know that I'm operating with a commitment to truth-telling. For most of my life, I've been a people-pleaser, and there's no place where I've wanted to please more than when talking with the nonadopted to downplay the effects that adoption—and the initial separation that preceded it—has had on me. Thankfully, I began to break these patterns through the process of publishing my memoir and speaking out through essays, interviews, and appearances as well as supporting other adoptees to write their truths, too, through the Adoptee Voices writing groups. Putting a happy face on adoption might help avoid hard conversations or worse—dreaded conflict!—but it doesn't ultimately serve anyone. Truth and transparency are of utmost importance if we have a genuine aim to better support adoptees' complete emotional well-being and ultimate maturation process. If I or my fellow adoptees interviewed for this book fail to sugarcoat or mince words when sharing about common struggles we experience, I ask for your grace. Don't let the sometimes-hard truths stop you from reading or discourage you. We adoptees ultimately need you to stick with us, no matter what.

Every writer brings their own biases, histories, and passions to each project. This is true for me, too. I'm thankful for close camaraderie with many trusted writers and adoptees and their review of early drafts of this section to help keep me in check, together with the thoughtful perspectives of my co-authors, Kelsey and Lori.

I'd also like to acknowledge the attachment-based, developmental insight that frames how I see adoption and how it influenced the structure of this part of the book—based on the work of child-developmental psychologist Dr. Gordon Neufeld, who I have had the privilege to study with for the last thirteen years. Dr. Neufeld is considered a foremost authority on child development and is the author of the bestselling book, *Hold On To Your Kids*,[1] co-authored with Dr. Gabor Maté. Dr. Neufeld has developed dozens of courses for parents, educators, therapists, and other caregivers as part of his life's work to help adults provide the conditions for children to flourish. His comprehensive theory of attachment includes six stages in the development of the capacity for relationship, and his model is inspired by early attachment theorists such as John Bowlby, Konrad Lorenz, and Harry Harlow as well as informed by other theories, current brain science, and the physical sciences.[2] Most of what I understand about the science of attachment has been learned through Dr. Neufeld, and at this point I've internalized his model so much that I tend to speak from my own place—from my head as well as from my heart—without precise memory of where this awareness first originated. I do my best to cite specific resources wherever possible and appreciate his time talking with me about this project and offering the psychological expertise and wisdom that helped shape these chapters.

Others who have provided much insight into mine and the adoption community's understanding of adoption include:

- Dr. Joyce Maguire Pavao has worked for fifty years in the fields of adoption, child welfare, family therapy, and more—in addition to being an adoptee herself. She is a lecturer in Psychiatry at Harvard Medical School, and she has consulted to various public and private child-welfare agencies, adoption agencies, schools, and community groups, as well as probate and family court judges, lawyers, and clergy. She has also worked closely with individuals and families affected by adoption, foster care, and other complex blended-family constructions[3] and is the author of *The Family of Adoption.*[4]

- Nancy Newton Verrier is a psychotherapist, adoptive parent, and author of the revolutionary book, *The Primal Wound: Understanding the Adopted Child*,[5] now considered a classic in adoption literature. Additionally, she is the author of *Coming Home to Self: The Adopted Child Grows Up*,[6] and an international lecturer on adoption issues and separation trauma.[7]

Since both of these intellects have been writing, speaking, and working in adoption spaces for so long, much of their work is now accepted as common fact and not always cited. In my studies of adoption, I, too, have absorbed their wisdom and may not even realize when I'm drawing upon their initial thoughts. I thank them for their contributions and insights, which have also played a role in this book.

For adoptees, the impact of adoption reaches far, wide, and deep. In hopes of creating some kind of order to help make sense of the many complexities, I have divided the "Adoptees Unfiltered" section into two key categories:

1. Emotional Responses to Separation (Chapters 2-5)
2. Systemic Problems in Adoption (Chapter 6-7)

EMOTIONAL RESPONSES TO SEPARATION

As mammals, attachment is our preeminent need and key to our survival. Thus, facing separation—experienced or anticipated—from those to whom we're attached is our greatest human threat. Dr. Neufeld says, "There is no experience that has more impact upon us as humans than that of facing separation."[8] What's interesting about this is the word "facing"—even merely *thinking* about being separated from the people we're closest to is an emotional threat that we perceive as more substantial to our survival than anything else.

The inherent nature and structure of adoption is founded upon the ultimate separation: between an infant or child and our first attachments to our biological mothers. Nancy Verrier says, "No matter how much the mother wanted to keep her baby and no matter what the altruistic or intellectual reasons she had for relinquishing him or her, the child experiences the separation as abandonment."[9] The separation that adoptees experience continues from that point forward and for the rest of our lives, regardless of whether we're in open or closed adoptions, or whether we ended up with "good" adoptive parents, or not. While the initial physical separation has passed, additional separation remains, keeping us from feeling close to our first attachments in the ways we long for and are wired for—and reminding us of a continual perceived or real threat of losing anyone else we attach to, making attaching feel inherently risky.

Therefore, it goes without saying that separation causes a significant amount of stress and trauma for adoptees manifesting in what Dr. Neufeld refers to as the three primal emotions of unbearable separation: pursuit/defensive detachment, alarm, and frustration—illustrated in Figure 3.

Figure 3

Part I

These are common emotions anyone can experience in varying degrees, since we are all built for attachment. But in Chapters 2-5, we'll look at how separation commonly impacts adoptees on an emotional level. Drawing on my studies of attachment and the privilege I've had to study with Dr. Neufeld, I'll explain each of these instincts further and share examples from my interviews with adoptees that help illustrate them.

SYSTEMIC PROBLEMS IN ADOPTION

My adoption took place at the tail end of what's known as the Baby Scoop Era—a term coined by Karen Wilson-Buterbaugh[10] to describe the decades between World War II and Roe v Wade when "hundreds of thousands of young, single American women were forced to give up their newborn children," as described by Ann Fessler in *The Girls Who Went Away*.[11]

My birth mother was among these women. After delivering me in the hospital, she'd decided to parent me. Her mother supported this decision and left to procure the necessary supplies to bring a newborn home. But plans were already in place. My birth father and his parents had pushed for adoption. Prospective parents had rushed through three states to pick up their baby girl, confused by a sudden, unexpected delay. The obstetrician, who had both a reputation as the "go-to guy for unwed, young mothers" and a professional connection to my adoptive family, needed the adoption to proceed. My young mother, left alone in her most vulnerable moment, didn't stand a chance when it came to advocating for herself and her first child, especially in a time when a patriarchal and religious culture shamed women for their sexuality, and most had already judged my birth mother as "bad," undeserving of the reward of her own child.

"I don't care about you," the O.B. told her. "We're done taking care of you. But that baby isn't going anywhere until you come to your senses."

With that, my destiny was sealed. My first mother—judged as unfit, immoral, and immaterial—receded into silence ... for nearly forty years. The cost? Both mine and my birth mother's long-term emotional well-being as well as the health of my adoptive family. The shame imposed on my birth mom clouded my parents' abilities to honor my roots, leaving us unable to have authentic conversations about adoption that could have led to closer, more fulfilling relationships.

Unfortunately, the Baby Scoop wasn't the first—nor the last—era of coercion in adoption. Questionable adoption practices are being exposed more and more, as adoptees and birth parents speak out, and as historians, scholars, and journalists dig deeper—uncovering problematic conduct and unethical practices in domestic and intercountry adoptions and sometimes outright human rights violations and child trafficking.

Adoption has been riddled with systemic issues for well over a century and many serious problems persist. Though not every adoption crosses ethical lines and there will always be a need for adoption, these systemic issues should concern us all whether we're connected to adoption or not.

In the aftermath of a hurricane, response crews must fly in to see the damage up close. It's the only way to know how to repair, rebuild, or start afresh with completely new construction. Similarly, we must study the wounds of adoption in order to address them. For this reason, Chapters 6-7 focus on some of the harm done through adoption from classism, racism, and religion.

I look forward to embarking on this journey together. Before we begin, I'll introduce you to the adoptee contributors who will be joining me as we share adoptees' unfiltered perspectives.

CHAPTER 1

Meet the Adoptee Contributors

ADOPTEES ARE THE CENTRAL FIGURES IN ADOPTION. YET IT IS rare that we lead conversations on adoption. Historically, adoptive parents and representatives from the adoption industry have been the dominant voices when it comes to adoption and adoptive parenting advice. Yet this has not served us because it misses the experience and wisdom that comes from decades of living adoption.

Just as with all parenting endeavors, we've learned a lot over the generations—about attachment, about brain science, about trauma—better equipping us to meet adoptees' developmental needs. This is helped by a more open society, where shame and secrecy around mental health is lifting. Adoptees, who in the past may have been silenced or afraid to speak their truths, are more open about their emotional and psychological struggles, in hopes of supporting future generations of adoptees and to normalize their experiences for other adoptees who may be living in isolation.

With a grateful heart for being connected to hundreds of such adoptees, I'm excited to introduce you to twenty-three of them whose perspectives have shaped this first section of the book. They range in age from their twenties to their sixties and collectively offer hundreds of years of lived experience with adoption—not to mention, a significant amount of emotional work and thought around adoption and how it has impacted them. While each

Chapter 1

adoptee is unique with individual responses to adoption, these voices express important commonalities and have much to teach.

Most of the adoptees I interviewed felt comfortable revealing their identities, and many of these adoptees work in various areas of education and adoptee support. I could fill volumes to include the full breadth and depth of their stories, and my hope is that by including information about their books and platforms, you'll seek out their work and hear more about what they have to say.

I've also included high-level details about their adoptions—whether open or closed, interracial or same-race, domestic or intercountry, private or through agencies, adoptions on the other side of foster care, and adoptions with heterosexual, same-sex, or single parents. Please allow these details to help you see the diversity and uniqueness of each adoptee—but don't discount examples that are not reflective of your specific experiences. We have much to learn from multiple voices and situations. Through my work, listening to adoptee stories through the Adoptee Voices writing groups that I lead, one of the things I've most loved is recognizing the similarities and broader dynamics that apply, regardless of the specifics of our stories.

If you notice gaps and inconsistencies as you read, please keep in mind that many adoptees have missing or falsified records and no access to birth family. Sometimes even basic information like birthdays and age at adoption isn't accessible, adding to the losses these adoptees experience.

Also note that I introduce each of these adoptees by the names they go by now, recognizing that names can be complex for adoptees—many of us were called by other names before our adoptions took place, and some adoptees have embraced new names as a way of reclaiming a part of their identity lost through adoption.

Lastly, I'd like to make clear that every adoptee is on a journey of some kind, complete with a full back story and character arc that's much more complex than a bio or quotes could possibly cover.

Meet the Adoptee Contributors

Amanda Medina is an interracial, intercountry adoptee born in Colombia sometime in 1984 and raised in Sweden. She is the host of the blog and podcast, *This Adoptee Life*, and creator of "The Adoptee Mantra"—a poster of affirmations for adoptees. Amanda's work is about vulnerability and community. She's built her platform by boldly sharing her journey toward healing as her understanding of adoption has unfolded, and she generously makes space for other adoptees' voices to be heard, too.

Astrid Castro's interest in adoption goes back to the age of four, when she and her biological sister were transracially adopted from Colombia. Astrid is the founder and CEO of Adoption Mosaic, an organization that offers adoptee-centered services, panels, and courses for adopted individuals and their families. Through her work, Astrid draws on her experiences as an adoptee, a woman of color, and growing up in a white family and community—as well as her degree in sociology with an emphasis in adoption. She's spent over three decades in the adoption field—working in both private and public sectors—presenting, consulting, and writing many articles on the subject of adoption and contributing to the book *Parenting As Adoptees*.[1]

Bonita Rockingham is a domestic, interracial adoptee, adopted with her twin sister when she was four years old. She grew up in a rural Mennonite community that upheld colorblind ideology and in a large family where she and her twin were the only adoptees and only Black children. Bonita is a speaker and writer, passionate about discussing the intersections between religion and adoption, and making clear the urgency to cultivate sustainable anti-racist systems and reform policies.

Carmen Hinckley was born in Brazil in the mid-1980s, adopted by a single mother. Though Carmen's was a closed adoption, with her mother's help she was able to experience reunion which helped heal some of the wounds of adoption. Carmen has been involved with Adoption Mosaic since 2012 and currently works for Holt International as the adult-adoptee community outreach coordinator.

Chapter 1

Cynthia Landesberg is an interracial adoptee born in Busan, South Korea and adopted at five or six months old by Jewish parents. She grew up in the suburbs of Washington, D.C., with an older sister who was domestically adopted. Cynthia is also an adoptive parent to two sons, both adopted from Korea (in addition to parenting her biological daughter). Cynthia blogs at *Adoption Squared* and her writing has been published in many spaces, including an Op-Ed for *The Washington Post*.[2] You will hear from Cynthia again, in Part III, sharing from her perspective as an adoptive parent.

Damon Davis is a domestic, same-race adoptee. He's the author of the adoptee memoir *Who Am I Really?*[3] as well as host and producer of the award-winning podcast of the same name. Since starting the podcast in 2017, Damon has supported countless adoptee listeners around the world process their own adoption stories. The podcast also helps nonadopted people grow in their understanding of adoptees' challenges and triumphs. In addition to parenting a biological son, Damon is an adoptive parent through a kinship adoption.

David Bohl, MA, CASC, MAC is the author of both *Parallel Universes*[4] and *Relinquishment and Addiction*[5] and is an independent addiction consultant. He was relinquished at birth and placed with his adoptive family seven days later. David is in long-term recovery from alcohol and nicotine addiction and now helps others navigate the journey of recovery from substances. He is known for his empathy and understanding around issues such as loss, grief, identity development, and low self-esteem.

Diego Vitelli, LMFT is from Colombia, adopted in 1979 when he was around four years of age. Following his journey of self-discovery, Diego sought a meaningful and rewarding way to support the adoptee community. He is a relationship and family therapist in the state of Washington, centering adoptees and their identity development through their lived experiences. He is also an Adoptees Connect facilitator in Seattle.

Meet the Adoptee Contributors

Donna Turner's story is a complex one of intergenerational trauma. She is a domestic adoptee whose birth mother was an international adoptee. Only as an adult did Donna learn that she had been conceived in a commune and that she lost her birth mother to suicide not long after Donna was born. Donna has experienced anxiety, depression, and suicidal ideation throughout her life and has devoted a lot of energy to healing through educating herself and managing her complex-PTSD.

Holly is an intercountry adoptee from Kanpur, India, adopted through Mother Teresa's Orphanage in New Delhi when she was one year of age. Holly grew up as the only adoptee in a White LDS family in Salt Lake City, Utah, with two older brothers and the memory of a would-be sister who had passed away before Holly joined the family. As an adult, she is herself an adoptive parent to a daughter, also from India.

Julian Washio-Collette is a Baby Scoop Era, domestic adoptee. He was relinquished and adopted into a closed adoption as an infant ... and relinquished and adopted in a second closed adoption at the age of nine. Julian currently resides in a small cabin with his wife, Lisa, behind a monastery in the coastal wilderness of Big Sur, California. He blogs occasionally at *Peregrine Adoptee* and writes about the intersection of adoption, healing, and spirituality.

Kathy Mackechney, LCSW was relinquished at birth and placed in foster care before she was placed with her adoptive family at ten weeks old. Today, she is a therapist who specializes in helping other adoptees and the people close to them. She works with adult adoptees, adopted children and teens, adoptive parents, birth parents, prospective adoptive parents, and the partners of adoptees as well as others who have had similar experiences for other reasons.

Katie Naftzger, LICSW was born in Korea, then internationally and transracially adopted. As a licensed clinical social worker in Massachusetts, Katie sees families, individuals, adults, and parents in her private psychotherapy practice. She offers a number of local and online groups for adoptive parents and adoptees as well

CHAPTER 1

as consults with schools, adoption agencies, and mental health facilities. She is the author of *Parenting in the Eye of the Storm: The Adoptive Parent's Guide to Navigating the Teen Years*.[6]

Kayla Zheng is an interracial, transcultural, intercountry adoptee from China. Born in 1998 under the country's one-child policy, Kayla was separated from her family in infancy and sent to an orphanage, ultimately adopted by White parents and brought to the United States. She grew up with two older brothers, biological to her parents, and eventually a younger sister, also adopted. Her writing has been published by InterCountry Adoptee Voices and she's participated in a number of adoptee panels, focusing on racial violence, cultural genocide, and surviving a White world as a non-White person. Kayla recently returned to her homeland of China to pursue post-graduate studies at the prestigious Peking University.

Lanise Antoine Shelley was born in St. Michelle, Haiti, as Lunise Antoine. Her future adoptive mother met two-year-old Lunise at an orphanage in Port Au Prince and, two years later, adopted Lanise and another young girl (not biologically related), raising them as a single mother in California. Lanise is presently an actress, director, and podcast host of *When They Were Young: Amplifying Voices of Adoptees*.

Lily P. McLaughlin was adopted from Yangzhou, China in the 1990s when she was six months of age. She grew up in racial isolation in a small Ohio town. She struggled academically and socially, never feeling a sense of belonging, even in Chinese adoptee groups she participated in during adolescence. Now an adult, Lily is the author of *Love Letters by LilyPearl*,[7] a story about her return to God, written in the form of personal narrative, poems, and photography.

Mar Meislin was conceived in San Francisco during what was called the "Summer of Love" in 1967. Their birth parents were both nineteen, Catholic, and unmarried. As was common for the era, Mar's maternal grandmother pushed her daughter out of the family and into an unwed-mother's home in order to keep her pregnancy a secret. When Mar arrived, they were adopted through an agency into a small Jewish family who had lost a biological daughter who was seven at the time of her death. As a person in long-term twelve-step recovery, Mar is on a path toward healing and integration of their Jewish and Catholic spiritual life.

Marci Purcell is a domestic adoptee, born in New Jersey to young, unmarried parents who relinquished her at birth. Due to a traumatic delivery, Marci was diagnosed with mild cerebral palsy, creating delays in her placement. She was a ward of the state and lived in foster care until adopted at age three. Marci grew up as one of six to eight kids, five of whom were adoptees, with an additional one to two temporary foster siblings. Supervision ranged from limited to nonexistent, making home life chaotic and unsafe. As an adult, Marci fights for adoptees' rights to access their original birth certificates (OBCs) with Support Texas Adoptee Rights (STAR) and advocates for systemic reform with Adoption Knowledge Affiliates (AKA).

Rich Uhrlaub, MEd was relinquished, adopted, and raised in Denver, Colorado. He has been an effective legislative advocate, support group facilitator, conference speaker and planner, contributing writer, and media spokesperson for over twenty years. He currently serves as president of the Coalition for Truth and Transparency in Adoption (CTTA) and Adoption Search Resource Connection (ASRC).

Sara Easterly is a domestic, same-race adoptee who came to her adoptive family through a private, "grey-market" adoption that took place at the tail end of the Baby Scoop Era in 1972. As the adoptee representative of this book and co-creator of the *Adoption Unfiltered* podcast, I include myself here for an easy reference, and out of recognition, that my experiences, too, will be included in the adoptee perspectives that follow. I am the author of the memoir, *Searching for Mom*,[8] and founder of Adoptee Voices—supporting adoptee storytelling through writing groups, workshops, and publishing opportunities. I'm also a staff member of the Neufeld Institute, supporting its children's literature book club and adoption/foster care courses.

Shelise Gieseke is an intercountry, interracial adoptee from South Korea who was raised on a farm as the only adoptee in her White family with three other children, biological to her parents. According to her paperwork, Shelise spent time in foster care before being brought to Minnesota and adopted at the age of eight months. Today she is Head of Operations for Adoption Mosaic and has over 10 years of experience in the adoption community as an educator, editor, and mentor.

Susan Devan Harness is a member of the Confederated Salish and Kootenai Tribes. She spent the first eighteen months of life with her birth family before being adopted by a White couple. Her story as an interracial American Indian adoptee is detailed in her award-winning memoir, *Bitterroot: A Salish Memoir of Transracial Adoption*.[9] In addition, Susan is a scholar with an anthropological perspective that is critically important—from both an historical perspective around the Indian Adoption Project as well as the Indian Child Welfare Act. Susan has appeared on the TEDxMileHigh stage and regularly speaks about the need for transracial adoption reform.

Tammy Perlmutter grew up in and out of foster care from the ages of four to eighteen, experiencing neglect and abuse in both her birth family and foster families that no child should ever have to bear. She openly writes and shares about her subsequent mental health struggles and faith journey as writer, editor, founder, and curator of *The Mudroom* and co-founder of Deeply Rooted, an annual faith and creativity gathering for women.

Tony Hynes began life with his mother, who suffered from schizophrenia and struggled to care for her son. Throughout his first year, Tony was often in the care of his grandmother or in an orphanage where he stayed from age one to three. Eventually a same-sex couple became his foster parents—and ultimately his adoptive parents in what became a court-ordered open adoption with Tony's grandmother, after an adoption appeal that went all the way to the Supreme Court. Tony is the author of *The Son With Two Moms*[10] and works as a Training Specialist at Center for Adoption Support and Education (C.A.S.E.). Tony completed his Master's thesis in Sociology on the psychology of children within the same-sex headed household and was awarded a full scholarship to begin his PhD studies in Language, Literacy, and Culture at the University of Maryland Baltimore County, where his dissertation-in-progress focuses on social connectedness among interracial adoptees.

Adult Adoptee Perspectives Are Key

Now that you've gotten to know these adoptees, you may be wondering why I didn't interview younger adoptees. Developmentally, it takes a lot of time for adoptees to process and understand the impact of early separation from our first families. When we were younger, any one of us likely would have said what we surmised our adoptive parents wanted to hear in order to keep them close.

Sadly, this is where a lot of adoptive parents glean their information—and then stop pursuing further input. This might feel reassuring to parents in the moment—and through the early years of parenting—but it doesn't ultimately serve anyone when the cost is having an authentic relationship for the long-term. Not to mention, later in life, adoptees may feel betrayed by too-quick acceptances of statements they'd shared before they started thinking more critically about adoption.

Myth-Busting

It may not always be easy to listen to adoptees. When adoptees are speaking adoptee-to-adoptee in a safe space, they speak truth. They aren't worried about hurting their parents' feelings. They don't hold back. If your primary source of information around adoption is to believe certain narratives our culture has been told for decades

Chapter 1

(by the nonadopted), then some of these perspectives may surprise or sadden you.

Critical thinking about adoption does not mean that these adoptees had awful adoptions or terrible parents. Some adoptions were gross failures and have resulted in necessary boundaries or estrangement, as can happen in any family with or without adoption. But many of the adoptees interviewed benefit from loving relationships with their parents—birth parents and/or adoptive parents. Some voices may sound angry, or a statement might land hard but if you can withhold judgment, a fuller picture of adoption may emerge. Similar feelings could one day come from an adoptee you know, whether it seems far-fetched at this time or not. All children, adopted or not, have feelings about their families, and adoptees are no different.

Thank you for reading and spending time with these adoptees' perspectives. It's an honor to know you're listening to what we share with an open heart and curious mind, and it's my sincere hope that our experiences shed light on how to better meet the needs of the adoptees in your life.

Chapter 2

Adoptees' Heartache and Pain

IF YOU ARE READING THIS BOOK, YOU PROBABLY HAVE EITHER A hunch or deep personal knowledge that there's more heartache and pain related to adoption than society leads us to believe. In the popular view, adoption is a win/win for everyone and a "beautiful" story of a child being saved. It's assumed adoptees feel nothing but gratitude. There's cultural dismissiveness, pushback, and sometimes outright anger when adoptees openly share about their pain and mental health struggles. Adoptee-advocates and influencers are often hotly debated when speaking up about the trauma inherent in adoption. In spite of an array of bestselling books on trauma that have been published in recent years, it's rare to find more than a line or two relating specifically to the traumas experienced by adoptees.

And yet, adoption is only made possible by the ultimate separation of attachment—between a child and the parent to whom they were first attached. Child developmental psychologist Dr. Gordon Neufeld explains: "Adoption is one of the earliest and primary disruptions in the continuity of connection which can last throughout life. It doesn't end right after adoption. That facing of separation is developmental and it will be there until the day you die."[1]

David says: "We were given up by our biological parents, and through that action, we have had the most crucial bond broken, and our idea of people and safety has been deeply altered."[2]

Rich agrees: "The impact of relinquishment and adoption is far greater than any metaphorical skinned knee, which hurts, bleeds, scabs over, and leaves a painless scar as a distant reminder of falling from a bicycle or skateboard."[3]

For many of us, our first mothers' stress and cortisol levels affected our brains in utero. Depending on when we were separated from our mothers, we experienced relinquishment and preverbal feelings of hopelessness, isolation, and loss. The deep wounding plays out throughout adoptees' lives. Donna says, "I think a lot of adoptees have this combination of developmental and complex trauma. I've never *not* known anxiety. I've really never *not* known depression."[4]

Donna isn't alone. Says Holly: "I don't think I realized how much adoption has affected me daily, and I didn't understand the emotional burden that had on me growing up. I look back and can now see the anxiety, the depression that I suffered from."[5]

With separation as adoptees' formative and lasting experience in life, how can we ignore or debate the pain in adoption? If we want to support the adoptees in our lives and meet their attachment needs from a developmental perspective, it's important to be aware of the pain points.

What about "Happy" Adoptees?

Parents and society have been known to dismiss adult adoptees' viewpoints about trauma, using "happy adoptees" as their supporting evidence to believe, "Not my adoptee!"

Part of the reason for the disbelief is that when adoptees are young, we often emphatically deny that adoption affects us.

In my case, I was a trauma denier until I became a parent and started considering my birth mother and attachment in new ways. Until then, I was such a good actor I could convince nearly everyone that I was unaffected by adoption. My parents, teachers, and friends bought it—I did, too! Even therapists (none of whom were adoption-fluent) would skirt right over adoption as if irrelevant to struggles I was mucking my way through at various stages of life ... though it turns out that the severing of my first attachment relates to just about everything—those struggles, naturally, as well as my outlook in life, career choices, relationships, parenting, spirituality, and more.

We deny trauma for varying reasons. For one thing, looking up close at the pain of adoption is akin to looking at the sun—it can burn. Some of us have to avoid it at all costs for protection—or so our brains have led us to believe. Some of us also learn to hide the pain from our adoptive families. When our survival depends on our adoptive parents, admitting to the full truth can feel like a risk we aren't willing to take—a risk that could lead to yet another severing of an important attachment. Some of us also feel protective of our parents, worried about hurting their feelings—maybe because we've picked up on insecurities (which Lori writes about in Chapter 16), or we've learned through the very setup of adoption that it's our job to meet our parents' needs (even if we're sometimes misreading the needs).

But just because adoptee pain is often hidden doesn't mean it isn't there. Some of us act out our trauma externally—perhaps out of rebellion, unconscious tests of love, or imagined reenactments that might make us feel closer to a birth parent. For others of us, signs of trauma may be hidden or look just fine—especially in a culture that values perfectionism, people-pleasing, neurotic organization, and compliance.

But as Diego says, "Whether we present as the happy-go-lucky adoptee or as the angry, lashing out adoptee, we are living in a trauma response." He adds, "Regardless, the happy adoptee is not removed from the experience of sitting in their trauma."[6]

LAYERS OF TRAUMA

The trauma around adoption isn't limited to the initial separation from our first families. Many adoptees experience additional wounding, such as in the following ways.

CHAPTER 2

Disenfranchised Grief

The profound grief that adoptees experience with the separation from our first mothers usually comes before we have either words or understanding of our incredible loss. We look to others to make sense of our situation, only everyone around us is celebrating—and nobody wants to approach what quickly becomes a taboo emotion: grief. To understand what it's like, imagine yourself now, losing a parent to death, and realizing the people closest to you offer no condolences or mentions of your loved one. Worse, they discount your sadness, or try to talk you out of it, reminding you how lucky you are now. As an adult, you'd probably get justifiably upset and recognize the callousness of the situation. To an infant or child without an understanding of words, the loss and continued lack of its recognition is incredibly confusing and can take decades, if not a lifetime, to verbalize and feel. This is the experience of disenfranchised grief.

Tony shares, "When we have children, especially for mothers, we are physiologically connected to that child's chemistry. Our bodies are literally making connections and attachments to our children. And so it's not easy, of course, it's very difficult to be separated, generally . . . to be told that you should feel okay about that is just completely opposite of what nature and nurture has really guided us to be."[7]

Mar says, "I was adopted into a family grieving the loss of their biological person. And I believe that my first year in that family was a combination of my grief and theirs. Although they were grieving the loss of a child, I was grieving the loss of my first family."[8] Of course, Mar is only able to recognize this now, well into adulthood. Growing up, the grief wasn't a topic of open conversation.

David says, "A baby has no concept of suffering emotionally or mentally and could not tell you that they're grieving. But the distress and the suffering are there."

The Pain of Operating Without a Voice

From an early age, many adoptees make sense of their situations through beliefs that can make us susceptible to silencing ourselves. We might infer that we exist solely to serve our adoptive parents. As naturally egocentric children often do, we decide we were relinquished because something was inherently wrong with us. We may fear being rehomed if we aren't "good enough." Even if these beliefs aren't shared or explicitly stated in our homes, at the deepest level they feel true and can work to silence adoptees, taking away our sense of agency and voice and ultimately pouring in more pain.

"Anytime I felt like I couldn't stand up and voice myself that added or maintained that trauma in some way," says Diego.

Lanise says, "It should be a given that we can be ourselves and speak freely and live freely but it's not for so many adoptees."[9]

In addition to losing agency and voice, many adoptees feel powerlessness from the ways their parents take over their stories and share their own versions of their child's adoption stories without consent. I experienced this—and Kayla did, too. She shares, "Countless times my adoptive parents would go up and start speaking about my adoption story, how they see it. No one ever once asked me, 'How did you see it?'"[10]

"My mom was always telling my story to everyone," Holly shares. "And that was hard because my narrative was, 'I was left and I was abandoned, and then they adopted me, and now I'm here.' And then everybody would say, 'Oh, you're so lucky.'"

Over time, the frustration of being spoken for and spoken over builds, often leaving adoptees feeling helpless, disempowered, apathetic, unimportant, and alone.

Expectations of Gratitude, Divided Loyalties, and Shame

Speaking of *lucky*, there's a source of more pain: the expectation that we adoptees need to be grateful for being so lucky. It's surprising how rampant this messaging is—from strangers, acquaintances, and loved ones. Kayla says, "People would come up to me with my parents, saying things like, 'Oh, aren't you so lucky? You have such amazing parents!'—right in front of me, right in front of my parents."

While usually not spoken, the implication everyone understands is that our first families were flawed and unworthy. Automatically this "lucky-adoptee" label and expectation of gratitude disrespects and judges our first families. Diego says, "It's inherently assumed that our biological family has problems."

Perhaps an unplanned pregnancy was indeed considered *a problem*, or other problematic factors lined up and led to the adoption. But the "lucky" label assumes our first families are forever less-than. Since we will always be attached to our first families in some way, even in the most closed adoptions and the most dire of family circumstances, this causes a split in our hearts and minds that's very painful.

Even though his was an open adoption, Tony experienced such a divide. He says, "There was definitely a time where there was a sense of dueling loyalties about which family should I be loyal to." He adds, "I didn't want to speak negatively, really, about either family. I saw positives in both of my families."

For David, the expectation of gratitude led to feelings of shame. "There was always the pervasive microscope and, of course, the guilt and shame over not feeling grateful enough, over not appreciating my wonderful fortune. I mean, on paper, everything looked absolutely perfect, and there should be no reason for me to be sullen about any of it."

Living in Isolation

In my work leading adoptee writing groups, I repeatedly hear adult adoptees express relief and joy upon meeting other adoptees for the first time. Astrid Castro, Founder of Adoption Mosaic, hears this a lot, too, in her work with adoptees. Considering she, too, grew up in isolation, Astrid knows how meaningful this kind of work is in bringing adoptees together.[11]

"The only other adoptee I knew was my sister, and the only other adoptive parents I knew were my parents," she says. "That adoptive family dynamic of isolation hugely impacted our lives."

When adult adoptees finally connect, their feelings and experiences are normalized, after years and years of keeping private worries at bay, including a general fear of being "crazy." But we shouldn't have to wait until adulthood to receive this kind of comfort. Isolation is not only lonely but keeps adoptees shrouded in shame and can be dangerous. As an adoptee who's struggled with suicidal ideation since adolescence, having an adult adoptee in my life when I was younger would have gone a long way—especially if the adult adoptee was someone who had a healthy relationship with their grief and a solid understanding of adoption and attachment to help me make sense of the confusing tornado of swirling emotions inside.

In addition to emotional isolation, many interracial adoptees experience racial, cultural, and spiritual isolation. Lanise says, "I didn't have any Black friends until middle school." Likewise, Shelise shares, "I only knew one other Korean in my elementary school."[12]

Hurtful Family Dynamics and Practices

Just as in any family, other kinds of wounding can take place in adoptive families and relationships with birth families. But sometimes these amount to additional trauma for an adoptee's already overworked alarm system.

For instance, commonly prescribed discipline practices—usually separation-based, such as time-outs or "cry-it-out" sleep-training methods—can close up a child's tender heart. But for an adoptee already saturated with separation, this can quickly become too much to bear. The adoptee learns it's unsafe to depend and, consequently, does not. Parent-child relationships can be quite strained, and later in life, relationships that require healthy reciprocation of caring can be compromised, too.

Chapter 2

Similarly, most sibling relationships come with a certain dose of comparison, score-keeping, and feelings of exclusion that can sometimes get ugly. But adoptees raised with siblings who are biological to their parents, or in open adoptions where birth parents are actively raising other biological children, may harbor a deeper core belief that they're not treasured in the same way. Since adoptees are already prone to feeling "not good enough," every family interaction that involves siblings is an opportunity to support that confirmation bias.

Many children grow up feeling unseen and unknown in their families. It may even be an existential experience, to some degree. But adoptees often get a double or triple dose—not feeling known by our birth families to the extent that we long for, or not feeling seen when our parents unknowingly discount our experience by telling or showing us that they don't think being adopted or a different race matters. Add to this our tendency to hide our authentic and true selves out of fear of rejection, and we learn that love is based on the false self we present outwardly; *if they really saw and knew the full us, they'd leave.* This can become a self-perpetuating cycle of never feeling truly known.

"Adoptees usually have issues because we haven't felt validated and seen. That's the root of it," says Diego.

Children in any family might experience these dynamics as painful. But for adoptees, the hurt can be punctuated because of the foundational trauma of separation from our first attachments.

All of this focus on heartache and pain—is it necessary? Yes, especially if we aim to better understand, honor, and support the adoptees in our lives—no matter their age and stage.

Besides, there's good news: our brains are made with great plasticity. Certain effects of trauma may be lifelong, but our trauma doesn't have to define us. With an understanding of attachment dynamics, there are ways for our developmental and attachment needs to be met—and it's never too late! With the right conditions, we can not only grow to maturity but come out the other side capable, resilient, and even thriving.

CHAPTER 3

In Pursuit of Love ... Or, Pushing It Away

WE WANT LOVE ... AND YET WE OFTEN PUSH IT AWAY. WE YEARN to feel safe in relationships ... and yet we can behave in ways that lead to a lack of safety.

These and other adoptee curiosities are explained by the primal emotion of separation-triggered pursuit—and its opposite, defensive detachment.

SEPARATION-TRIGGERED PURSUIT

Pursuit is one of the primal emotional responses to unbearable separation, with a purpose of "closing the separation gap," as Gordon Neufeld refers to it, "doing whatever it takes to close the gap, including changing one's shape or one's form."[1] In the last decade, many have come to describe this as the "fawn" response to trauma, a term coined by psychotherapist Pete Walker as an expansion of instincts commonly referred to as "fight, flight, or freeze."[2]

Katie describes this dynamic in saying, "I think adoptees inadvertently, or maybe overtly, try to stack the odds in our favor. We want to do what we can to not be abandoned, rejected, fail, or disappoint—or any of those things that might put us at risk of ending up alone, not being taken care of, not being remembered, or not being special to people."[3]

Chapter 3

What follows are some of the common ways that separation-triggered pursuit manifests for many adoptees.

Compliancy

Many adoptees, as adults, recognize and self-describe themselves as compliant adoptees. In childhood, they felt they needed to be "good" in order to keep their parents close. Our definition of "good" can vary, depending on what we instinctively perceive as valued by our families.

Shelise says, "I was very compliant. Compliance was my thing ... I was kind of my parents' star child. I was outgoing and did a lot of activities and I got good grades. They never had to bother me and I never got in trouble. I just did the things they asked me to do. I rarely complained but that was just part of wanting to please them."[4]

For Shelise and many other adoptees, this need to be "good" is rooted in both the initial mother-child separation of adoption as well as an almost constant facing of additional separation. We typically feel we don't truly belong in either of our families and need to ensure we do whatever is needed to guarantee a place. Even if the adults in our lives give us nothing but messages of belonging, the lack of genetic mirroring—through thousands of genetic differences between us and members of our adoptive families, both subtle and glaring—tells us otherwise and serves as a perpetual reminder of more potential separation looming.

Shelise says, "I don't have any memories of anyone in my immediate or extended family ever challenging whether or not I was a part of the family. I don't have any memories of my siblings ever saying, 'You're adopted,' or 'You're not my sister,' or, 'We're not actually related.' And yet internally, I was always needing to create more security—doing more, being good more—so that no one could challenge it, even though no one ever had. But I feel like there was always this anxiety for me that that could somehow happen."

Presenting a False Self and Secret-Keeping

Since none of us can be good all the time, it's no wonder compliant adoptees often get stuck presenting a false sense of themselves to the world. There's no awareness or malice around this; we do this because keeping our families close is of utmost importance to our brains and the quest for survival. The instinct to sacrifice and hide our true selves to present a different image to our families and others we seek closeness to can be so deeply buried that many of us don't have the faintest idea who our true selves are. That inner self within is an enigma, and our instincts to hide can lead to stuckness when it comes to identity formation, authenticity, and maturity and individuation.

Amanda describes a dynamic of her younger self as "always keeping myself in check, always playing small, never fully just being me." She adds, "I grew up with a feeling that if I didn't live up to a certain character, then I would be put to the test or questioned. My life constantly felt like a house of cards that could come crumbling down. You don't know what's going to be exposed because you don't know yourself."[5]

As part of hiding our true selves, many adoptees feel they need to keep secrets. For example, Shelise's inner world was a complete secret to others. "No one close to me knew anything about the internal part of me. External Shelise was happy and outgoing and funny, loved to dance, was in the musicals, and all of those things, but nobody knew how lonely I felt."

My big secret was that I missed my birth mother. I harbored a rich fantasy life in which I desperately hoped my first mother was looking for me and watching me from afar. Outwardly, though, I feigned disinterest in her and pretended to be perfectly content that I was adopted, presuming this was my parents' desire and expectation of me. I made assumptions (that may or may not have been accurate) in whether they could handle my true feelings. By keeping my yearning for my birth mom private, I "closed the gap" to keep my adoptive parents close. Even admitting to myself that

I missed my birth mother pushed me into more separation, as it felt like a betrayal to my adoptive parents, and I didn't want to lose them.

When we keep secrets, such as hiding significant parts of ourselves, we're automatically ruling out deeper levels of attaching. We can't feel truly seen and known and experience the rest that comes with that—the tragic downside of presenting our false selves to those closest to us.

People-Pleasing
A lot of what drives adoptees to be compliant and "good" comes down to our instinct-driven tendency to read rooms, situations, and people to perceive the needs . . . and then meet them. This is commonly referred to in our culture as people-pleasing, and many of us have been raised to be people-pleasers. For adoptees, this can be an ingrained way of being as we deal with unbearable separation.

Donna says, "As a safety mechanism, I will, under stress, go into sort of freeze or fawn and say to myself, 'How do I make everything okay so I can get out of here safely?'" Incidentally, people-pleasing felt so natural to Donna that she pursued a career in a caretaking field. "I think that's one of the ways that it feels safe for me to do attachment. If I take care of a person or if I can be helpful, then that seems like a reasonable way to have a connection."[6]

Fantasy Attachments
Many adoptees secretly harbor detailed and intense fantasy attachments to imagined birth parents or with a birth parent they know.

Tammy, who lived in foster care and group homes from age four to eighteen, shares, "The only thing I knew about my mom was that she loved Elvis. That was the fantasy. I think I read something about Elvis comforting his kids when they were scared and how he'd looked under the bed for the monsters. That stuck with me, and so the idea of my mom and Elvis marrying and taking care of me was my fantasy for years."[7]

When I was an adolescent, the math added up enough for me to believe Madonna was my long-lost birth mother. Her busy music career explained why she couldn't keep me, I'd surmised. Over several decades, I psychologically attached to several other dreamed-up mothers, some more realistic than others.

This is not a dynamic exclusive to adoptees in closed adoptions. Even adoptees who grow up in open adoptions can spend a lot of energy thinking about what an idealized life would be like with their birth mothers. These fantasies can compete with deeply attaching to our adoptive parents, keeping us at an arm's length from them because there's so much energy directed toward fantasy mothers or imagined "other life" situations.

Perfectionism, Winning, Achieving

Many adoptees seek emotional safety through striving to be perfect. Messages we tell ourselves include, "If there hadn't been something inherently and deeply wrong with me, my mother would have kept me," or "If I never make a mistake, I won't be abandoned again." Because of this deep wounding and the instinct to "close the gap," messing up, not looking good, not winning, not being seen as "the best" or the "most special," or not being chosen can tap primal places inside of us that face us into that life-or-death emotional experience of separation.

Lanise vulnerably shares: "I have an issue with proving my value, proving my worth, and I have a fascination and an addiction to achievement. For example, I'm going to get these two fellowships. And I ask myself, 'Why? You already have four fellowships. Why do you need a seventh and an eighth? Like, who does that?' But I do. And I think it does stem from this need to prove myself constantly. I don't know when it will be enough. But I do know that it is because I'm adopted that drives me to prove my worth constantly."[8]

Chapter 3

As an adult, Lanise is working to "clean up her perfectionism," as she says. As a podcaster and actor with a public persona, she yearns to be relatable. She's also cognizant of how perfectionism hurts her. "I'm not perfect. And the problem is that once you allow people to perceive you as perfect, you have to hold that up. That is where the anxiety resides, the constant balancing it up in the air all the time."

When we influence the outcome through being compliant, presenting a false sense of ourselves, people-pleasing, and myriad other ways of "closing the gap" to feel loved, cherished, adored, and safe, we reinforce patterns that don't serve our emotional health and well-being for the long-term, as Lanise articulated. Success is temporary and doesn't last. Like a drug, we will need another hit. And another. And another—and before long, these are depersonalized pursuits that are no longer specific to finding closeness with key attachments but a more generalized need to be attractive, to win, to measure up, to impress, to help, to charm, to obtain status.[9]

We may feel additional shame, grief, and confusion that's hard to pinpoint and name—inherently knowing that we're not being true to ourselves and we're lying to others. We may also feel selfish for the masks and coping mechanisms we don in order to feed an insatiable attachment hunger. The shame cycle continues because we can believe that our needs don't matter—or that they rank last in priority. After all, adoption often delivers the subtle and not-so-subtle message that our job as adoptees is to meet our parents' needs—those of our birth parents, to solve the dilemma of an unwanted pregnancy; and those of our adoptive parents, to solve their childlessness or perhaps their savioristic desires.

Sadly, when adoptees work to "close the gap," short-term successes such as winning the smiles, feeling loved for our achievements, basking in the adoration associated with being admired or seen as "special," reinforce these and other self-limiting beliefs.

Defensive Detachment

When separation becomes unbearable, our brains take care of us by reversing the attachment instinct of pursuit. This is a dynamic Dr. Neufeld refers to as "defensive detachment." This protective state can be proactive, with adoptees resisting getting close or backing out of relationships with potential to wound us. Defensive detachment can look like losing our caring feelings. Or we may come across as oppositional, hostile, fearless, controlling, or preoccupied with dangerous or taboo activities.[10] Defensive detachment can also look like shyness in reverse.

Resisting Closeness

Because of the high levels of separation adoptees experience and our brains' natural tendency to move into defensive detachment, it can be a struggle to attach deeply to our parents. To be clear, this is not because we are flawed or broken people, and please do not confuse this with a diagnosis of "reactive attachment disorder" or other stigmatizing labels. Besides, attaching to our parents is not a child's responsibility or duty. It is the job of the caring adults in our lives to make it safe enough for us to depend on and attach to them. Unfortunately, many parents do not have the insight, skills, patience, or perseverance to create safe enough conditions for those of us with deep separation wounding to seek closeness with them. The result, sadly, is the cost of our hearts.

Amanda says, "I just never really felt connected to my adoptive family. It's more like we were just four people living in the same house."

Julian echoes Amanda's sentiments as he reflects on the relationships he had with both sets of adoptive parents. "I don't think I ever really bonded with them.... I don't think there was ever any real bonding."[11] This makes sense, considering Julian and his sister were relinquished not once, but twice, allowed no contact with his first family or first set of adoptive parents and family members, and suffered from abuse at the hands of his second adoptive family.

Likewise, as she considers her relationship with her adoptive mother, Holly shares, "I don't feel like we bonded or ever had a chance to. It was really sad, because I feel like I never had that connection with her."[12]

I experienced a similar disconnection from my adoptive mother, which didn't begin to resolve, sadly, until she was dying, and I divulged a long-held secret. My mom responded by offering me a sense of unconditional love that I never imagined I could experience. Even though I was forty-one years old, until then, the compliant adoptee in me hadn't tested my mom's love in such a way that allowed me to rest in it and deeply attach to her. Since adolescence, when intrinsic separation and individuation tipped the scales for me into separation that felt overwhelming, I'd been flatlined in a state of almost constant emotional numbness—which I successfully hid through the false self that I presented as her daughter. In the days before her death, I basked in what had at last become a deep attachment to my mom, which helped me forgive her wrongdoings as a parent and led me to flourish in many ways since. But even in her death, where my personal spiritual beliefs assure me that she's transformed into "the perfect mother," and even with my knowledge of defensive detachment, feelings of connection to my mom waver. Feeling secure and safe in close relationships—especially when the stakes are high—is fleeting and still a journey in progress.

Backing Out of Relationships

For many adoptees, backing out of relationships can be a deeply instinctual response—an unconscious attempt to leave before being left. Our brains, after all, rightfully declared the initial separation from our birth mothers as a serious threat to our survival and work overtime to take notice of potentially dangerous (real or perceived) relationships to avoid more separation going forward.

Relationships with our adoptive mothers can feel especially fraught since we've already learned mothers leave. This can extend to relationships with other females, or generally to any relationships where closeness could lead to future abandonment. Outside our awareness, we might back out of these relationships—or feel an overwhelming desire to run away from them.[13]

Lily says, "I was just always fighting, always trying to protect, and always trying to hide or push away. I think it's something adoptees don't like to discuss because it can sound shameful."[14] Offering hope to parents, she says, "If adoptive parents understand that this can be part of their journey and seek help, rather than try to fix or control their kid, it might better serve the adopted child."

Defensive detachment can look like disinterest in, or pulling away from, our birth parents, too. Children in open adoptions may show resistance to visits with their birth parents or might appear apathetic when in their presence. Adoptees may insist they have no interest in knowing their birth mothers, denying Nature's connection to one's roots and ancestors. Adoptees in open adoptions or reunion can lash out at birth parents or cut off ties seemingly out of the blue.

Shyness in Reverse

Even as adoptees and foster youth resist closeness with their caregivers, some of us can be indiscriminately affectionate with strangers. We might come across as outgoing and at ease talking to almost anyone, or we may be promiscuous. "I was acting out all over the place. I was acting out with guys. I was acting out with girls," Tammy shares.

The reversal of shyness can be baffling to those closest to us, who may wonder why it's so hard to win our hearts when we can give them so easily to strangers. But it's important that we're not pathologized, since labels often miss the underlying attachment emotions—all driven instinctively due to the impact of separation.

CHAPTER 3

When adoptees are operating in defensive detachment, especially if we get stuck in it, we can be challenging to parent. It's not an easy road caring for a child who has a hard time depending on you, requiring an enormous amount of patience, perseverance, gentleness, and trust in the developmental process, even if it might take years or decades to see results.

Further complicating matters, adoptees' instincts—there to protect us from unbearable separation—can inadvertently create a cycle where more separation ensues. For example:

- Parents and educators often employ separation-based strategies or shame to discipline us, but these approaches only add more separation into our already saturated systems, creating a spiraling of alarm (I share more about alarm in the next chapter) and leading to more defensive detachment.
- Sometimes our prickly behaviors activate our parents' own defensive detachment instincts causing them to react apathetically, in anger, or in other ways that feel like we're being abandoned again.
- Uninformed parents can leave us to our own devices, thinking we're stronger and fiercer than we really are and taking our instincts at face value, especially when they lead us to say (or scream) things like, "I don't care!" or "I'm not scared!" and "Adoption doesn't affect me." Or, to act on the thought, "I'll leave you before you can leave me." But parents' believing these outbursts is experienced as giving up on us—which, to our brains, reads as more rejection and loss—putting adoptees in a separation pressure cooker with overwhelming emotions of alarm and frustration bubbling over and leading us to more defensive detachment.
- Birth parents can be driven to defensive detachment, themselves, as they try to cope with the overwhelming separation from their child lost to adoption. It's no wonder

that adoptee-birth parent relationships can be strained, or at least, incredibly complicated and often leave adoptees feeling even more alone.

Instinct-driven emotions abound in adoption—created by a vast sea of separation for all. Let that not discourage us, though. Hope lies in the naming and understanding of these dynamics. When they remain outside our awareness and misunderstood, it leaves adoptees in isolation, fretting over our sanity and worth; stuck instead of maturing; feeling unknown and thus not fully loved by those closest to us; and rarely or never experiencing the security that could be a balm for our separation wounds.

Adoptees cannot be expected to make sense of these emotional instincts and attachment dynamics as children, so we need the adults in our lives to understand them and better support us. With regard to our separation-triggered pursuit and defensive detachment, this looks like parents who don't take our natural instincts personally and show us, over and over, that they're big enough to handle the full range of our emotions and that they are one-hundred percent committed to the challenge of meeting our attachment needs.

I'll share more ideas for supporting adoptees in later chapters. As we continue to look at common struggles related to separation and adoption, we'll turn next to alarm and frustration.

Chapter 4

Living Anxious and Alarmed

I'VE LIVED WITH FEAR AND ANXIETY MY ENTIRE LIFE. AS A CHILD I couldn't sleep in the dark. I'd often get stranded at the top of escalators, afraid of taking the required leap of faith onto the monsterlike teeth of the moving stairs. Fireworks terrified me, and I never understood how thousands of others could relax on blankets at the park, enjoying the spectacle, while I cowered in fear, plugging my ears and burying my head from the sparks I believed would burn us all. Now that I'm an adult, my fears have expanded to an array of grown-up worries both large and small, seen and unseen. I confess that I still rely on a nightlight to sleep . . . and avoid fireworks and escalators whenever I can.

My intense fears stood out in my adoptive family, not only making me feel different and isolated as the only person not genetically related, but also generating much shame. Nobody around me understood the roots of my anxiety—let alone grasped that my fears were driven by the underlying emotion of alarm. They laughed at or worried about me, which reinforced a message I already held due to my experience of relinquishment: that something was wrong with me. The task of making sense of my anxiety, and its associated shame, was left solely to me . . . and took decades.

Even though I grew up knowing nothing about the science and psychology behind alarm, feeling ashamed because of my intense fears, I now know that I'm not alone. "Alarm problems are extremely common," says Dr. Gordon Neufeld, "There are very few of us who are not afflicted by an alarm problem of one kind or another, or at least at one time or another."[1]

What's more, a significant number of adoptees struggle with anxiety, which Dr. Neufeld describes as "alarm without eyes"—in other words, alarm without insight into its source.

Donna shares, "I've constantly had anxiety. It's the air I breathe and the water I live in."[2]

"My underlying experience throughout my entire life until recently has been fear," says Amanda, "fear of rejection, fear of judgment. That manifested for me as hypervigilance. When you're a baby losing your mother, you don't have the language for it, but you know the loss. How do you survive that?"[3]

Katie describes growing up with hypervigilance too. "I was certainly one of those adoptees who did not say a lot but was thinking a lot, and my anxiety was more in the form of guardedness. It didn't look or feel like anxiety, but it was more of a vigilance."[4]

Alarm is an important primal emotion that serves the main purpose of avoiding separation by moving us to caution. As explained in the previous chapter, facing separation is our greatest human threat and so it makes sense that alarm enters the scene and takes center stage.

When our alarm system is functioning well, moving us to caution is our brain's way of taking care of us. Since separation cannot always be avoided, our alarm system also helps us adapt and grow resilience. That is, when it can develop in healthy ways. "The alarm system is notoriously oversensitive and requires activating in a context of safety to become properly calibrated,"[5] says Dr. Neufeld. If we're chronically alarmed, as adoptees tend to be—often without our awareness—it can lead to alarm-system problems.

There can be a continuum of experience in how alarm problems manifest, commonly presenting as anxiety-based, agitation-based, or adrenaline-based.[6] Examples of each include:

- Anxiety-Based Problems: Digestive issues, phobias, obsessions, clinginess, trouble focusing, incessant worrying, having a hard time making decisions, becoming overly conscientious or controlling, panic attacks.
- Agitation-Based Problems: Difficulty learning, trouble sleeping, restlessness, recklessness, acting hyper, scattered attention.
- Adrenaline-Based Problems: High-risk behavior, a perverse attraction to what alarms, adrenaline-seeking.

For adoptees, our propensity for alarm-system problems can begin as a physiological predisposition due to our prenatal circumstances and birth experiences, further impacted by the psychological effects of separation. We'll take a closer look at both.

ALARM AND ITS PHYSIOLOGICAL ROOTS

It wasn't until recently, when trying to understand why I verge on panic attacks in hospital-like settings that I fully reflected on my first experiences out of my birth mother's womb. How distressing must it have been for newborn me, lying in a hospital untouched immediately after birth. I was presumably fed by nurses—strangers who smelled and sounded nothing like my mother—but I never saw my mother or felt the comfort of her arms. I missed the first "gaze interactions between infant and caregiver that motivate the infant to attach to the caregiver."[7]; such was my welcome into this world and for the first two days of my life, a time of critical brain growth that affected the development of my neural pathways. While I don't have actual memories of this time, my body remembers it, as Bessel van der Kolk describes in his book *The Body Keeps the Score*.[8]

Entering the world alone affected me deeply and is explained by Dr. Bruce Perry in his book with Oprah Winfrey, *What Happened to You?: Conversations on Trauma, Resilience, and Healing*: "Our earliest developmental experiences . . . are organizing experiences that help create the infant's 'worldview.'"[9] Separated from my mother after nine months in her womb, it makes sense that my default view became that the world is inherently unsafe. After all, "proximity to the mother confers psychobiological regulation as well as safety."[10] states trauma therapist Dr. Veronique P. Mead.

Going back further, like many adoptees, I am the product of an unplanned and unwanted pregnancy. "Women reporting low pregnancy wantedness would be at higher risk for anxiety," report Kimberly A. Tremblay and Elizabeth Soliday in their study on the *Effect of Planning, Wantedness, and Attachment on Prenatal Anxiety*.[11] My mother's stress hormones were likely flowing to me through the umbilical cord. Dr. Arthur Janov states, "An anxious mother is delivering stress hormones to her baby/fetus. And so the baby can be said to be born with a tendency to anxiety, as well. One way we know this is that mothers who are anxious seem to raise the cortisol levels in the amniotic fluid surrounding the fetus."[12] He also says, "Newborns of a depressed mother show a profile that mimics the mother's prenatal state, including her physiologic state. This includes higher stress hormone levels, lower levels of dopamine and serotonin, and greater right frontal brain activity."[13] Considering how and when our alarm systems develop, it is easy to see the beginnings of future problems with alarm. "The alarm system begins operation by the sixth month in utero," says Dr. Neufeld. "Your alarm system will still bear the legacy of your mother's alarm system in this way."[14]

This flies in the face of the concept of "tabula rasa," the idea that babies are a blank slate—often a philosophical rationale in support of adoption. On the contrary, "The prenatal time and the first hours and days after birth are part of a sensitive period when babies and mothers are primed for bonding and are especially impacted by their environments," states Dr. Mead.[15] She also states that, "Children are most vulnerable to trauma during prenatal life and in infancy by virtue of their complete dependence on others. . . . Events in the earliest stages of life have a larger impact than at later stages."[16] In a related book, *Adverse Babyhood Experiences (ABEs)*, Dr. Mead states, "Our experiences in the womb, at birth, and in childhood also guide the formation of nerve pathways and the ability of our nervous systems to help us settle and rest, calm ourselves down, recover from fear, pain or grief, and experience a sense of safety and connection." She adds, "Early experiences also influence whether our bodies will function with extra care and caution because they are primed for survival and are highly sensitive to stress."[17]

ALARM FROM A PSYCHOLOGICAL STANDPOINT

Again, alarm is an important emotion that serves the purpose of avoiding separation. The problem is that we live in an alarming world where we're constantly faced with separation. It's fast-paced, competitive, and full of shocking news that seems to constantly remind us of the threat of losing our loved ones to violence or disease. What's more, many of our lives are over-scheduled and full of stimulation and high expectations. We simply cannot escape the emotion of alarm. This is true for adoptees and nonadoptees alike.

But alarm can be exacerbated by our experiences of relinquishment and adoption. Adoption and foster care are not possible without separation from our first attachments (even in open adoptions) and so our alarm system, already working to keep separation from taking us down, can end up staying in the "on" position to ensure we're never caught off guard again.

David says, "We put so much pressure on ourselves as human beings, but adoptees have those pressures in spades!" He shares, "Imagine living like that, never being able to relax fully and wondering when I was going to make some grave mistake that would perhaps have me relinquished again."[18]

Not all adoptees are conscious of the fear that we might be relinquished again. Our brains can land on other things as the source of the alarm, because it's too much to look at the real losses of adoption directly. Even if we're living in caring, stable adoptive families, remaining ever on the lookout for future abandonment can become our brain's standard, leaving us feeling chronically insecure in specific relationships or generalized to all close relationships.

As Dr. Neufeld explains, "You can be in the midst of plenty, but it has to do with your confidence that it will be there tomorrow. It doesn't matter how much contact and closeness you have—it could be 24/7, it could be continually for a child, but if they can't take it for granted, there is no rest. They are constantly seeking. To be insecure is to be alarmed by default."[19]

Katie says, "When we're talking about trauma and anxiety, in a way, 'anxiety' doesn't even really capture it. Because when I think about that kind of anxiety, it's more like terror. It's terrifying to get close to someone and depend on them, or terrifying to be alone, or terrifying to feel abandoned, or to be abandoned again." She adds, "The stakes can feel so high all the time."

As adoptees grow up in this dark shadow that follows the initial separation from our first attachments, there are many other common hidden sources of alarm that can be layered on in unique ways for adoptees, some of which are described as follows.

Shame

Most of us intuitively know that children are prone to blame themselves for adult problems such as divorce. As previously mentioned, many young adoptees decide early on that there's something inherently wrong with them that explains why they weren't "wanted." We must not have been "good enough" to have been "kept," we reason. From then on, we might live a highly alarmed life trying to be "good" going forward. While this might seem like a wonderful trait to our parents and teachers, making us easier to raise, it comes at a high price given the extreme levels of alarm and adrenaline constantly flooding our systems.

Complicating matters, our feelings of shame can be compounded if we're disciplined with shame, or treated or diagnosed in ways that make us feel like a "problem," or "too much to handle."

"Therapy was another source of shame. I would have to leave school early to go to therapy," shares Tammy. Teachers and peers knew Tammy was being picked up by a social worker for therapy. Not only did Tammy believe she was a problem, which the need for therapy reinforced, she felt embarrassed that others thought so, too. "It was a horrible experience," she says.[20]

A Sense of Separateness
Even if we're assured that we belong in our adoptive families, adoptees are usually aware, even if only at an unconscious level, of genetic differences that leave us feeling like outsiders. Racial and cultural differences can leave adoptees feeling more disconnected from their primary caregivers and the communities in which they live, significantly adding to the alarm experienced.

Nancy Verrier says, "It's very difficult growing up in a family where you have very little in common. That's fine as long as everybody understands that and everybody is allowed to be themselves. That's not always the case, unfortunately."[21]

Secrets That Could Divide
As shared previously, many of us long to be closer to our birth parents but are afraid to express this deep truth to our adoptive parents. Doing so can feel like a betrayal and faces us into additional separation by threatening the connection we have with our primary caregivers, upon whom our survival depends. "It's highly alarming to have a secret that, if out, could cause divisiveness," says Dr. Neufeld.[22] *Will my parents get jealous? Will they be hurt if they find out how I really feel? Will they send me back?* These are the kinds of alarming thoughts that can constantly haunt us, whether or not they are realistic.

Lack of Control
It can be alarming knowing that we have little to no control over our lives. After all, from the moment of relinquishment, others

have been "playing God," making decisions over which family we're placed in, and determining our futures in ways that differ from those who aren't adopted.

As we grow, we also discover that we don't always have agency over when and how our adoption stories are presented. Sometimes relatives know more about our adoptions than we do. Parents often overshare when talking with friends and acquaintances, unaware of crossing the precarious line between their adoption stories and ours. For those with obvious racial or other genetic differences, even being seen next to their adoptive parents tells their adoption stories—yet another matter out of their control.

Some of us may react by working to control our environments and the people around us (anxiety-based), while others flirt with danger (adrenaline-based). Tammy shares, "I didn't like that feeling of being out of control and yet I placed myself in danger all the time. I was constantly walking train tracks alone. Or, I'd know I was being followed and just wouldn't care what happened to me at all."

Like Tammy, many of us experience a swirling of big emotions that we don't always understand—that can sometimes erupt without warning—adding to the number of things out of our control that can saturate adoptees with alarm. Gabor Maté explains, "lack of essential information about ourselves and our situation is one of the major sources of stress and one of the potent activators of the hypothalamic-pituitary-adrenal (HPA) stress response." He goes on to say, "stress wanes as independent, autonomous control increases."[23]

Emotional Isolation

Because of so many big emotions and a lack of insight into them, many adoptees grow up in emotional isolation. Donna recalls, "I have this memory of coming out on the playground as a little kid and looking around and feeling like, *I don't see how everybody else is just able to go through recess and be okay with it.* I remember

Chapter 4

thinking, *Okay, if I sit on the swings, I can just get through this.* What kid is suffering through recess for no reason?"

When Donna shared this story with me, it resonated. I, too, felt similar isolation during elementary school recess. But we didn't have each other as fellow adoptees to console or commiserate with on the playground. Many adoptees grow up without knowing other adoptees who could help normalize such experiences. Even if we do have adopted friends in our circles, developmentally it takes years and years for adoptees to process adoption to be a source of understanding, compassion, and insight for another adoptee, so peer relationships can't always provide the support young adoptees need.

Unfortunately, alarm can further escalate—especially when an alarmed adoptee's pervasive experience that *something is wrong* is met with messages, no matter how subtle, by well-meaning but insensitive caregivers, that *something is wrong with me*. (It is in this way that the typical alarm that comes with simply being an adoptee can turn into a crippling sense of shame.)

Tammy articulates this through a memory of wishing her caregiver could see her and better support her: "I remember *trying* to get her worried about me, so that something would click and she would figure out there's something going on with me. She couldn't ever get it. And that left me feeling even more lonely."

Not only did Shelise grow up aware of racial differences between her and her adoptive family, she also lived in emotional isolation around dealing with racism she experienced. "Without being able to name it, I just knew that my dad was racist. He had said racist things, and I'd heard him and his friends say racist things. And so I decided, or simply figured out: *I am on my own*."[24]

Comparison

As discussed in Chapter 2, another big source of alarm can come through comparison. For adoptees raised with siblings who are biological to our adoptive parents, we may live with another ongoing source of alarm: worrying whether blood matters more and whether our siblings are cherished more than we are. Adoptees in open adoptions or in foster care may experience similar alarm when comparing their lives to any siblings their birth parents are actively raising. In families with multiple adoptees—each with different birth parents—adoptees may experience alarm when comparing their experiences of contact and closeness to those of their siblings.

While Tammy spent the bulk of her childhood in foster care, her brother returned to live with their mother. Eventually their mother had another child. "She has another kid that she keeps. It was super painful," Tammy shares.

Dynamics such as these can face us into additional separation and continually cycle us through feeling shame and disconnection from our families, piling on more alarm.

The Long-Term Consequences of Alarm-System Problems

Dr. Perry explains that "anything that can cause unpredictable, uncontrollable, or extreme and prolonged activation of the stress response will result in an overactive and overly reactive stress response."[25] As one can logically ascertain, there are long-term consequences to a sympathetic nervous system that starts out and remains chronically activated—affecting our physical and emotional health.

Alarm's Impact on Our Physical Health

Our sympathetic nervous system is meant to ebb and flow with the parasympathetic nervous system. But when we're chronically alarmed, the sympathetic nervous system is in overdrive, and activities required by the parasympathetic nervous system, such as digestion and sleep, can suffer.[26]

We can be more susceptible to chronic illnesses and immune system problems. "Because the baby can be born with higher than normal stress-hormone levels, and because the immune system works in seesaw fashion with cortisol (high stress, low immune function), the fetus has possibly set the stage for a lifetime of immune problems," states Dr. Janov, speaking to our prenatal and birth experiences, adding, "high stress in the fetus will affect those areas with genetic vulnerabilities."[27]

Dr. Nadine Burke Harris stresses the impact of alarm on developing children. "Children are especially sensitive to this repeated stress activation, because their brains and bodies are just developing. High doses of adversity not only affect brain structure and function, they affect the developing immune system, developing hormonal systems, and even the way our DNA is read and transcribed."[28]

Dr. Neufeld explains, "If you're highly alarmed, your immune system is highly activated, because the whole system is part of the alarm and looking for what is threatening."[29]

Moreover, recent epigenetic research indicates that the effects of alarm-system problems can reach down our genetic line. "Stress, emotions, nutrition—the environmental influences of a human life—can modify the genes we carry," states Dr. Thomas R. Verny adding, "life experiences don't just change us; they may affect our children and grandchildren down through many generations."[30]

Alarm As It Affects Our Emotional Health

One major long-term result of alarm-system problems is that it can be difficult to come to a place of emotional rest. Donna articulates this well, saying, "When your whole experience of life is that everything inherently feels unsafe, and you move through the world trying to manage everything and control all of the things, there's no resting place. There's no sense of safety or security." She adds, "It creates a higher susceptibility to stress and stressful events and transitions and just makes everything a little more difficult to deal with."

"The cost is joy and authenticity," says Katie. "If you're constantly in survival mode and strategizing about how to position yourself, or when you've worked to stack the odds in your favor, that doesn't really bring a lot of joy. It just means you're dodging bullets."

Just getting by, whether it's surviving recess or evading all of the metaphorical bullets life throws our way, doesn't always lead to emotional fulfillment.

It can also be harder for those of us in chronic alarm to depend on others. We may learn that it's best to rely only on ourselves. This may not bode well for relationships where dependence is needed, such as with parents, teachers, and therapists—and can create a cyclical problem. Taking charge and assuming responsibility for everything so much of the time, instead of relying on our caregivers, can reinforce that we're alone, leading to more and more alarm. This can become habitual and ingrained, affecting intimate relationships later in life, which require a healthy exchange of depending and caring.

I would not be sharing this if there wasn't hope—hope, that is, in the spontaneous nature of healing, if conditions are conducive. Studies in neuroscience remind us that the brain has great plasticity and that we're wired for resilience. "Our bodies and brains are designed to be influenced by interactions with our environments," says Dr. Mead.[31] And because we've had so many futilities to adapt to, adoptees can be among the most resilient people around. As Dr. Joyce Pavao proudly states, "We're adopted and we're adaptive!"[32]

If nothing else, may we take comfort in remembering that while specifics and underlying causes may differ, these dynamics are not exclusive to adoptees. I share this not to make light of a population suffering from alarm problems, but to remind us that we're not alone . . . and that healing is possible and evidenced in abundance. There has always been human suffering, and at the same time, an internal human essence that propels us toward healing.

I'll talk extensively about adoptee healing in Chapters 21 and 22. But first, let's turn to the third primal emotion in response to separation: frustration.

Chapter 5

Full of Frustration, Light on Feeling

So far, we've looked at pursuit/defensive detachment and alarm. Now, let's focus on frustration.

If I could suggest a prerequisite to reading this chapter, it would be watching Dr. Gordon Neufeld's twenty-three-minute overview of frustration from an attachment perspective. Among the insights is this refreshing gem: "Frustration is one of the unsung heroes of the emotional brain, whose work is often camouflaged and reputation tainted."[1]

Seeing frustration in a positive light isn't the norm. That's because instead of seeing frustration we usually respond to its eruptions such as tantrums, hitting, blaming, fighting, throwing, sarcasm, insults, put-downs, yelling, screaming, suicidal impulses or other forms of self-attack, and more. The world is full of these and other signs of frustration—especially as we continue to emerge from a years-long global pandemic. We've all been on both the expressing and receiving side of frustration and can agree that frustration is . . . well, frustrating.

But there's a point to it! Dr. Neufeld describes frustration as a "first responder" to input, with a purpose of scanning for what isn't working—and then either effecting change, leading us toward adaptation and transformation, or, if thwarted, driving us to attack.

The next three figures are inspired by the "Frustration Traffic Circle" in many of Dr. Neufeld's materials. Figure 4 illustrates

Full of Frustration, Light on Feeling

Figure 4

frustration pouring in, and our tendency to eliminate it through effecting change—either through fixing or changing situations or others' minds—and sometimes going to great lengths and spending a lot of time and energy trying to change ourselves.

But change isn't always possible. "Attachments not working is the primary source of frustration,"[2] says Dr. Neufeld. Since adoption can't occur without severed attachments, and adoptees continue to experience separation throughout their lives, it makes great sense that we're often filled with frustration. Examples of some things inherently not working for us can include:

- Not living with our biological families (no matter the reason);
- Not feeling invited by our first attachments in the ways we yearn to be;
- For interracial adoptees, not having control over our adoption stories because standing next to our adoptive families says it all;
- Not feeling the same as our adoptive families—looking different, having different interests or mannerisms, etc.;

CHAPTER 5

- Not feeling a sense of control over our fates;
- Not knowing or regularly hearing our complete origin stories;
- Not having access to our medical information and original birth records;
- Not feeling as though our adoptive families honor our birth families, leading us to question if our whole self is accepted and loved.

These are just some of the *massive* futilities that adoptees typically cannot change, so as we maneuver through the frustration traffic circle, Nature's desire is to change us from the inside out (Figure 5), through feeling our sadness and adapting to the unchangeable.

ADAPTATION
WHEN CHANGE IS FUTILE AND IF THAT
FUTILITY IS FELT (I.E., AS SADNESS,
GRIEF, OR DISAPPOINTMENT),
DEEP TRANSFORMATION OCCURS,
LEADING TO RESILIENCE.

Figure 5

Full of Frustration, Light on Feeling

You may now wish to cue *The Serenity Prayer*: "Grant me the serenity to accept the things I cannot change, courage to change the things I can, and wisdom to know the difference." To get to acceptance, we need to feel our sadness for frustration to do its job of deep transformation. As Dr. Neufeld shares, "Frustration has to be *felt* to be managed."[3]

Adoptees' significant futilities are incredibly difficult to face, and we often instinctively respond by building up defensive walls. Imagine bricks and mortar, a knight's iron-clad armor, or The Adoption Fog, which we described in the Introduction—any of these metaphors help us visualize the defenses that can protect us from feeling adoption's many losses. After all, our brains don't want us taken down by them. We have lives to live!

Not only are the defenses in place, but it can also be very hard for adoptees to feel safe being vulnerable—so, often there's a cyclical combination of the alarm I wrote about in Chapter 4, the defensive detachment I shared about in Chapter 3, and sometimes, due to the ways caregivers respond to us, a piling-on of more alarm, pursuit/defensive detachment, and/or frustration. The tender emotions of sadness or disappointment, needed to drain our frustration, can become even harder for us to feel.

This doesn't take into account all the other frustrations every human encounters—big and small—so it should be no surprise that adoptees are often loaded with frustration. If not tempered by mixed emotions—an ability to hold two opposing feelings at the same time—the frustration turns foul and comes out as attack (Figure 6).

While we won't get into all expressions of foul frustration (there are simply too many), let's hear from adoptees about three of the common ones that tend to arise for us:

CHAPTER 5

Figure 6
ADAPTED FROM HANNAH BEACH AND TAMARA NEUFELD STRIJACK, *RECLAIMING OUR STUDENTS: WHY CHILDREN ARE MORE ANXIOUS, AGGRESSIVE, AND SHUT DOWN THAN EVER—AND WHAT WE CAN DO ABOUT IT* (PAGE TWO BOOKS, 2020), 160–61.

- Anger and Outbursts (attacking energy going outward)
- Suicidal Impulses (attacking energy goes inward)
- Addiction (the temptation to seek a different route out of the traffic circle)

Anger and Outbursts

While Shelise may not have known about the traffic circle when we spoke, she seems to have an understanding of how in her younger years she'd spin through it, looking for a way out, either through change or attack. "I think when I was younger, I probably expressed a lot of rage—that passion-fueled anger that tries to help you think you can convince other people to think your way,"[4] she says. The conundrum, of course, as Shelise experienced, is that attacking others doesn't usually bring about change; attacking only escalates the frustration."

As she ages and her parents do, too, Shelise describes the adaptation that comes through feeling certain losses. "I often have that feeling of helplessness and powerlessness, like time now has taken away my parents' ability to progress or transform. And that feeling is sadness."

What can be scary about anger is that when it erupts outwardly, it affects those closest to us. This can lead to a lot of shame—and face us toward more separation, worried whether our loved ones could reach a tipping point and stop loving us or leave us. Not to mention, we care about our loved ones. It's frustrating when, in spite of our love and best intentions, anger hurts them.

Amanda shares, "The hardest thing to deal with is the anger. With anxiety, I can deal with the crying and the pressure in my chest and the tingling in my body and the restlessness. But the anger is what affects the people around me. I'm in a stage where if things are just too overwhelming, I have to protect myself or I attack." She adds, "I can get so upset, but more like a dark anger. That's the best way I can describe it. That was hard, and it's still hard."[5]

While it may be a challenge for others to see, sometimes attacks on our loved ones reflect a certain amount of safety in the relationship. Amanda shares, "Growing up, my anger came out toward my adopted parents or my siblings. In close settings, with people I knew well, I would attack. But in other settings, where I didn't necessarily feel comfortable acting out in anger, it would just be shutting down."

Foul frustration is obvious when anger goes outward. But sometimes it's not safe to be expressed and goes inward. Such was the case for Julian. His second adoptive mother was emotionally abusive. Expressing frustration-related anger was definitely unsafe and had to be kept private. "I listened to angry punk rock music all the time," he says.[6]

While Julian is healing his adoption wounds in significant ways, including through writing, he still often finds himself circling through the frustration traffic circle. "I wake up in the morning and I feel this tension in my body, this churning in my belly," he shares. With a great deal of natural intuition, he adds, "You can call it rage. You can call it grief. You can call it a lot of things, because it is a lot of things."

As I picture Julian riding through the traffic circle, I envision him doing what we all do—seeking release by trying out all three roundabout exits. He wrote an essay that shows his mixed feelings keeping his attacking impulses under control and thus offering him power: "My rage is my own. I claim it! Therefore, I no longer need to be driven by it. Do I want to continue to live inside of rage? Do I want to continue to bind myself to people, situations, and institutions that have not earned the privilege of inhabiting my heart? Now I get to choose."[7]

Mixed emotions come with age and maturity. Developmentally, young children don't have the capacity for both/and feeling until ages five to seven—and often longer for the especially sensitive (and I would argue that ALL adoptees are sensitive due to the early trauma we have experienced). Some adults, for that matter, have trouble holding onto two conflicting emotions at once.

Having mixed feelings isn't set in stone, either. Even when we can usually hold two opposing emotions together, we all have moments where this isn't possible. Tony articulates this reality well, "I'm not going to say that anger is dissipated or gone. And I don't think it's healthy for us as adoptees to discuss our issues as, 'Oh, I *was* going through this but now I'm just in this great place in all areas, and I'm just perfect.' That's not genuine and that's not how life works for any of us, whether we're adopted or not."[8]

It's also important to note that anger isn't to be judged as a bad thing. Sometimes anger leads us back around the traffic circle to effecting change, as Kayla says, "I want to proudly say I am an angry adoptee. Anger is a natural reaction to injustice, and you can use the anger to fuel your passion, fuel your research, fuel your advocacy and education."[9]

Suicidal Impulses and Ideation

A statistic widely shared among adoption advocates, including myself, is that adoptees are four times more likely to attempt suicide than nonadoptees.[10] This is of grave concern. Simply knowing this can be incredibly alarming, and it goes without saying that experiencing suicidal ideations is alarming, as it faces us into separation that is final.

For adoptees like me who struggle with suicidal ideation, recognizing that it can be a common response to overwhelming separation diffuses some of its power. Understanding that it's another form of attack—a route out of the traffic circle which goes inward, instead of out—also helps. To be clear, cognitive awareness is useful, but isn't the answer to frustration, because "The brain needs to *feel* its way through the maze of life. Adaptation is an emotional issue—not a cognitive issue,"[11] says Dr. Neufeld. At the same time, I find that when these dynamics are illuminated, insight can ease my alarm as can realizing I'm not alone. As the statistic conveys, many adoptees struggle with suicidal impulses or other forms of self-attack.

Donna says, "I probably have experienced suicidal ideation since around sixth or seventh grade, and I now see it as a part of me that wants to protect me from chronic emotional pain when it gets too severe and too intense."[12] She describes a similar sense of relief in knowing she's not alone. "When I came out of the fog and started connecting with the adoptee community and reading trauma books, there was something helpful in learning that this is more common with adoptees . . . even though it's crushing, too."

Holly reflects on experiencing suicidal impulses in her younger years. "I remember getting really low to the point that I felt so upset that I just needed relief from it,"[13] she says.

Kayla shares, "It's always present, especially as adoptees. It's not that I want to die, it's that I don't want to be alive. It wasn't that I was looking to kill myself, it was that I was looking to escape a place of pain."

Each of these adoptees articulates the issue: looking too close and grieving the inherent frustration and losses that come with adoption's many futilities can seem like an emotional impossibility. Unbeknownst to us, we have so many emotions—all three of the primal emotions of pursuit/defensive detachment, alarm, and frustration spinning around inside of us like a washing machine off balance—which can become so overwhelming that we tend to bury or press down upon (the literal meaning of depression) them ... until it's built up so much that we can no longer contain it. The safest, closest, or only outlet can lead us to taking it out on ourselves.

Tammy shares, "I was so depressed and I began cutting more. I was passing notes to my friends about wanting to die."[14]

Just as I have experienced, insight has helped diffuse some of Donna's alarm around impulses toward self-attack. When she sought reunion as an adult, she discovered that her birth mother, also an adoptee, died by suicide. "It very much felt like, 'Oh, this is just my heritage.'"

It is too bad that she hadn't known this about her birth mother when she was younger, as having this kind of introduction to herself may have helped Donna learn to navigate her own emotional complexities sooner.

This understanding also led Donna to feeling vulnerable emotions. "Learning more about her story and the significant traumas she had experienced gave me perspective for what happened to her. I have a better understanding, and also a lot of grief for her not having resources and support."

When we speak of adoptees and suicide, Katie reminds us that "in adoption, we usually talk about abandonment. But really, it's a survival story."[15]

It's true. We have already survived the worst. Feeling our way through the losses can't hurt us in the same ways again ... and in fact, feeling is our pathway to freedom.

Addiction

Self-attacking impulses are one way to escape the depths of our sadness. Addiction is another way we can run from it. I don't mean to suggest that these are choices we ponder and come to logically. Our flight from feeling is anything but conscious. It's only from an adult perspective, peering through a lens of attachment and brain science, that I and others are able to reflect upon some of our instinctive emotional responses.

David aims to do just that. An adoptee in recovery, he runs an addiction and adoption constellation support group through the Celia Center. He shares, "Adoptees/relinquishees are definitely more prone to struggling with addiction than the general population. A study, 'Substance Use Disorders and Adoption: Findings from a National Sample,' found that 'the proportion of adoptees was 14 times higher than expected in two SUD (Substance Use Disorders) treatment programs. In a national U.S. school survey, adopted adolescents had higher smoking, drinking, and drunk scores than nonadopted adolescents.'"[16]

In recovery himself, David has personal wisdom to share. "When I found substances, I was able to put my worries aside. I established surface connections with people through partying and drinking and taking on a persona that was gregarious, extroverted—happy even. But I was just acting. The real me was a little lost boy, hiding deep down inside me, afraid to come out and to be hurt again—or worse, abandoned."[17] He adds, "That first drink or first hit is like that soothing touch of the mother who never was. It's warm and it's ever-encompassing, and it feels loving. You no longer feel grief. It's been pushed down; or you no longer care about it. Your suffering is temporarily relieved."

Not only did Mar live with grief related to relinquishment, they also feared additional rejection that drugs and alcohol could help them forget. They share, "I was afraid of losing control. But at the same time, I needed something to fill a place in me that I didn't know how to deal with. That had to do with my fears

CHAPTER 5

of being found out for being gender-different—what I ultimately came to see was nonbinary. I was very afraid of being rejected by my adopted family if they were disappointed in me, and I turned to alcohol very young as a way to cope."[18]

Addiction isn't always to drugs and alcohol. There are many addictions that can help us avoid vulnerable, sad feelings. One of mine is an addiction to work, which can appear noble or important, perhaps "professionally sanctioned" and not always identified as a flight from feeling. For Holly, it was food. "Food was an addiction for me, and sugar is definitely a trigger for me, too," she shares. "I was very much using delicious food to fulfill an emotional need."

David reminds us, "Not every adoptee will develop a substance use disorder or even mental health issue, but we are particularly vulnerable to it, and this should be taken into consideration by all involved in the adoption community—the biological parents, the adoptive parents, the agencies involved, and the relinquishees themselves."

We don't have to grieve every single thing that's not working in our lives. But being able to tap into our sadness, disappointments, and losses is how we adapt and grow.

Reflecting on his childhood, David shares, "I wasn't angry. I was deeply wounded, and I was grieving." He adds, "I had to hide it. I didn't even know what I was hiding. I just knew that there was something wrong with me and that it had something to do with my beginnings."

What young David needed was an open invitation for his sorrow, an adult to come alongside his grief and help him wade through it. Parents often want to *effect change* when their children are hurting. But once adoption has occurred, parents, too, have futilities to grieve: that the hurting will always be there. In this way, everyone in adoption is called to *feeling* in order to get out of the frustration loop and move closer toward healing.

CHAPTER 6

The Tentacles of Classism and Racism in Adoption

AS A WHITE PERSON AND SAME-RACE ADOPTEE, I'LL ADMIT THAT I am uncomfortable writing about adoption and racism. But I am also uncomfortable *not* writing about adoption and racism—especially in a book examining many of the struggles of adoption. The reality is that we live in a racist society and interracial adoptees experience racism early and often, including from within their families.

Race has played a significant role in shaping adoption practices in the United States, just as it has shaped other American institutions as well as our cultural belief systems and biases on individual and systemic levels. We all bear a responsibility to look at racism and join the movement to dismantle the ways it's embedded in adoption. Bonita says, "It's important to make clear that the adoption system, like any other system, does not function outside of systems of oppression but instead often works in tandem to perpetuate and exacerbate systems of oppression."[1]

In telling the story of racism in adoption, I aim to do my best as an ally and to keep myself in check so as not to inadvertently resort to my own form of saviorism in sharing the stories of interracial adoptees whose perspectives need to be elevated and heard. The adoptees who trusted me to share their experiences did so with candor, grace, and emotional labor. The honor of listening to and sharing their voices is not lost on me, nor should it be on you. May this chapter lead you to seek out the perspectives of many interracial adoptees, several of whom have books, blogs, podcasts, and other platforms that we include in the Resources section.

HISTORICAL EXAMPLES OF CLASSISM AND RACISM IN ADOPTION

A look at the history of American adoption reveals the many ways adoption is founded upon classism, racism, and colonialism often cloaked in saviorism:

- In the late 1700s, racism was apparent when "adoption became a mode of reproduction intended to metaphorically and literally contain Indian bodies within expanding territorial borders."[2]
- Children's literature published in the 1800s portray dynamics of classism with adoption stories that "provide sentimental accounts of children saved from homelessness"[3] and "often portray birth parents in black-and-white terms, either as morally reprobate and neglectful of their children—often because of drunkenness—or as loving but financially unable to provide for their children."[4]
- In the early 1900s, both racism and classism in adoption can be evidenced in the Child-Rescue Campaign, whose founder carried "fears about immigration, race suicide, and the social threat posed by uncontrolled, undisciplined, un-American youth."[5]
- Between the 1920s and 1950, classism enabled Georgia Tann to steal babies and children from poverty-stricken families, homes deemed as "less-than," to sell them into more affluent and influential families, standardizing adoption and normalizing the movement of children from the poor to the prosperous.[6]

- Between 1958 and 1967, racism and saviorism led the Indian Adoption Project, "a government program designed to save the government money and dismantle tribes—all under the guise of integrating Native children more fully into American society."[7]

Recent Adoptions: Classism and Racism Amplified

Over the past seventy-five or so years, the demand for infants has surged, fueling an adoption industry that has exploited racial and class divisions for profit. (Kelsey and Lori write more about these dynamics in Chapter 11 and Chapter 18, respectively.)

With advancements in reproductive rights in the 1960s and 1970s, such as easily accessible birth control, the domestic supply of infants dropped lower than demand. The adoption industry looked abroad, ushering in an era of intercountry adoption that exploited the balance of power between developing and developed nations. National and international news outlets have been shedding light on some of the nefarious issues with adoption in countries that include Ethiopia,[8] Guatemala,[9] Uganda,[10] Haiti,[11] the Marshall Islands,[12] Chile,[13] China,[14] South Korea,[15] Romania,[16] the DR Congo,[17] Scotland[18] and other parts of the UK,[19] and in the United States with "America's Murky Private-Adoption Industry."[20]

Less newsworthy, but just as problematic, examples of classism and racism in adoption include:

- Failing to address or fund socioeconomic factors and programs that could work toward pregnancy prevention and family preservation;
- Deeming poverty-stricken, "lower-class," or single mothers as "unfit" and shaming or coercing them into giving their children "a better life"—a subtle-but-not-subtle statement about wealth, Whiteness, and in many cases, religion;
- Differentiating adoption fees based on skin color and ethnic background and charging higher fees for White infants,[21]

CHAPTER 6

often related to parental preferences for children who might easily pass as "matching" in terms of skin color;
- Marketing interracial adoption as saviorism, with emphasis on the child assimilating into White culture.

While it may be tempting to dismiss these as historic or outlier situations, when looked at as a whole, we clearly have a problem. Dr. Joyce Pavao says, "We have to stop seeing adoption as a business and an industry or a mission and realize that we are manipulating individuals and families, and we are causing a great deal of loss, trauma, pain, and distrust."[22]

Racism and classism aren't broader adoption issues reserved for newspaper headlines and courtrooms—let alone this specific chapter in this specific book. These issues play out every day in countless, deeply personal ways. Let's turn to the voices of interracial adoptees, who have important things to say.

RACIAL ISOLATION

As previously mentioned, racial isolation is common in interracial adoption—most often with people of color living in Whiteness—and impacts emotional health in significant ways.

Kayla says, "I grew up in a predominantly White environment and lived in racial and cultural isolation. Growing up, I do not remember ever seeing an Asian adult. I'd never seen anyone who looked like me."[23]

Holly experienced racial isolation growing up in Salt Lake City. "The whole neighborhood was White American with big families of kids, where all the siblings looked like each other. I always felt different,"[24] she says.

At many points in life, we all feel different, and certainly many people of color, adopted or not, describe how living in largely White communities can leave them feeling othered. Racial isolation adds more complexity to the adoptee's already fractured sense of identity, when fitting in can be a matter of life or death.

Belonging is Complex

An underlying assumption in adoption is that an adoptee can find belonging in a different family and culture than from which they were born. This can be a challenge, though, when race-based cues abound, leaving many adoptees wondering whether, where, and how they belong. In interracial adoption, racial and cultural mirroring doesn't come from within adoptive families and communities, so it might seem like same-race communities would provide that mirroring and sense of belonging. Yet many interracial adoptees describe that it's complicated.

Lanise shares, "Once I found Black friends in middle school, it was hard. My White friends said things like, 'Oh, so you're going to be Black now?' And based on the stereotypes people draw from, my Blackness always felt like it was on trial—and still is—because of the way I speak or the things I do."[25]

Susan experienced similar complexities as she tried to straddle two racial worlds. "Other kids would say things like, 'So can you talk Indian to me?' 'Do an Indian dance for me.' 'Do you guys still live in teepees?' These things were informing me of *all* that I didn't know about who I was supposed to be, and it was embarrassing not knowing who I was." She adds, "When I got into college and tried to run with the Indigenous crowd there, their perception was that I was actively turning my back on the Native community and trying to 'White my life up' because it was embarrassing to be Indian."[26]

Many people of color talk about code-switching, or changing the way they present themselves in order to conform to different cultures. Shelise says, "For interracial adoptees, it feels intense because people often value you for your racial difference. And yet internally, you're trying so hard to be a part of Whiteness."[27]

As Shelise touches on, living in Whiteness, absorbing cultural and race-based messages about beauty and how to belong can lead to internalized racism that affects a sense of belonging. She further explains: "I really wanted to look like my adoptive family because that's such an easy way to indicate to others that you belong.

Chapter 6

Growing up, I was very unaware of racist microaggressions. I just knew that my appearance was somehow problematic."

Colorblindness Isn't the Answer

Race is a social construct, rather than a biological one. Perhaps this is why many people are tempted to say things like, "Race doesn't matter," or, "I don't see color." Shelise explains how she came to see colorblindness as an issue: "A lot of interracial adoptees talk about this evolution from when they were younger, when people would say, 'Well, I don't see you as Korean. I just see you as my daughter or my friend.' For a time, that feels really good. And then as your own identity and adoptee consciousness develops, you realize, 'Oh, that means they're denying a major piece of me.'"

Kayla adds insight into the problem with ignoring, or pretending not to notice, racial differences: "It felt like whiplash, trying to navigate this White world as a person of color, as an Asian woman. On the one hand, no one would recognize I was different, or acknowledge my race and how that challenged me in the world. But, at the same time, White people would randomly come up to me and say things like, 'I have two grandchildren who came from the same place you did.' They'd bring up my race to connect with me about a race I couldn't even connect to on my own because of the racial isolation."

Another problem with colorblindness is that it's not typically bidirectional. When White people say they don't see color, it is related to unconscious biases and expectations that people of color assimilate into Whiteness.

"The forced assimilation that I experienced was an added layer of trauma," says Diego. Coming from Colombia at age four or five, he already spoke the language of his people when he came to the United States. "My language was taken away," he shares. "I didn't know that it was being taken away. It was just an experiential thing that happened. And the trauma that got layered on was the reminder, 'To fit in here, you don't get to speak your language.'"[28]

Racism and the Family

People of color who aren't White-passing are often subjected to racism in predominantly White countries and communities. In same-race families of color, there is typically built-in, second-nature support for children around handling racism on emotional, practical, and life-saving levels. This doesn't always exist in interracial adoptive families with parents who may not know what they don't know—making it difficult to effectively guide adopted children or keep their own racism from causing additional isolation and hurt.

As an example, when Shelise experienced racial name-calling at school, she didn't feel she could go to her parents for support. "If my dad was using the N-word, why would they think the word 'Chinkmaster' is bad?"

Susan grew up very much aware of her adoptive father's racism. "By the time I was five years of age, I knew every ethnic slur for every European group. When I was a teenager, I realized if he's calling them names, I know he's calling Native Americans names."

Similarly, Tony says, "When I went over to my birth grandmother's house, there were a lot of instances where she questioned the validity of Mary and Janet, my two adoptive moms as parents, where she would say, 'Those White people don't know how to parent you.'"[29]

Racism isn't always so blatant. Sometimes uninformed gestures can hurt as much as outright racist remarks. Kayla shares, "My adoptive mom is very much into scrapbooking. She's great at it. She made a scrapbook for me, but the stickers in the scrapbook portrayed Japanese culture. I'm from China, and she didn't know the difference. Another time, she gave me a gift basket of snacks, knowing I love gift baskets. But they were ninety-percent Korean snacks so she didn't even get it right there."

Such racist attitudes and unconscious behaviors can wound to the quick—leading to more pursuit and desperation to try to belong, more alarm, and more frustration. Ultimately this boils down to more isolation and separation when not feeling fully supported, seen, known, and accepted.

LACK OF VALIDATION AND SUPPORT

Sometimes racism that comes from outside immediate family relationships calls for corrections or drastic measures to protect adoptees. Children need to know that their parents are in their corner—no matter what. When this doesn't happen, more unbearable separation can ensue. Lanise shares an email she received from her adoptive grandmother when she was eighteen, which read, "'Your mom brought you into her family and you are unworthy and undeserving of this.'" Unfortunately, Lanise didn't feel supported by her mom in the ways that she needed. "At the time, my mom brushed it off. She said, 'Oh, she loves you.' It was doubly traumatizing because my mom did not stand up for me."

No child should have to protect themselves from their family, or feel they are completely alone in navigating the complexities of racism. Shelise sums this up: "It's weird to have to protect yourself from your own family."

Teachers should be a source of protection, too, but sometimes aren't, as Shelise experienced. "When the boys started calling me 'Chinkmaster' in fifth and sixth grade, I told the teacher and received a response wrapped in a 'sticks and stones may break my bones, but words will never hurt you' message," she says. "In reflection, I really needed somebody to acknowledge that actually, that does mean something."

As an adult, Lanise has had some hard conversations with her mom in an effort to help her understand, once telling her, "You have never protected me. You've never protected me from your family or guarded me from this world." Lanise believes this is because her mother "never had to face the hardships that I have to. She's never had to question her identity, have her identity on trial, never had to go into circles where she is the minority and thrive in those circles. It's one thing to go to another country and try to colonize it. It's another thing to go to schools, churches, group meetings, and other institutions and be the minority in every single situation that you're in. My mom has never felt that."

Exacerbated Differences
It's important to know that race and cultural differences, especially when layered on top of racial isolation, influence self-esteem and self-worth—already so precarious for adoptees. As Lanise shares, "Those of us who are intercountry, interracial adoptees are at a deficit. We have to catch up to cultures. We have to catch up to language. We have to catch up to just the nuances that other people are born into. And then it becomes increasingly complex if we're a different hue than our parents." She adds, "Coming into an English-speaking culture, I always felt that I was dumb. However, I was marked immediately as a gifted child. I was in all of these advanced placement classes, but I never felt intelligent."

"I wasn't good academically, so I didn't fit the stereotypical Asian narrative," says Lily. "I wasn't really succeeding at anything ever. I was very different and I remember feeling left out all the time."[30]

The Dangers of the Rescue Narrative
Self-esteem issues may also stem from unintentional messages that come with the rescue narrative that's so common in adoption. Susan explains: "Any time you decide you're going to save a child, that child gets put another rung down the ladder. Not only were they defective enough to be saved, but they came from a group of people defective enough to be saved from."

She adds, "Due to the white supremacy in transracial adoption, we still have this idea that children of color and in Third World countries are not adequately parented. Americans can come in and feel good about themselves by making sure that these children have a good upbringing, however you want to define that. And the more they talk about how the child has nice clothes and goes to good schools, they're diminishing everything that child came from."

Another problem with the rescue narrative is that it can lead adoptive parents toward "wanting to be the 'good guys' who won't abandon their child," says Katie. "So that's what they say: 'We will never abandon you.' And that really is a double-edged sword for those of us who hold *all* parents close to our heart, even if we don't ever know them, because they're basically saying, 'We will never abandon you like your birth parents did.'"[31]

There's inherent judgment in the rescue narrative that doesn't honor birth parents, birth cultures, and in turn, adoptees.

THE GRAY AREA: PRIVILEGE

Making matters more complex (as if adoption wasn't complex enough!), in certain cases there may be some reality behind the rescue narrative. Many children adopted through foster care do, indeed, feel rescued, and adoptees in other situations can feel this way too. For example, because she'd been labeled as delayed and disabled, Marci was considered "hard-to-place." Her adoption took several years and included a financial incentive. She shares, "Adoptees are often told we've been rescued from foster care and should feel indebted because our parents took us in. It's not healthy to grow up with that gratefulness narrative. But for adoptees with disabilities, there was no waiting list, there was no price tag. It makes it harder for us to break through that problematic messaging because it actually is true. Adoption is a long shot for us."[32]

Other adoptees have learned to hold multiple conflicting emotions and perspectives around "rescue." On one hand, it's a judgment against one's roots, and thus also a judgment against an adoptee's first attachments and whole self. On the other hand, adoption into higher classes may result in certain privileges when in close proximity to Whiteness.

Astrid says, "It's been clear to me my entire life that I came from a certain class. I was born into one and I was adopted into another. And I don't think I ever took that for granted in my entire life."[33]

"I have received benefits from my adoption. As adoptees, we need to acknowledge that," says Susan. "The thing is, though, we paid a high price for those benefits."

Supporting Interracial Adoptees

When reunion is both possible *and adoptee-led*, adoptive parents should provide ample support to meet and build relationships with birth parents—even in closed, intercountry adoptions. "I would say that having the opportunity to experience reunion helped to greatly heal my wounds from adoption," shares Carmen. "Before reunion, I didn't feel whole, like something was missing."[34] Reunion can be difficult in intercountry adoptions, where records may have been fabricated, lost, or swapped, or parents may be unknown or deceased. But easy access to DNA testing and our increasingly interconnected world are making reunion—with birth parents and other birth family members—more feasible. Holly dreams of system-wide support to better facilitate such connections: "Especially with intercountry adoption, I wish we had one central place where all countries could upload information, where all families who have lost a child can search, and where adoptees could submit their DNA."

Whether or not reunion is possible, parents can support interracial adoptees through continual honoring of their cultures. When supported with intention, honoring helps lead to a healthy and whole sense of identity. Carmen says, "My identity as an adoptee from Brazil has changed in that I've learned more about the culture and am figuring out how to engage with different aspects of it, such as music, films, politics, and learning Portuguese."

Cultural knowledge requires substance. "When I was in my thirties, I joined the Indian community here and learned how to do bead work," Susan says. "It felt like I was being inauthentic because I was learning the cultural traditions without the depth. Becoming Indigenous is not like becoming Lutheran."

For this reason, Susan advises, "If you're going to adopt a kid from a different ethnicity, you need to give that child a community—one that is theirs, which you can share as a parent and participate in, while remembering that it's not your community." She advises, "Raise that child and provide that child resources and care that they may not have received there. But take them back to that community regularly so the community can welcome them home and remember who they are. That is the adoptive parents' responsibility."

This counsel is important, because keeping adoptees connected to their first communities is a means of creating the safe adult attachments, mirroring, and cultural continuity that children of color need—including support on matters from hair care to police safety to race-based violence. Lanise says, "Interracial adoptions are so precarious, because how does a White person prepare a Black person to exist in this environment right now? You can't. How can you prepare them for what is ahead? You cannot. And it's essential that they're prepared."

Awareness of racial issues is a must, of course, and this includes a willingness to consider ways racism exists on individual levels, too. "I recognize that my adoptive parents love me to the best of their ability. However, they can only love me to the extent of their white supremacy," says Kayla.

Adoptees of color do not get to opt out of the impact the construct of race has in their lives, so White parents shouldn't opt out, either. "My parents are probably thinking, 'Why do you talk about race all the time?' They aren't pausing to reflect and say, 'Shelise must be making some really difficult decisions about race and racism in her life by knowing us.' They aren't considering the sacrifices I'm making just to be in a relationship with them and not feel abandoned."

These are just some of the important ways to support interracial adoptees when it comes to the long tentacles of classism and racism. Many interracial adoptees are active in adoption spaces, speaking out and offering education and resources, including Patrick Samuel Yung Armstrong, Rebecca Carroll, Astrid Castro, Nicole Chung, Torie DiMartile, April Dinwoodie, Aselefech Evans, Shannon Gibney, Katie Gagel, Shelise Gieseke, Melissa Guida-Richards, Susan Devan Harness, Jade Henness, Kevin Hoffman, Tony Hynes, JaeRan Kim, Jia Sun Lee, Lynelle Long, Amanda Medina, Harrison Mooney, Stephanie Oyler, Rhonda Roorda, Lanise Antoine Shelley, Cameron Lee Small, Ferera Swan, and Angela Tucker, to name a few and risk leaving out many.

More suggestions for supporting interracial adoptees are shared in Chapter 21, Supporting Adoptee Maturation. Next, we'll walk around another systemic issue: the entwining of religion and adoption.

CHAPTER 7

Religion's Pain Points for Adoptees

THERE IS A LOT THAT CAN BE WRITTEN ABOUT RELIGION AND adoption. Much has already been written—with examples ranging from the Judeo-Christian story of Moses, the first abandoned baby mentioned in the Bible and Torah (Exodus 2), who ultimately saves the Hebrew people, to more recent works like Kathryn Joyce's *The Child Catchers*,[1] and adoptee-scholar Erin M. Heim's *Adoption in Galatians and Romans*.[2] I'd add to this short and noncomprehensive list my spiritual memoir, *Searching for Mom*,[3] which shares my personal journey as it relates to mothers and mothering, being an adoptee, and coming to hear the voice of God, which had been drowned out for the first forty or so years of my life—largely due to my experiences of relinquishment and adoption.

As a young adoptee, I sensed rejection everywhere. Even though I had little information about my adoption to go on, I felt that my first mother had rejected me. I must not have been good enough to keep, I reasoned, and felt sure that I'd be rejected by my adoptive family, too; especially if I didn't behave as they expected, failed to please others around me, or dared to reveal my true and full self.

Whenever adoption came up in my adoptive parents' circles, it seemed to reinforce the sense of rejection I felt. A lot of this took place (and often still does) in Christian spaces, where:

- Christians often gush about the "beautiful" story of adoption. My losses, and more nuanced experience of adoption—even with loving and devoted parents—remained unseen.
- Friends would admire my parents for their selflessness, unaware of the implication, which I believed, that I was broken and required saving.
- I'd bristle whenever talk of adoption came up, inevitably feeling like a sinner as I pretended to be grateful, which I'd surmised as the only acceptable response.
- My first parents seemed villainized for engaging in premarital sex. As their by-product and someone who, like most people, cared about my family origins, I took on that shame.
- People remarked that we're all adopted by God, dismissing the significant loss and trauma inherent in adoption.
- The mission work of "rescuing children" and "orphans" was regularly presented to the congregation, without eyes to see, understand, acknowledge, or address the widespread classism, racism, saviorism, and history of corruption in the profit-making adoption industry that has preyed upon both vulnerable families and hopeful and well-meaning prospective parents.
- Adoption was presented as a holy, win/win alternative to unplanned pregnancy and abortion. A heavy focus was placed on the suffering of fetuses, without interest in hearing about or supporting adoptees who can experience lifelong, serious effects of separation trauma such as anxiety, depression, addiction, and suicidal ideation.
- The importance of family preservation is touted when it comes to divorce, and yet this value often gets forgotten in the realm of adoption.

- Adult adoptees who speak up or search for their first mothers and/or cultures can be treated in unholy ways: shunned, called "spiritually lost," or labeled "ungrateful."
- Adoptive and foster parents can be overheard complaining about their parenting challenges, while others respond with sympathy and reminders that they are doing "God's work."
- Adoptive parents often lament over why their adult adopted children haven't found Jesus, without reflection on the ways the church and prevalent approaches to adoptive/foster parenting can push adoptees out of the Christian message and silence them, making these spaces and thus God, feel unsafe.
- Many Christian authors and influencers use their adopted children for social media likes, affirmations, and a performative commitment to multiculturalism. Combined with the reality that many turn to adoption to solve fertility issues, adoptees are sent overt and covert messages that they are tools to serve our parents' needs. What's more, these influencers inspire others to pursue faith-based adoptions based on misinformation, so that nearly every Christian space has a large percentage of adoptive parents and their friends pursuing adoption for questionable reasons and treating adoptees as described above.

Because so much of this adoption-related wounding happened in "God's house" when I was younger, it wasn't a big leap to believe God had rejected me, too. Maybe God was mad at me—for not being good enough, grateful enough, not measuring up, not being perfect, not having enough faith to conquer my confusing emotions or the behaviors that stemmed from my deep attachment wounds. Surely I was the problem, my shame-saturated self believed.

It wasn't until later in life that I learned how flawed these beliefs and actions were. Such beliefs muffled the voice of God, who had other things to say. In my faith tradition, such words include: "I will not forget you . . . I formed you in the womb" (Isaiah 44:21, 24). And, "Not a man, not a mouse, slips through the cracks" (Psalm 36:6). Also, "We're not keeping secrets; we're telling them. We're not hiding things; we're bringing everything out into the open" (Luke 8:17).

I'm not alone in feeling confusion and pain over the ways religion and adoption are often entangled to the detriment of adoptees. Now that you've heard some of my story, let's listen to other adoptees share their experiences.

DOES GOD ORDAIN ADOPTION?

Bonita felt heartache over messages she received in her family's Mennonite church. "Adoption was often talked about—at least with strangers—as a miracle from God. It is difficult to fully articulate the layers of this inference but as a child what I felt was that my separation from my biological family was something God ordained. These messages were painful and violent—and *are* painful and violent." Just as I'd inferred certain messages as far as religion and adoption went, Bonita did, too. She says, "While I want to be clear that no one explicitly told me these things, I also would argue that no one had to. I was meaning-making all the time."[4]

Cynthia, who was raised Jewish, also grew up with discomfort—and a good deal of worry—around the intertwining of adoption and religion. "The God in the Old Testament is not particularly kind. To me, he's a vengeful and authoritative God, and I grew up questioning what role he played in my adoption. Was this his plan?"[5] On her blog, Cynthia reflects further, as related to Moses' story: "On the day I became a Jewish adult, I exulted a God who left an adoptee abandoned, excluded, and alone, a perpetual outsider, torn away from his Egyptian family and kept from his Jewish one, all because he showed doubt. If that can happen to

Moses, the greatest prophet in Jewish history, then what hope was there for me?"[6]

Rich also grew up wondering what was and wasn't God-ordained as it related to his adoption. "I had to reconcile my story with my faith. If the Judeo-Christian God I had been raised to believe in loved me, how could He allow me to live in so much pain, disconnectedness, and insecurity?" Rich's perspective has since evolved, and he's found healing and strength through embracing a spiritual framework. He shares, "Though friends, family members, and government officials may not 'get it,' Jesus understands the impact of being forsaken, and Hebrew and Christian scriptures are steeped in the importance of bloodline and heritage."[7]

RELIGION CONTRIBUTING TO DIVIDED LOYALTIES

Like many adoptees, Kayla grew up absorbing "God-ordained" messaging in the conservative Christian home in which she was raised, often told things like, "It's the Lord's will. You were meant for your family from the very beginning." This is a message adoptees commonly hear, but it can lead to shame and split loyalty in ways like Kayla describes: "I internalized this narrative, that this was always meant to be, telling me I wasn't worthy of being with my birth mother or my birth father."[8]

Whether through an open or closed adoption, this is fact: adoptees have at least two sets of parents. It's important for parents—whether or not they believe in the biblical call to "honor your parents"—to realize that adoptees need space to honor *both* sets of parents, and to feel as though their parents honor the other set, too.

Mar was raised Jewish, but always knew their birth mother was Catholic. Though Mar was drawn to both religions, at times it was a challenge to reconcile the religious differences. They share, "So much of what I was learning about religion made Catholicism and Judaism obviously mutually exclusive. If I chose Jesus to be my Lord and Savior, I would be going to heaven . . . and my adoptive family would *not* be going to heaven. The idea that I had to choose between heaven or being separated from my immediate family in the afterlife was too much for me to bear. I was devastated by that."[9] Knowing what we do about the effects of facing separation, it's understandable to consider how alarming this would have been for Mar.

Mar says, "I never had an encounter with someone who said, 'You don't belong to God,' but learning about the Holocaust was confusing because I was afraid I came from Jew-haters." What's more, Mar says, "My adoptive mom kept emphasizing that I was not Jewish by birth. The worst part was when she said to me, 'If the Nazis come to the door, I know they won't take you because I'll be able to tell them that you're Gentile.' She meant it as a comfort. But I heard it as, 'When the Nazis come, they'll take you because you're one of them.'"

Something Mar's family did well was to make room for Mar to integrate both religions—sending them to Catholic school, for example. Later in Mar's life, their mom sang in multi-faith congregations, modeling an "openness around worship and theology that these could coexist without being mutually exclusive," Mar shares. "My parents wanted me to be able to choose what faith I wanted or how much I wanted to be involved in the Jewish community. They didn't want me to be forced into religion. They wanted to give me a chance to choose."

Now that they are an adult, Mar integrates both religions into their life. "It remains complicated for me how I relate to both religions, but they're both very important to me." They add, "There's something really beautiful about being an outsider among Catholics and an outsider among Jews. Living with contradictions is a meaningful part of spiritual life."

THE IMPACT OF RELIGIOUS ADOPTION MESSAGING ON MENTAL HEALTH

Many children are told that they are blessings to their parents, but adoptees seem to hear this much more often than the nonadopted.

Chapter 7

Growing up, Kayla heard this a lot. "Adoption was seen as a gift. *I* was seen as a gift," she says. Perhaps because the adoption process can be so emotionally and logistically trying for adoptive parents, when an adoptee has finally joined their family, the payoff may very well feel like an otherworldly reward. While much religious messaging revolves around giving thanks and seeing the blessings in one's life, when applied so vocally to adopted children, it can reinforce a core belief that adoptees are merely tools to meet our adoptive parents' wishes and needs. In addition, this messaging can wreak havoc on our inner lives, driving us to try to become an idealized image of "the perfect gift" in many of the ways covered in Chapter 3; such as perfectionism and people-pleasing which don't ultimately serve our healthy development.

Tragically, Kayla's experiences of religion repeatedly caused her a great deal of pain. Worse, religious beliefs stood in the way of supporting Kayla with important mental health support she desperately needed during adolescence. "I was definitely suicidal in middle school which peaked at the end of high school. I finally got the courage to ask my mom to see a therapist, and she said, 'God's your therapist. Go pray to him.'" Once in college, Kayla sought a therapist on her own, and as an adult, has created for herself a large emotional support network where there's room for "hours of talking and crying and holding space for my anxiety." Years later, she tried letting her mom know how hurtful it was not to have received therapeutic support. "She told me, 'Because we knew your religious views, your father and I didn't feel comfortable financially supporting you to see a therapist who wasn't Christian.' That reinforced to me that even though my life was at risk for dying by suicide, my life did not have as much value to my adoptive parents because I wasn't Christian." That moment, she says, "really hurt, because as an adoptee, I was already questioning my worth and value."

As previously covered, adoptees can be prone to feeling isolated, confused, anxious, depressed, and misunderstood. Religion should not sacrifice adoptee mental health in order to uphold what has become an idol of adoption. For adoptees growing up in religious homes, they need spaces where they are not silenced, used, and spiritually bypassed. They need space for their losses within their families and faith communities to better support their mental and spiritual health.

Religion, Race, and Adoption

As covered in the last chapter, adoption and racism often go hand in hand, and religion can be a destructive force in that already corrosive mix.

Bonita reflects on inferences she made as a child in her White Mennonite church: "As a kid, I was hearing the following implied and dangerous messages: Black people are people only if White Mennonites think they are: (1) worthy of salvation; and (2) have experienced a physical disaster that can be eased through Mennonite fiscal support."

The meanings Bonita made in church were "subtly providing me with an analysis of who 'belonged' in church and who did not, and they were also impacting how I began to know 'God.' I use 'God' in quotes because as I got older, I began to identify that this 'God' wasn't 'God' at all, but an idol of white nationalism, white supremacy, and patriarchy."

For Cynthia, a lack of racial representation impacted her sense of belonging, too. "I was the only non-White person in my synagogue, and it added a layer of otherness to the otherness that adoptees already tend to feel." Cynthia continues, "I already had the racial otherness from my family, but then to have it also from my spiritual community was really challenging."

In both Bonita's and Cynthia's cases, the hurt they experienced related to religion, race, and adoption has driven them to make important contributions and needed headway, both personally and professionally. Bonita says, "The glaring lack of Black representation in leadership positions in my insular Mennonite community—combined with the almost imposed posture of gratitude that 'nice White Mennonites' would reinforce with comments like, 'Aren't you so glad you were wanted?'—encouraged me to begin (and propelled me on) my own journey of developing critical analyses." As an adoptive parent, too, Cynthia regularly publishes her writing which powerfully weaves together her experiences as an intercountry adoptee from Korea with her experiences raising two sons, also adopted from Korea. (For more on Cynthia's thoughts as an adoptive parent, see Chapter 18.)

WHEN RELIGIOUS BELIEFS INFLUENCE ADOPTION OUTCOMES

Religion can be a driving factor in adoption from the very beginning of an unwanted pregnancy. Evangelicals who oppose abortion often suggest to "Just adopt," as if it's a simplistic and straightforward pro-life alternative. (At this point in this book, politics and personal beliefs aside, hopefully by now we can all agree that adoption is anything *but* simple.) To this day, Christian churches actively encourage adoption, and a large number of adoption agencies are faith-based.

Diego says, "I look at religion as one of the biggest systemic problems that contribute to why biological parents—birth mothers in particular—find themselves having to relinquish because religion has placed a stigma on being an 'unwed mother' or to just be somebody who has had sex outside of a marriage." He adds, "There's no support. It's just 'We will help you find somebody else to raise your child while you somehow cleanse yourself of your sin.'"[10] Kelsey shares more about this dynamic as it relates to birth parents in Chapter 9.

For adoptees, religious beliefs—or imagined beliefs based on widely communicated religious convictions—can continue to influence adoption journeys later in life. Mar had been raised with assurances by their adoptive mum that when Mar turned eighteen, they would be able to meet their birth mother. "And then I started to realize I was gay. And I started to notice I had gender differences, though I didn't know how to describe them at the time," they share. "But the reason I did not search when I turned eighteen is I was afraid my Catholic birth parents might be homophobic." Eventually Mar overcame this deep worry. While reunion always comes with complexity, they ultimately discovered birth parents who accepted their sexual and gender identity.

Awakening to Corruption

Beyond looking at how religion can influence adoption, it's important to wake up to the corruption that can exist in adoption—too easily masked and dismissed when it's touted in God's name. While the point of this chapter is not to delve into the history of corruption in adoption, which I wrote about in the previous chapter, it's important to know how religious systems have historically preyed upon the vulnerable through adoption. This includes the Baby Scoop Era, largely driven by a patriarchal and religious culture, and the booming intercountry adoption industry that began in war-devastated Korea in the 1950s, led by Christian adoption evangelists like Harry and Bertha Holt who turned saving children and converting them to Christianity into large-scale missions.[11]

Since the early 2000s, American evangelical churches have been rallying around a perceived "orphan crisis," even though our western definition of orphan differs from that of other cultures and many of these children have at least one family member caring for them. Poverty-stricken parents unable to read English are often lied to or otherwise manipulated into relinquishing their children, thinking they're temporarily sending them away for food or education rather than signing away permanent rights to their children. Adoptive parents may also be lied to through falsified papers and stories that capitalize on their idealism to help vulnerable children, their eagerness to build a family, and their deep pockets and/or fundraising savvy as they spend tens of thousands of dollars to adopt. Lori shares more about this in Chapter 18.

While not every adoption begins with corruption, our westernized, religious view has excused human-rights abuses in order to promote a message of saviorism around adoption. As Alice Stephens and I wrote in a book review, "The result? Christians can come across as uncaring, hypocritical, and self-serving—not exactly persuasive traits of conversion. What's more, many adoptees extend our experiences and feelings of abandonment to our spiritual understanding, deciding that if there is a God, he's a God who abandons. Or, he's a callous God who doesn't ache alongside us over the injustice of one of the most sacred of bonds—between mother and child—being torn apart."[12]

HONESTY AND REPENTANCE AS A PATHWAY TO REFORM

Christians speak often about repentance. As a Christian-identifying adoptee, my soul knows right from wrong, and it hurts that the Christian education that helped nourish that soul still fails when it comes to the practice of repentance in adoption.

It's not for any of us to judge what and when and how we repent to God—or that we repent at all if religion is not something we embrace. Regardless, we should all care about how we relate to one another. Do we know how to give a heartfelt "I'm sorry?" Are we willing to set aside our egos, ideals, and religious fervor to show the people we've wronged through adoption that we empathize and care? Do we know how to change course when our systems oppress and marginalize? Can we recognize our complicity in gushing over the "beautiful story of adoption" and speaking with authority about God's will (that just so happens to repeatedly favor affluent White couples)?

Yes, adoption can result in some truly heartwarming stories. Love abounds, even from ashes—I join many others in the adoption constellation in being proof of that. But are we willing to talk honestly about the devastation and ruin, too, and then work to turn the corruption around?

Looking at the ills of adoption requires rethinking long-held beliefs. This will be difficult, especially when it comes to a long perception of adoption as nothing less than holy. Repenting requires both refining and expanding our views of pro-life. Adoption is not a clean pro-life solution to abortion if it's founded upon coercion, manipulation, deceit, marginalization, patriarchy, classism, racism, colonialism, and commercialization. And bringing adopted children to God—as is often the stated or implied goal—does not erase the complicity that comes from an unwillingness to see the corruption of adoption.

While the need for adoption will never go away, the adoption industry demands reform to save families from being unnecessarily torn apart and children from growing up with the long-lasting wounds of separation trauma. Making headway will not be easy because it involves tackling systemic societal ills such as poverty, youth or accidental pregnancy, child neglect, and more—each complex matters with no simple solutions, making it hard to know where to begin.

Bonita poses some important questions as a starting point: "What if our adoptive parents begin attending churches that are committed to intercultural competence? Could that impact the kinds of messaging adoptive children might hear?" she asks. "What if churches outside of the adoption constellation were also doing the work of unpacking the entwining of adoption and religion? Could it model to the community that they take seriously that beautiful Audre Lorde idea that our liberation is tied up with each other's? I suspect it might."

As always, honest acknowledgment and a sincere apology are a good starting place for the seeds of change: *I'm sorry. What happened wasn't right, and I'm committed to doing better.*

WE CAN DO BETTER!

If you're reading this feeling remorse or worry—perhaps fretting over things you've said that may have inadvertently hurt other adoption constellation members in the past, or wondering whether you've unknowingly contributed to some of the abuses of religion and adoption—thank you for your caring. It offers a solid starting point for doing better. Reform is necessary and includes a willingness to let go of previously held beliefs to make space for new ones. I love the way Bonita puts it: "I'm not saying everyone who says these messages is a horrible person. Not at all. What I am saying is that it would be important for those of us working toward reform to think seriously about what these messages can reveal, and work together to develop sustainable strategies that address both root inequities and future possibilities."

I'm confident that if we each start with a commitment to listen and communicate from a place of deep empathy, the answers will become clear and we will indeed find language, policies, structures, and adoption practices that are ethical and more sensitive, honoring, and inclusive.

Now that we've walked around adoptees' common struggles, next, let's listen to the experiences of birth parents.

PART II

BIRTH PARENTS UNFILTERED

WELCOME TO THE SECOND SECTION OF *ADOPTION UNFILTERED*, written by Kelsey Vander Vliet Ranyard.

Our society loves to hear two stories about birth parents: first, the story of our "selfless" choice and second, the reunion story that occurs around twenty-five years later. No one seems to believe that the time in between matters, but they are wrong. The birth parent experience is a crucial story to be told, no matter how our world tries to write us out of the narrative. How we exist, cope, grieve, find joy, and heal, are all important stories. Culturally, adoptive parents have been sharing their stories for decades. Recently, more and more adoptees are changing the narrative. Some birth parents are speaking up, but we have more headway to make. It's intimidating to speak up about our experience. We know that there is so much at stake if we say the "wrong" thing. Adoptive parents have the power to close off contact, and adoptees in reunion could become spooked by us either coming on too strong or not strong enough.

Both the birth mother and birth father face scrutiny but often the birth mother bears the brunt of critical remarks, such as, *no mother in their right mind would give their baby away.* It's a curious decision—to relinquish one's child for adoption.

Part II

Whether a choice made through her own free will or without any choice in the matter at all, placing a child for adoption is a devastating one. From the outside looking in, it may be complicated to understand why or how a mother could choose adoption for their child. For birth mothers attempting to understand their own decisions, it's often no less complicated. However, one thing is for certain: like any person, birth mothers have a burning desire to be loved and understood. There are barriers to reaching acceptance of our decisions within our communities and even our families. Sometimes these barriers are simply us, standing in our own way. Whatever the obstacles are, how do we give birth mothers the embrace they need and deserve? I hope to cover that within Part II.

One of the most important conclusions I reached on this writing journey was this: I am not just a birth mother. There is so much more to me. Birth parents often wonder, *If I hadn't given them my baby, would the adoptive parents still care about me as a person?* We all want to be valued without conditions, and it's not surprising that we struggle finding self-worth after relinquishing our beloved children. Birth mothers don't always feel they have a voice or a listening ear. I hope that as you read through these chapters, you are mindful of the strength they carry in telling their stories.

For these chapters, I incorporated snippets of my own experience as a birth mother in a domestic open adoption, but I also interviewed eighteen different birth mothers, all from varying demographics representing a wide range of adoption experiences. None of these birth mothers are the same in any way, except that they all relinquished a child for adoption. All eighteen of them used their voices courageously and gave their own unfiltered take on what it's like to be a birth mother and how it feels to sign away parental rights to their own flesh and blood. And even more challenging, they spoke candidly about what it feels like to live with this decision for the rest of their lives and how they have sought healing as their post-placement lives develop. While these chapters speak from the perspective of domestic adoption, many of the emotions related to relinquishment would be similar for intercountry adoptions, where there may be even less post-placement support and openness is less likely.

As you read Part II, I hope you see these birth parents as the humans they are. Moving beyond the simplicity of *what* a "birth mother" is, I hope you discover all the complexities of *who* these women are. There are no rainbows and butterflies here, but there is wisdom and power and most of all, love and perseverance for a better future in adoption.

Chapter 8

Scarcity

Unbiased Information and Post-Placement Support

Before birth mothers get the chance to ask for help they ask for mercy. On a hot day in September, I sat on the cold tile floor of the bathroom in my parents' house, disbelieving eyes fixated on a positive pregnancy test. *This can't be happening to me* was the only thought racing through my head. My hands, which once held dreams and ambitions, were now white and ghostlike from their stiff grip on a little plastic stick that held a fate I didn't ask for. The day before, I'd been making plans for an escape from my hometown to the West Coast wondering what freedom would feel like. But now, a much different scenario was in play, and suddenly, freedom had been whisked away before I could even taste it. An unexpected pregnancy is not always devastating, but for many it is exactly that. Vulnerable, expectant mothers who weren't planning to become pregnant face similar circumstances every day. Nothing would ever be the same.

Not every birth mother starts this journey not wanting to be pregnant, however. Some may rejoice seeing a positive pregnancy test; the signal of a promising upturn in their life, a purpose they had been searching for. Perhaps the prospect of motherhood was unexpected but not necessarily unwelcome. Nevertheless, the fleeting forty weeks of pregnancy may not prove enough for this expectant mother to transition her life, especially if she has little support or stability. With each heavy reality pushing against her—financial, housing, lack of support from a partner or family, substance use disorder, or mental illness—her plans begin to crack. Unfortunately, there are few safety nets available and when she comes up short she begins to look for outside support, maybe even a permanent alternative. She may discover she isn't the only one coming up short. There is a scarcity of real help for expectant mothers considering adoption.

HIGH STAKES: COMPETING FOR THE CALL

For whatever reason an expectant mom begins to consider adoption for her child, most turn to the same place for answers: the Internet. In fact, even her loved ones are likely to turn to the Internet, despite holding the belief that the Internet is the least trustworthy source for adoption information.[1] From the moment someone searches for adoption information, the advertisements and search algorithms guide her like an unseen current. The Internet is shark-infested waters for women considering adoption, and pregnant moms are without a boat. With adoption numbers sinking dramatically in recent years and a free-market framework with little regulation and virtually nonexistent enforcement, expectant mothers considering adoption are easy prey for unscrupulous adoption professionals. Trustworthy adoption professionals exist, but they aren't typically the ones showing up in search results because those who offer the best services cannot afford to play the search game. The more one pays for prominence in Google advertisements, the more likely they are to appear at the top of search results, drawing the searcher to the advertiser's lair and away from accurate and nonpredatory information, helpful services, legal representation, and more. As most expectant mothers turn to the Internet for adoption information, it becomes a territorial warzone with adoption entities fighting for coveted calls from women in crisis and seeking help.

Chapter 8

Expectant mothers just beginning to explore adoption are at the mercy of their geographic location and what professionals pay to appear in the Google search. The road ahead is typically unknown to her, so she must rely solely on what search engines deliver. An expectant mom who searches "pregnant need adoption help" in Boston may get very different results than if she were in Los Angeles. But even more frightening, she could get the very same results.

Adoption in the United States is unique in that states lack the oversight, and apparently the spine, to prevent unlicensed individuals and entities from opportunistically meddling in the adoption field (and let's be clear; if an unlicensed entity is preying on expectant moms, you can bet it is also preying on people eager to adopt a baby). Currently, twenty-eight states prohibit unlicensed professionals from providing adoption facilitation services, but few states have taken action to enforce these laws. Unlicensed adoption brokers show up on the first page of search results in nearly every state. These brokers have no qualifications: no educational prerequisites, no license to practice, no social work or legal certifications, nor are they subject to oversight, regulation, or discipline by any governing authority. In other words, there is no accountability for bad actors who practice out-of-bounds. Further, unlicensed brokers appear at the top of every search results page because, simply put, they can afford to. Unlicensed brokers have few overhead costs, provide no meaningful services, and charge prospective adoptive parents anywhere from $8,000 to $30,000 per match. If an expectant mother in Dallas finds a deceptive ad from a broker that says, "adoption agency in Texas" or "financial assistance for birth mothers," she clicks, trusting that she'll find a licensed adoption agency in Texas. To her dismay, she may later discover that the entity served to her by the Internet was *not* a licensed agency or attorney after all. She finds this out only *after* her signed adoption consents have become irrevocable, having gone through the entire process without a qualified professional. This can be devastating, realizing that she could have been receiving false adoption information, fraudulent legal advice, and in the worst cases, choosing a family that viewed the adoption as transactional and the birth mother as dispensable.

Unfortunately, the adoption field is not split into easily identifiable good guys and bad guys, into simple categories of licensed and unlicensed professionals. There are also dangers in working with some licensed adoption professionals. Expectant mothers could also click on an advertisement from a large, corporate-licensed adoption agency in a different region of the country that is unable to meet her face-to-face or offer her local services or referrals. There are licensed professionals who act in bad faith without many consequences, as well, making it difficult to shine a light on a specific group of culprits. In the United States' current landscape, there are no federal laws governing domestic adoption, but rather fifty sets of state laws. An unregulated adoption field with a lack of oversight and enforcement creates an environment filled with inconsistency and instability which is unlikely to offer safeguards for already vulnerable expectant mothers. A system that fails to serve mothers also fails to serve their children.

Nonexistent Neutral Support

Even when expectant mothers get lucky with a reputable, licensed, adoption professional, it is unlikely that she is being shown the full picture of adoption. To keep moms on the path of adoption or preserve matches with prospective adoptive parents, information that would be helpful to them may be concealed. Instead of providing moms with neutral spaces for options-counseling, properly informing them of what grief may look like, or informing them of their responsibilities in an open adoption, it's easier for professionals to just say, "You are doing a wonderful thing!" or "You are a hero!" There is not much guidance online for a mother walking through this process, either. From most professionals' *Frequently Asked Questions* web pages, one can easily draw out the loaded questions they're framing for her to ask:

- "Can I get paid for an adoption?"
- "Can I be housed if I choose adoption?"
- "Do I have to do an open adoption?"
- "Do I have to hold my baby in the hospital?"
- "Do I have to tell the birth father?"

If a mom isn't informed what adoption will require of her in the long term, or how she may grapple with her decision, it's likely because the professionals leading her through the process haven't given her any information of substance. How will she get answers to the questions she isn't asking? Better yet, what *should* she be asking professionals? Start with these questions from the *Thinking About Adoption* podcast:

- Who are you?
- What are you?
- Who do you represent?
- What services do you provide?
- How much do you charge?[2]

While these questions may seem basic, a professional who cannot clearly give an answer to a basic question may not be the best to provide adoption services to a vulnerable expectant mother. Neutral support is scarce, even when one is not considering adoption.

As soon as the two pink lines appear on a pregnancy test, others begin to mark their territory on the trajectory of her decision. An expectant mom may be accompanied by people like the baby's father, her family members, or members of her church, who may have their own agendas which keep her from calling the shots during her own pregnancy. Without a neutral liaison at any point in her pregnancy, she is led through the dark by individuals and entities with an emotional and financial stake in her final decision.

Many professionals are afraid to offer pre-placement counseling for fear of leading her away from adoption and are similarly hesitant to prepare her for the grief that awaits her post-placement. In this way, modern-day adoption cannot avoid being transactional. The sad truth is that keeping a mom in the dark keeps a professional's lights on.

FINDING UNTAINTED ADOPTION INFORMATION

The road to relinquishment has a serious problem with informed consent. Expectant mothers generally are not informed of the procedural process of adoption. It is typical for an expectant mother to not have their own attorney or even be offered one. Only one party having an attorney is specifically an adoption problem. Normally when there are two parties in a legal arrangement, with one party signing their rights away, they *both* have their own attorneys. Contrary to the hesitations of many, birth mothers having an attorney to represent them serves many benefits including being informed how state laws will affect the birth mother, drafting a post-adoption contact agreement, and answering questions moms may not know to ask. Emily says, "I was not told that I could have a post-adoption contact agreement. They also never told me that I wasn't limited to only my agency's waiting adoptive parents, that I could have a chance to look at more families if I wanted to."[3]

From an emotional perspective, expectant mothers are never told that they will likely think about their children every single day for the rest of their lives. No one tells them that the pain may become so intense it could extend beyond emotional effects to cause physical pain and health issues. Professionals don't inform her that she will need to show up to this open adoption relationship even when all her natural reflexes are telling her to run. Ashley placed her son for adoption sixteen years ago and resonates with this, saying, "I was not told how hard open adoption would be. I was not told that my child would want and need to be part of my life. I was never supported in how to process things as they come up in open adoption. I had to figure it out on my own."[4] Adoption professionals do not tell expectant mothers to prepare for the questions their growing child will ask someday, or how to keep the adoptee centered in the relationship, even in seasons when sadness and suffering are festering below the surface. No matter what she is not told before placement, she will eventually discover it to be true after placement; although, she will likely have to trudge through these checkpoints of understanding without support from an expert.

Post-Placement Support

The day a birth mother walks out of the hospital with empty arms is the most sorrowful day of her life. Birth mothers exit the hospital with even less than an empty womb and arms. In many instances, birth mothers leave without resources, a follow-up call from their professional, paid maternity leave, stable housing, and so much more. Further, they leave without an understanding of how open adoption works, what their new role and responsibilities are, and how to navigate the heavy grief stemming from the loss of a child who is still alive.

It is impossible to know exactly what relinquishing a child feels like beforehand, but it is much worse when birth mothers have not been alerted about what to expect. For many, relinquishment engages a flight response; in my career, I have seen countless birth mothers ask for an early discharge from the hospital and even change their phone numbers afterward. A birth mother who leaves the hospital in a frenzy is often misunderstood as someone who doesn't care, but she might just be desperate to escape the anguish of the experience. Though, even when she sticks around for a proper discharge, is her professional scheduling follow-up casework or an appointment with a therapist? I hope so.

Even so, six months later, when she searches for a therapist on her own accord, she rarely lands on someone who is savvy with loss associated with relinquishment and adoption. Even searching through an online therapist directory for adoption-fluent therapists isn't what it seems. Many therapists who claim to be adoption-fluent are proficient in therapy for adoptive families and adoptees but not versed in what it's like for the ones who relinquish. On the occasion when the agency or adoptive parents do offer to cover the cost of adequate mental health support, birth moms are still left to jump the hurdles of having the time, capacity, and transportation to attend therapy sessions. Telehealth has made this more accessible but again, that's if they are able to find a therapist who is fluent in birth parent issues.

So much of the post-placement support that currently exists has the potential to do more harm than good for the birth parent's healing process. Turning to the Internet once again, birth mothers may find any number of Facebook groups or online forums that claim to be support groups but often are without any structure or curriculum, thus resulting in a mass amount of trauma-dumping without tools for grief and healing. This is a recipe for confusion and another barrier to the healing these birth moms are desperate to find.

However, the Internet can also be a great resource, especially for birth mothers who reside in more rural areas where there are less options for adoption-fluent therapists and in-person support groups. While there is a scarcity of resources in many areas, there are more solutions available in the digital age and community can be found in unlikely places. It is unarguably best practice that birth mothers are offered a set of options for healing, including counseling, post-placement casework, support groups, and more, no matter where they live. Shonda, a birth mother in Montana, attended a year of counseling from a third-party therapist, and an in-person support group, and has had post-placement casework by her social worker who is also a licensed counselor. "I have met with her a few times a year in the seven years since I placed. Having that person to talk to is an amazing resource."[5] About the birth mom support group, she says, "To know we all experienced the same life-changing event was key to feeling less isolated. I felt so stuck and so many people in my life just kept moving on. Connecting with other birth moms was so comforting to me."

Erika G., a birth mother in Northern California, lives in a much more populated area than Shonda, where current law requires two counseling sessions before placement and one session after. Erika knew this would not be enough, and the attorney who facilitated the adoption did not connect her to any additional resources. However, her son's adoptive parents paid attention to what Erika was experiencing in the aftermath of relinquishment. Erika says, "My son's adoptive parents could see that three sessions weren't adequate and continued to pay for my therapy for several months until I felt ready to pay on my own."[6] Erika got lucky that the adoptive parents recognized her need but this isn't always the case. Adoptive parents may not notice her needs at first, but they will realize later—when they see how a birth mother's unresolved trauma may impact the adoptee and the open adoption relationship.

It is the job of the adoption professionals to spot these needs. The absence of post-placement support as standard practice in adoption leaves the birth mother to do the heavy lifting of a life event that she has not yet fully grasped. The responsibility of acknowledging the need for mental health support after relinquishment rests on those in power, namely, the adoption professionals who are paid to provide services. We talk more about the need for reform in Part IV.

The pathway to placing a child for adoption is murky. The unpredictability of the Internet, lack of regulation and oversight of adoption professionals, neglect of informed consent, and inadequacy in post-placement support all layer veils over the mother who is considering adoption in a crisis. Only when the ink dries on the adoption consent forms do these veils begin to lift to reveal the shaky ground before her. Birth mothers always deserved more.

CHAPTER 9

Making the "Right" Choice

Religion's Role in Relinquishment

I GREW UP ATTENDING AN EVANGELICAL CHURCH EVERY SUNDAY morning. My little brother and I sat between my parents on wooden pews, doodling on the weekly church bulletins while the pastor delivered his sermon. We learned about Jesus's undying love for us, simple and steadfast. The messages about Christ's forgiveness were gentle and warm. We sang, *Oh, the blood of Jesus, it washes white as snow.* As I grew older, the messages about God became more serious and I became more afraid. Looking back, I know I was just fumbling through life the same as any adolescent, but at the time, I fostered a paranoia about meeting a tragic fate if I continued to forfeit the "right" choices for sinful choices. I also paid attention to the hypercritical gossip over coffee and donuts after Sunday service, the mean-spirited finger-pointing commentary about congregants who had fallen from grace, and I eventually joined in on the chatter. In my young adulthood, I came to realize that maybe being a Christian involved two different things: (1) Jesus, and (2) going to church, but it became increasingly difficult to tell which was which.

I was taught that it was immoral and sinful to have sex before marriage. There was no nuance to the subject of premarital sex. Nonetheless, I grew into a young woman who engaged in consensual sex with multiple partners throughout college and beyond, and spiritually, I vacillated between if that was terribly wrong or just fine. I was a woman who enjoyed having sex. I didn't want that to be wrong, and truthfully, it didn't *feel* wrong but something in my mind told me I should feel ashamed. But I simply did not. This only changed when I became unexpectedly pregnant at twenty-two without a ring on my finger. I had been caught. A myriad of conflicting thoughts ran through my head: *Am I a bad person? Does God love this baby but not me? Was premarital sex the sin, or is being pregnant the sin? Have I just sealed my fate in Hell's Unwed Mother Hall of Fame? Will I be washed white as snow? If so, when?* Exhausted by the mental gymnastics of purity culture and the toll it took on me, I shut myself out from the world for the duration of my pregnancy. I accepted my fate as a shameful sinner, the girl who got pregnant by her summer fling. *How irresponsible of her to let a man knock her up like that*, I imagined churchgoers saying if I had been foolish enough to show my face.

Christianity is not the only religion that has played a part in adoption, but by and large, it has had the most significant impact on adoption in the United States and the world. From the Christian narratives crafted for adoption, which Sara wrote about in Chapter 7, to the massive presence of faith-based professionals and adoptive parents, Christianity has made a lasting mark on adoption as we know it. However, religion and spirituality can have different impacts on birth moms. While some birth mothers are vocal about the harm inflicted on birth mothers by the church, others express finding solace and comfort in their spiritualities and religious communities. Although in my interviews with birth mothers, no matter if they were currently practicing Christians or not, most of them recognized Christianity's oversights and negligence in adoption.

THE FALLOUT OF PURITY CULTURE

Purity culture has branded women with the hot iron of a frightening, patriarchal god, and many birth mothers have the scar tissue to prove it. Trying to make sense of the reception and fear surrounding my premarital sex and unwed pregnancy was like forcing the grooves of my brain to play a game of Twister. Mellisa remembers growing up and hearing about the dangers of premarital sex, recalling how this mental framework and internalized shame led her down unfortunate paths, "I was taught that premarital sex was bad and if I had it then I would go to hell. I remember my parents giving me a chastity ring for my birthday at a certain age but after they learned I was no longer a virgin they took it away from me. I was shamed so badly and made to feel like I was unworthy of love. My promiscuity became worse as I grew older. I started to use it to control others and to feel accepted."[1]

Sarah grew up in an evangelical church and recalls how many purity culture narratives she absorbed by the church's messages, "My sin would become a blessing if I chose adoption. I was choosing to create a family for someone else. It was God's will that I have this baby for them. I was a vessel to fulfill their parental wishes, and God was using me to give them their dreams. Jesus would honor my decision and redeem me. Then, in the aftermath, I was used as the poster child for what redemption could look like for single, sinful women like me to be restored in the eyes of God, in the church, through placement."[2] In purity culture, unwed pregnancy and parenthood carry much greater shame for women than men, just as premarital sex does. Erika G. believes this is indicative of deeper issues, saying, "Purity culture aims to normalize adoption in the effort of vilifying pregnancies that happen outside of marriage. It is a narrative that very conveniently benefits those profiting off the notion that it is wrong for someone to raise a child outside of marriage."[3]

How does this narrow ideology translate to adoption practices? The market is saturated with faith-based agencies and many expectant moms receive adoption services from them. Experiences with faith-based agencies widely differ, as some professionals take the Christian mission of love and aid seriously, and others use it only as a label to signal their loosely held religious beliefs, demanding trust they are unworthy of receiving. There is a longstanding history of sending expectant mothers to faith-based maternity homes beginning in the postwar Baby Scoop Era. As will be referenced in Chapter 11, maternity homes were mostly filled with White expectant mothers as Black mothers were not accepted. Detailed in *Wake Up Little Susie* by Rickie Solinger, "approximately two hundred licensed homes were scattered across forty-four states" and "about twenty-five thousand unwed mothers each year spent the final trimester of their pregnancies" in these maternity wards.[4] The environment was often punitive, with a history of prohibiting anesthetics during childbirth and enforcing strict rules and curfews. Now, maternity homes do not exist in multitude as they once did, but they still have a small presence. While not every birth mother has had a bad experience in a maternity home, many have left feeling infantilized, without help, and unheard. Mellisa stayed in a maternity home in the 1990s after the birth father ended their relationship and she had nowhere else to go. She says, "The maternity home was strict and did not seem to demonstrate much grace to those of us living there who were navigating complicated situations. I was kicked out after about two months and was not given options where else to go."

Adoption as "God's Plan"

Sometimes adoptive parents and others describe adoption as "God's plan," ignoring the profound loss inherent in separating families to rebuild others. Emily, a Christian and birth mother, finds this description troublesome and uncomfortable. She says, "Adoption wouldn't exist in a perfect world—the world which God intended in the first place—therefore I don't think adoption, which includes layers of emotion, pain, and grief no matter the outcome, should ever be distorted with such simplicity by saying it was 'God's plan.' Using this term simplifies adoptees' and birth parents' loss and pain, and just as detrimental, it leads to labeling

God as cruel and without compassion."[5] If adoption is God's plan, then God is an exclusionary deity, picking blessings off vulnerable mothers and redistributing them to more financially able families.

There are many "Christianese" phrases that get tossed around the adoption sphere from "adoption is the gospel," to "adoption is redemption." These terms manage to cement birth families at the bottom rung of the adoption hierarchy, the sinners in need of radical atonement. Mellisa's story echoes this. "Adoption was a way I could redeem myself for becoming pregnant at nineteen and being unwed." Religion was a large part of Ashley's adoption story as well, but these phrases fail to encapsulate her experience. She says, "I believe that there is redemption in my story throughout my journey but 'adoption as redemption' is misusing the Bible to meet an agenda of professionals and adoptive parents." Ashley continues, "You will never convince me that God's plan was for me and my son to be separated just to build a family."[6]

FINDING COMFORT IN SPIRITUALITY

While many have had harm inflicted on them by religious communities and the church, many birth mothers have found solace within their religious spaces and spiritualities. For the birth mothers who were met with acceptance, support, and love instead of shame, judgment, and punishment, community and God's love has been received with warmth and welcome. Emily says that amid the chaos of grief in adoption, she finds rest in her relationship with Jesus. She says, "I've found it's okay to not have every answer and to continue to question. As I've read and learned about Jesus's understanding of pain, I've found there is room for all I bring to the table."

Erica S. details the love she has found in her healing journey after relinquishment, "I see the hard things working out for the better. I see richness and growth, cultivating tenacity and strength, and deep, feel-it-in-your-bones love I wouldn't trade for anything. I see beauty in ashes."[7]

Chapter 10

Emotional Health

The Residue of Trauma and Grief

During my pregnancy, I pictured the birth and placement of my child as checkpoints to pass through. As many mothers do, I, too, counted down the days until the pregnancy was over. However, I never came to terms with how different my postpartum experience would play out in an emotional way. In the final weeks of pregnancy, I was numb and dissociated—preparing and protecting myself for the moment of detachment. I assured myself that if I could just make it across the finish line, I could finally breathe. I had no idea that the wind would be knocked out of me as soon as I permanently placed my baby in someone else's arms. From an outside perspective, it seems rational that the decision to relinquish a child would cause emotional distress—adoption is an unpopular choice for a reason—mothers don't ordinarily wish to part with their children. However, for the individual experiencing the pregnancy in crisis, the path traveled is enveloped in a thick fog. I never thought I would be living through this seemingly impossible scenario, so I was no expert on what was to come next.

In the days, weeks, and even months after leaving the hospital empty-armed, I woke up every morning to the cruel, stabbing realization that my baby was gone. My body ached for my little one, the one who was, just days prior, entwined with my body and knew no one else but me. I vomited from extreme stress and wept until my eyes were sore. As jolting and despairing as these days were, this was the beginning of my grief process. There was no finality to the process, no logical rhythm or boxes to check as I moved through each agonizing emotion. I desperately wanted to move forward and have a fresh start, but the chronic pain of relinquishment had branded my heart with a hot iron; I would never be the same again. I soon realized that the only option I had was to find a way to live my newly transformed, abnormal life in tandem with the grief over the loss of and separation from my child.

ANTICIPATORY GRIEF

Relinquishment is a unique experience; while some life events display parallel side effects, there are no identical experiences and accompanying outcomes. Because of this fact, combined with other factors discussed further in the chapter, birth mothers don't possess a strong forecast of what is to come, but they can certainly guess. It's possible that these mothers will experience some form of anticipatory grief, which is grief that occurs *before* the loss happens, commonly found in people who have a loved one facing a long battle with a terminal illness. Anticipatory grief can be displayed through separation anxiety, denial, and the overall preparation for the loss and subsequent life without that person.[1] Some birth mothers who parent other children may have a hypothetical notion of what it might feel like leaving the hospital without their baby by imagining the opposite of their own experience. However, it's safe to say that only one group of birth mothers knows what to anticipate after placement: birth mothers who have already walked the walk. Birth mothers who have previously placed a child generally know what emotions and grief to expect. However, this does not exempt them from having to encounter the process all over again.

Sarah placed two children within a span of nineteen months. She explains that while she generally knew what to expect, it did not ease her process and pain. Sarah details the exacerbation of grief in placing twice: "It's double the loss and grief. Double the unrealized-becoming-realized trauma. Double the missing out on their lives. Double the feeling of not having felt enough or capable of being a parent to either of them. Double the amount of time I wasn't provided post-placement care or counseling. I didn't fall through the cracks once, but twice. And I paid doubly for it over the years as I attempted to find healing from decisions I made for them. It also took me twice as long to believe I deserved any help, community, or support because I had willingly chosen this twice. Everything was doubled down, and compacted, especially when I finally unearthed the actual weight and magnitude of my decisions."[2]

Even when a birth mother anticipates her grief, it is unlikely she is prepared to cope with this new trauma. Many birth moms are *counter-prepared* due to the misleading boosts of self-esteem given to them by adoption professionals who neglect to inform them of the emotional realities to follow. Many an expectant mother is told by adoption professionals, adoptive parents, family members, and others within their community how selfless and heroic she is for choosing adoption. It's no wonder when she leaves the hospital in emotional and mental ruin she feels conflicted for daring to feel the inevitable heartbreak. Her grief comes to a crossroads: if she did such a wonderful thing, why does it feel so excruciating? Now, she is not only grieving without resources, but also having a mental conflict leading her to participate in her own grief disenfranchisement.

TRAUMA NOW, GRIEF LATER

Whether birth mothers allow themselves to feel the effects of grief immediately or delay it until years down the road, grief lingers, waiting to come into frame. Muthoni recalls unconsciously delaying her grief after relinquishment and coming to terms with that fact after attending her first therapy session, two years after the placement of her daughter. "As soon as I started therapy and confronted my issues, I realized that a lot of my process that led to choosing placement was wrapped up in my fear of being a terrible mom. And I hadn't once truly considered any of that before attending therapy."[3] After finally entering her delayed grief process over the relinquishment of her daughter, she revisited the vivid, painful moments of losing her daughter just the same as she would have two years prior. Muthoni found that there was no detour around grief; she had to travel through it.

Birth mothers only have one thing in common: they relinquished a child for adoption. How these moms got to this point varies greatly. While birth mothers can experience any number of trauma-inducing circumstances; relinquishment trauma is unlikely to be the first encounter with life's challenges. They may have come to this decision due to the compounding isolation and paralyzing fear of unplanned pregnancy, a changing body on display, the weight of shame and self-blame, the coercion of others, lack of familial or partner support, or all the above. Many birth mothers may also face a constant backdrop of traumatic life circumstances, such as poverty, housing insecurity, substance use disorder, domestic violence, various abuses, mental illness, or more. Lastly, women may also decide on adoption because they don't feel ready to parent or they don't want to be a parent. Whatever their reasons for placement, they will experience the trauma of relinquishment, loss, and separation in one form or another. More importantly, these additional traumas do not disappear when she returns home from the hospital; her adoption trauma simply adds another layer of complexity to her already present difficult circumstances.

Ambiguous Loss and Disenfranchised Grief

Everlasting grief from the loss of a child who is still alive sparks bizarre feelings. Finding internal acceptance in these feelings is often accompanied by the acknowledgment that few others can relate to the experience, and it may be easier to not share it with others. Even for birth mothers who have an open adoption and visitation privileges, the feeling of visiting with a child whom they love deeply and think about daily may kindle impostor syndrome. The discovery that maybe this child does not really know them at all is painful to reconcile. While the pull from the feelings of innate connection is strong, the push from the feelings of unworthiness can unfortunately be stronger, and more callous. These kinds of contradictory emotions cause birth mothers to second-guess their relationship with both the adoptee and the adoptive parents, and at times cause them to feel rather stupid for attempting to find belonging in their own adoption constellation.

Many birth moms experience layered complications in the grief process but the first of these is ambiguous loss. Ambiguous loss is one that results from a life event that produces a loss without closure. A birth mother's loss is like death in many ways, but the absence of closure is a defining difference. Many times, in the loss of a loved one through death, people receive closure one way or another. We don't host a wake for a person who is still alive, and we certainly don't host a funeral when a new arrival is being celebrated elsewhere. Mothers who relinquish a child for adoption don't receive a day of mourning as it is not only unusual but also typically unspoken loss. Relinquishment is a loss in which "the normal rituals of support that accompany death loss do not apply and therefore are unavailable."[4] Even when others respond to a death with hurtful comments such as, "At least they're no longer in pain" or, "Finally, they are at peace," at the very least, they have acknowledged the loss. With no intention to diminish the pain of death and loved ones leaving us too soon, grief stemming from the relinquishment of a child exhibits contrasting elements to grief stemming from death. Birth mothers are aware that their children are out there, somewhere, and yet, they may not have information beyond that. Even in open adoptions, while birth mothers may know more regarding their children, there are significant gaps they are left to fill through their imagination. In place of closure, there is only a series of mysteries that birth parents are socially or emotionally permitted to solve.

It can be challenging for a birth parent to find stability in their emotional well-being, considering their adoption choice generally invites the critical opinions of family members, friends, and basically any other human who has a pulse. When surrounded by people who have expressed adamant opposition to their adoption choice, birth mothers may hesitate to share their pain for fear and trepidation of hearing "I told you so" and receiving a merciless scolding. On the contrary, for those who have a hyper-supportive community, birth mothers can feel as though they are trapped in a continuum of faux happiness. Hearing "You did the right thing" playing on a loop, they may feel unable to discover acceptance and answers to simple questions that would otherwise be found in early phases of grief. Even birth moms who find themselves somewhere in the middle suffer from the spins of the yeas and nays that are counterproductive to their grief and healing processes.

It's fair to assume that at least some people in a birth mom's life do not equate her emotions with grief. The experience of grief over relinquishment produces helpless feelings like free-falling in the night sky. Enduring deep, dark, disenfranchised grief in public is humiliating; the visibility of the struggle seems to make everyone else uncomfortable. Nobody knows what to say or do to help. The clearest message birth mothers receive from a stiff audience is that they're waiting for her grief to cease. It's easier for society to pretend the loss isn't authentic than to confront the ugly realities of a loss they know nothing about.

When birth mothers have a lack of support in their own familiar communities, it may be common to consider seeking some form of emotional support from the adoptive parents of their child. However, sometimes this thought remains an idea and nothing more, due to their desire for boundaries or fears of revealing weakness or initiating inappropriate conversations. Some birth mothers do feel comfortable sharing details about their grief with their children's adoptive parents but many do not. While adoptive parents generally recognize that birth mothers will grieve the loss of this child, they may also struggle to accept that despite a welcoming invitation, the probability that they would seem like a safe place for a birth mother to confide might be naïve. However, as the open adoption relationship develops and a foundation of trust is established, it can be possible for more open communication to occur. Sarah was afraid of revealing too much about her struggles to the adoptive parents stemming from a fear of being cut out of her kids' lives. She says, "I knew I was in a very small minority of birth moms who hadn't been shut out completely by the time my child was five." As her relationship with her children's adoptive mother developed over time, they began to have more nuanced, transparent conversations about Sarah's experiences as a birth mother. "I am grateful that we can have hard conversations now without worrying about our relationship being at risk."

Triggers, Post-Traumatic Stress Disorder, and Complicated Grief

As life progresses for birth parents, so does their grief. Loss follows them through new life experiences, especially experiences that mimic the motion of their prior pregnancy and relinquishment, such as the birth of another child. The constant reminder of their traumatic pregnancy and relinquishment may diminish the excitement that a growing family might otherwise bring. Birth mothers may feel unable to bond with the children they parent, mirroring a phenomenon called "emotional cushioning" observed in women who have previously experienced perinatal loss.[5] Emotional cushioning is "a conscious or subconscious mechanism that serves as emotional self-protection from pregnancy anxiety, specifically the potential emotional pain and hurt of another loss." Ashley gave birth to a daughter four years following the relinquishment of her firstborn child and experienced reluctance to bond. "I knew how to give birth, but I didn't know how to parent. It took months after my daughter arrived to find peace and trust that my baby wasn't going anywhere and that it was safe to bond with her."[6] These stresses also affect birth mothers beyond the infant stages of their parenthood. Amy E. went on to parent four children after placing her firstborn for adoption when she was a teenager. She explains the pressures of being a "good mom" that has been further inflamed by the shame and insecurities resulting from relinquishment, and how they have affected her parenting and stoked her fears of rejection. She says, "I have recurring fears that they will decide to leave and not come back."[7] Detachment may leave unrealistic anxieties to fill the empty space.

Relinquishment is not the norm for mothers, making it an adverse birth and postpartum outcome. Birth mothers may be at higher risk for experiencing Postpartum Depression (PPD), which affects thirteen percent to nineteen percent of childbearing women, with the strongest risk factors being prenatal depression and current abuse.[8] It is estimated that 3.17% of women experience PTSD after childbirth, as the highest factor of vulnerability "most strongly associated with birth-related PTSD [being] depression in pregnancy."[9] Additionally, when severe separation anxiety is present, complicated grief may develop, which is "characterized by continued severe separation distress and by dysfunctional thoughts, feelings or [behaviors] that are related to the loss that complicate the grief process."[10]

In a perfect world, the entire experience of relinquishment and adoption would not exist. However, in a slightly better world, the adoption, mental health, and healthcare professionals would work to create infrastructure to mitigate the negative outcomes of PPD, PTSD, and complicated grief and provide accessible mechanisms for healing. A birth mother's surrounding community would be supportive, therapeutic, and inclusive in their acknowledgment of the separation and loss experienced. Finally, a birth mother would be equipped with the awareness and acceptance of grief as well as with useful techniques for coping and healing. It's safe to say there's room for improvement.

The Metamorphosis of Grief and the Need for Community

As time passes grief changes. Birth mothers adapt and find ways to coexist with loss. New life events and relationship dynamics with the adoptive family and adoptee will challenge a birth mother's balancing act time and time again. It is important that birth mothers are not left alone to cope and stumble through this complicated evolution. Finding a community after placing a child for adoption can be lifesaving for mothers dealing with the aftermath of relinquishment, even decades later. When one birth mother finally meets another birth mother with a similar experience of relinquishment, it is often described as feeling like freedom. As it turns out, it isn't just a feeling. Research shows that healing can happen in communities of biological parents with shared experiences, and group treatment contributes to alleviating the effects of disenfranchised grief for birth parents, because "their loss is normalized and validated" in a group setting.[11] Support groups, while before lacked widespread presence, are more prevalent than ever before. Now there are multiple birth parent support groups that exist both online and in-person in several locations across the United States. Some monthly groups, such as the ones sponsored by Lifetime Healing Foundation, have monthly curricula that offer birth mother attendees healthy coping strategies, storytelling, and critical education for trauma and life events that extend far beyond adoption. There are also birth mother retreats like the ones sponsored by the On Your Feet Foundation and Concerned United Birthparents (CUB) that provide a haven of support and respite. Barriers to accessing this type of group support still exist, but the disenfranchisement is removed from view in a community with shared experiences; creating a sense of safety and trust for birth mothers to exist freely as they are.

Accepting the Invitation of Grief

Grief is boisterous, unruly, confusing, and twisted, but grief can and should be welcome in birth parents' post-placement journeys.

It is natural to grieve after the loss of a child through adoption. Birth mothers will and should continue to grieve this loss even when their surrounding communities decline to recognize it and also when they voluntarily chose this path. With the tools, resources, and supportive community, there is an opportunity for healing. We eventually learn that when we accept grief's invitation to dance, the steps become easier to learn. When we agree to waltz with grief, someday we may find it easier to learn to tango.

Chapter 11

Power Dynamics

Race, Class, and the Hierarchy of Adoption

I FELT A TINGE OF INSECURITY WHILE WRITING PART II DUE TO my lack of everyday relevance within the constellation. I am an outsider to the mundane aspects of adoption. I certainly think daily about the child I placed for adoption, but I don't play a main role in their life. I stay behind the curtain carrying on with my own life and waiting patiently for my cue. However, when I am called to enter the stage, I do so with vigilance, acutely aware of the sensitivity to every move I make or word I say and how my actions may be perceived. It's important to note, *this is nobody's fault*. Rather, this is just the result of adoption. More narrowly, this is the result of the power dynamics inherent in adoption.

There is a substantial power imbalance in all adoption arrangements. If everyone in the adoption constellation were to sit at a theoretical family gathering, adoptive parents would be at the adult table. Adoptees would be at the kids' table, no matter their age. Birth parents would be standing on the porch looking in through the front window with a casserole that's gone cold. This is not to say that just because one has a seat inside the house they have a louder voice but simply that adoption naturally puts birth parents outside. We don't always have a developed understanding of what's going on inside the gathering. We may see silhouetted figures moving behind the sheer curtains in the windows, but we can't hear the conversations or share our own thoughts in the moment.

Generally speaking, birth parents recognize that access to a relationship or mere contact with the adoptee and adoptive parents is a privilege, not a right, because we literally forfeited those rights. There are a variety of factors that birth parents may face which affect their access or ability to maintain contact. These factors add a range of nuance to the entire adoption experience. Factors such as socioeconomic class, race, ethnicity, culture, age, family support, financial stability, housing security, mental health status, etc., may not be permanent or self-defining, but they do carry weight in forming a lasting image of the birth parent. Throughout this chapter, we examine how a few of these factors affect the power imbalance, birth parents' adoption experiences, and what can be done to mitigate the harm done and make the adoption relationship more equitable.

THE ROLE OF RACE IN THE BIRTH PARENT EXPERIENCE

Adoption agencies have historically charged lesser fees for the adoption of Black children than for the adoption of non-Black children.[1] In 2010, *The Economist* published that it cost approximately eight thousand dollars less to adopt Black babies than to adopt White babies.[2] While many adoption agencies have phased out this disturbing practice, it is still the standard in many agencies to this day. By putting a price, as well as a discount, on an infant's head before they are born, are adoption professionals also correlating the services provided to Black mothers while pregnant? In other words, does less "profit" translate to less care and fewer services for a Black client than for a White client? It's a question with no systemwide answer. For now, it is simply a thought for adoption professionals to consider. What we do know, however, is how the culture in the United States has historically viewed Black, unwed mothers. From a stigma that didn't just place shame but blame, to labeling them "welfare queens," and in the most heinous cases subjecting these women to widespread forced sterilization, Black women in America have faced unwarranted hatred and hostility at every turn.[3] When pondering the answer to how adoption professionals may treat Black expectant mothers and birth mothers, the analysis is incomplete without the examination of the extra cards stacked against them.

The experience may be dependent on the birth mother's comfort with their caseworker and how cooperative and adaptive they may be. Muthoni built a close relationship with her adoption caseworker, feeling supported. However, in later years she reflected upon this saying, "I think I had such a positive experience because I had a good caseworker but also because I was treated as the 'model expectant mother.' I didn't need *too much help* from the agency. I was always cooperative and didn't make waves."[4] Because birth mothers do not share any definitive experience that bands them together besides relinquishment, the "good ones" are vulnerable to tokenization.

Many Black expectant mothers who are considering adoption often ask to be shown the adoption profiles of Black or biracial families when searching for an adoptive family, and many times they are told there are either none available or very few to choose from. There is a wide range of misinformation about whether Black families adopt and why they aren't as prominent in the sea of waiting adoptive families as White families. Informal adoption, or kinship adoption, has a longstanding history in the Black community.[5] But perhaps more significantly obstructing them from formal adoption is that prospective Black adoptive families face substantially more barriers to domestic infant adoption than White parents,[6] leaving Black birth moms with mostly White families to choose from. In the Baby Scoop Era, legal adoption was not a realistic option for most Black mothers, as mother-baby homes refused entry to the majority of unwed Black mothers and White families expressed little interest in adopting Black babies.[7]

This was mainly due to overt racism but was also due to the secrecy of closed adoption and White adoptive parents' desire for their adopted child to blend in and resemble their family.[8]

Not only do Black birth mothers find more limited choices when choosing an adoptive family, but many also report facing scrutiny from their own communities after choosing adoption which can isolate them from the desperately needed support in post-placement. Allana says, "The challenges I faced and am currently facing are gaining acceptance in the African American community. It is known that we don't place our children for adoption. There is someone in the family who will help raise your child. . . . I'm still praying and trying to find better ways to break this stigma."[9]

The added stigma for Black birth mothers can be a hindrance to finding support and acceptance for their circumstances, choice, and grief process. This stigma may be more significant for those who choose to place their child with a White family. Muthoni echoed Allana's thoughts, "I have experienced some shaming from the Black community because of my choice to place. Kinship adoption is accepted in Black culture, but my choice to place with a White family is problematic to a lot of people." Muthoni believes, however, that there is hope and community with education and understanding, adding, "I've come to see some acceptance and I've had some Black friends express how reading about my experience has given them a new view on my decision to place my daughter." Birth mothers of non-White children who placed their children into a White family may struggle to watch their children grow up detached from their birth culture. As Sara touched on in Chapter 6, the complexities of simply existing as a minority in America will likely be a steep learning curve for White adoptive families. Unfortunately, this may be a harsh reality for adoptive parents who hadn't considered these matters until they have already brought a child into their home. For birth mothers who are already an outsider to the adoption arrangement, verbally addressing some of the cultural shortcomings of White adoptive parents may feel risky.

CHAPTER 11

GAPS BETWEEN SOCIOECONOMIC CLASSES FEED THE ADOPTION BEAST

The overarching adoption hierarchy is intensified by socioeconomic class differences. A system that profits off the misfortune, extreme inequities, and general policy failures of our society, and furthermore, declines to invest in the long-term betterment of birth parents and adoptees contributes to the widening of the gap between the haves and the have-nots. When asked about the long-term effects of class disparities and adoption, Erika G. responded, "When one birth parent places their child for adoption because they don't have the resources to care for their child adequately, that family has now been dismantled because of immoral economics."[10] Not only does one family become severed, but the gap of relatability and class solidarity between the biological and adoptive families may expand further. In open adoption and reunion alike, classism may pose a barrier to having genuine relationships with one another. Birth moms who struggle with the feeling of class inferiority may feel mentally blocked from showing up to open adoption and having an authentic relationship with the adoptive family and the adoptee.

A question that is often posed in adoption circles is that if an expectant mother is considering adoption mainly due to financial reasons, why can't the prospective adoptive parents just give her the money they would have spent on the adoption? While at first this sentiment feels like the missing puzzle piece, it's more practical and realistic to view the unsolved financial solution as a policy failure rather than the failure of an individual couple to empty their life savings to help someone else support their family.

As a result of class differences, birth parents also deal with negative stereotypes, as well as being subject to degrading public commentary. Erika G. says, "Those who place their children because of disadvantages such as poverty, housing insecurity, and lack of resources are so often vilified and dehumanized, while those adopting children out of those conditions are glorified and celebrated. This is all happening in a space where very little is being done to solve the real issues at hand."

THE POWER OF CHOICE

The power held in adoption constellations is in the firm grasp of adoptive parents. From the very beginning, they choose to adopt, and they write the checks. However, while they hold the power, they are certainly not bound to it. People in power have choices, after all.

A disparity of power allows a continuation of boundary trespassing and lack of honesty because birth parents may not feel as though they have the privilege to speak up and establish their own parameters, or communicate openly with the adoptive parents. Yet, adoptive parents have the option to cultivate the space for a birth parent to determine and set their own boundaries and partner together in building a relationship.

Amy S. was able to meet up with her adult son's adoptive mother to iron out their own relationship that has been affected by power imbalances over time. "I wanted to reset the power dynamic," says Amy, "to reclaim my space and to show up as a full participant in our relationship, which is part of my own life and my son's life, no matter my regrets about adoption. She responded with open arms and shared her own ambivalence about adoption as a practice in the United States and her grief as an adoptive mother."[11] The notion of two separate parties living out two very different adoption outcomes, dwelling in two drastically different power stances but choosing to meet eye to eye and truly see one another is difficult to imagine for every situation but so necessary to benefit the child. Adoptive parents and birth parents do not have to come to the same conclusions about everything, but they do need to agree that the child must be kept at the center.

Finding balance in adoption power dynamics is not possible in entirety, but that doesn't mean that fighting for more equitable relationships is a lost cause. Erica S. gives this insight, "If adoptive parents don't make a conscious effort to level things, the imbalance will tip even further for them. That dynamic does not foster true openness or a healthy relationship."[12] Erica adds, "You have to be really brave to fight through that feeling and/or have an incredibly vulnerable and loving adoptive family that is eager to level the playing field to combat this power inequity."

Erica is right. Striving for equity within the adoption relationships takes great courage. Holding on to power with a tight fist may stem from fear or insecurity, but it is not to be mistaken for strength. Rather, it is a weakness that may cause our children to feel anguish in choosing sides and insecurity in themselves, as Sara shared in Part I. Choice grants us all the opportunity to grow deeper in our relationship with one another. Adoptive parents have many choices. At the family gathering, they can choose to allow this adoptee to graduate to the adult table, form opinions, and make their own choices. Adoptive parents also have a choice to invite birth parents into the house to partake in the gathering, or not. Because man, it's cold out here! And I make a damn good casserole.

CHAPTER 12

Birth Parent Challenges in Open Adoption

WHILE WRITING THIS CHAPTER, I WAS SORTING THROUGH THE contents of my desk. I found a letter I wrote to my unborn child, dated November 25, 2015, the day I officially chose adoptive parents. While the letter was well-intentioned and written with so much love, to now view the words my twenty-two-year-old self scrawled onto that page makes me feel disconnected with that version of myself. I had no idea what this open adoption would look like, clueless about how much work it would take to cultivate a healthy relationship for the sake of this nameless little person to whom I was writing.

As the adoptive parents and I got to know each other over monthly lunches, we made vague plans about open adoption, based on the little information we knew about openness as well as our growing comfort with one another. We didn't fully realize it, but we were building a foundation for a trusting relationship. After being discharged from the hospital the following spring, I had no official plan in place for contact. I knew they would send me pictures and that, eventually, we would set up a visit because this is what they said they would do. Honestly, I had zero expectations for what was to come. If I had chosen another set of parents who weren't sincere about wanting an open adoption, this could have had a devastating outcome. Luckily, my child's adoptive parents were indeed the "go with the flow" type and five weeks after leaving the hospital, they asked me if I would like to stop by, so I did. Without thinking too deeply about what was about to happen, I walked into their home and rejoined the same baby I had placed for adoption, except he was five weeks older than when I last saw him. As I held his peaceful, sleeping little body and watched his chest rise and fall, I was propelled forward in time, blurring the weeks in between when we had been apart. This moment sparked a realization that would culminate over time, showing me that I owed this child so much of myself and that my job as a birth parent was not over. I owed him my wholehearted effort, heart, and humility but at this moment I was unsure of how or when it would be needed. It would be some years before I would gain clarity around this. I anticipated that I would continue to wade through the thick mud of grief for the rest of my life but wasn't sure what that would look like. Regardless, I was committed to the journey.

On my way home from my second visit a few months later, I concluded that I was completely alone in this post-placement journey. During the two hours of driving home on the highway, my vision of the road was fogged by tears that would not stop. My chest felt tight like it was closing in on me; my body's center was feverish, as though my heart had been doused in kerosene and a match tossed inside my rib cage. The subsequent separation brought familiar helplessness and aching pain. Birth moms in open adoptions often say that leaving a visit sometimes feels like being back in the hospital all over again. Not only do they feel the intensity of that memory, but they may also be shocked to be dealing with this at all, as so many believed that having an open adoption would make relinquishment less painful. Considering the depth of this wound and the damage it can inflict on our spirit by reliving the moment, it takes a lot of gumption and blind faith to willingly step back into in-person visits, without the certitude of the effect it will have on us and how long we will be down as a result.

Though not all, most birth mothers who place a child for adoption do so without a birth father counterpart involved in the process or post-placement. In these cases, birth mothers are solo as they walk against the wind. Even in healthy open adoption relationships, by nature, open adoption may sometimes *feel* like two versus one. Are these feelings justifiable? Possibly not, possibly so but building trust, fostering communication, and working to nurture this relationship are all important actions to alleviate this response and create a healthier space for all. Simply put, birth parents are an important part of the makeup and life of this child, and this should be echoed to birth parents and adoptees through actions and words.

Defining Open Adoption

Open adoption is defined in different ways mainly due to the divergence between how open adoption is marketed and how it develops over a lifetime. A modern-day open adoption is typically recognized as one that has ongoing communication, an exchange of identifying information, and in-person visits. However, "openness" is a wider concept than just going through the motions of communication as Lori explains in Part III. Birth mothers who enter an open adoption after relinquishing their child typically have little knowledge of what the journey entails. This is partly because there is truly no way to know how all these individuals will grow over time. Still, it is perhaps more significantly due to the apprehension or outright refusal to educate expectant mothers. Pre-adoption education for adoptive parents gets a few things wrong about open adoption and leaves many questions unanswered, but pre-adoption education for expectant parents who wish and plan to become involved birth parents is often bypassed altogether.

A major falsehood that many adoptive parents and birth parents initially believe about open adoption is that post-placement communication is done as a favor for the comfort of the birth mother and her emotions. Holding the belief that open adoption is a courtesy to the birth mother is a fair indicator of a fundamental misunderstanding of openness and, in turn, the ignorance of the magnitude of the role adoption plays in the life of an adoptee. It is reductive to describe open adoption as the basic act of allowing a birth parent to watch their child grow up from afar. Jessie has had an open adoption since 2011 but believes the agency's failure to educate both her and the adoptive parents properly on openness caused them to approach open adoption with trepidation. "I had no guidance and little support when it came to navigating an open adoption. Because we were so focused on following the "rules" and the checklist provided by the agency, progress has been slow. No one encouraged us to have tough and potentially awkward conversations at the beginning; no one encouraged us to get to know each other better."[1]

Adoption education makes a huge difference. During pregnancy, both Allana and the birth father, Jamaal, who is now her husband, wanted only semi-open adoption contact. However, after getting support from her agency and having the space to get to know the adoptive parents, she saw the benefits of openness and never looked back. "Updates and pictures turned into the adoptive parents supporting us at our college athletic events. Now Jamaal and I get to support our daughter at her athletic events."[2] Open adoption, and openness as a broader concept, greatly impacts the health of adoptees: our children and descendants. Of course, people don't know what they don't know, so they may coast along in safety for a while until they are ambushed by a seemingly common obstacle that lies in wait. When birth mothers are not alerted to the responsibilities that open adoption requires of them, their world can be swiftly turned upside down.

I Scream, You Scream, We all Scream for Boundaries

One of the common conversations surrounding open adoption is the concept of adoptive parents establishing boundaries with birth parents. Instituting healthy boundaries early on is critical and mitigates a lot of potential hurt down the road but rarely are boundaries spoken about reciprocally. Birth parents deserve to have boundaries too, and in my work I have seen many instances of adoptive parents crossing the line with birth parents. Mutual respect is important. From respecting how differently a birth mother parents her other children, to refraining from judging her lifestyle, please honor her boundaries.

Like other facets of life, social media has complicated the landscape of open adoption. In case any adoptive parents or birth parents need to be dispelled of their blissful ignorance of anonymity, yes, they have already found you on social media. Some adoptive parents and birth parents choose to become friends on social media, some don't. Establishing boundaries for personal lives extends to the online world. Further, it extends to how both parties, adoptive parents and birth parents, display the adoptee on social media without their consent, especially when they are too young to give proper consent. Many people don't give it a second thought to post their children on social media. We're proud of our kids. We want to show our social bubbles how much they've grown and what they're up to. However, as with all things, there is a line, and many people in the adoption world, me included, have crossed it. It is essential that we are careful and consider the adoptee in all things, even and especially when posting pictures and words on the Internet.

COMMON FEARS

Writing about open adoption while currently participating in an open adoption is very frightening. I know that I do not have the power in this relationship and that anything I say about this relationship is subject to misinterpretation, misunderstanding, and hurt feelings, even though my intentions are never to that end. I don't think I will ever breathe easy when speaking about the challenges of open adoption, for fear of upsetting the other parties in my own, despite being one of those with a positive open adoption experience. It's likely that other birth mothers feel similarly.

Fear is ever-present for birth mothers in open adoption, no matter how steady the relationship may be. Referring to Dr. Gordon Neufeld's words found in Sara's introduction to Part I, "There is no experience that has more impact upon us as humans than that of facing separation."[3] When asked about their worst fears, many birth parents in open adoption—me included— would answer without hesitation, "being cut out." For all birth mothers, the threat of separation has already become a reality through relinquishment. For many birth mothers, the promises of open adoption vaporized at some point after placement, making separation a helpless reality, no longer a threat. At some point, the line item of open adoption was undervalued, discounted, and ultimately cut out of the "love makes a family" budget. Erin placed her daughter in a semi-open adoption, wherein the adoptive parents committed to semi-annual updates and photos. Erin says, "I felt some sense of agency in the process, because I was determined to be actively involved and discerning in finding the right parents for my child."[4] However, she felt the colossal dynamic shift after placement, noting that over time, her stance in the power dynamic fizzled away. "I felt I had less leverage and less visibility. The correspondence became less frequent over the years, until eventually almost none. I felt powerless, never wanting to overstep anyone's boundaries. My only option was to wait."

To have a successful relationship with any person, healthy communication is key. Open adoption relationships are no different, but they are joined by barriers to communication. Many birth mothers sense trepidation when faced with the task of communicating openly and honestly knowing that if they make the wrong move or say the wrong thing, their open adoption arrangement could collapse. They may misrepresent themselves as an act of preserving the thin lines of communication that they do have.

With red flags and warning signs comes our intuition and built-in reflexes. Open adoption tests and triggers those reflexes repeatedly. Every instinct I learned up to the point of relinquishment and placement had to be specially altered for open adoption. Normally in circumstances where I feel uncomfortable, or as if I don't belong, I immediately exit. I do not voluntarily enter spaces where I feel like an outsider. However, open adoption comes with different stakes. The child I carried is on the other side of my insecurities and uncomfortability. What if they need to see someone who looks like them, or ask a question about where they came from, but I left because it felt uncomfortable? At the beginning of open adoption, and especially in the moments where there is the slightest nonalignment between adoptive parents and the birth parents, everything in our bodies signals us to flee the scene. Raquel is in an open adoption and has experienced persistent fears, saying, "I've feared offending my daughter's parents for the majority of our relationship and still have to remind myself that we are allowed to hold different viewpoints, and I am not bound to submit to theirs in an effort to keep the peace."

When Ashley placed her son, she was convicted that her decision was the *right* choice. When her son was six months old, she received a letter from her son's adoptive parents, along with pictures of him. Ashley said, "I didn't recognize this boy. He was six months older than the baby I knew, wearing clothes I didn't dress him in. I felt totally disconnected from who he was."[5] This prompted her to make an unwarranted confirmation that her baby was meant to be with the adoptive parents and thus she did not need to interfere with their life. Even though that was not a notion the adoptive parents were placing on her, she reached this conclusion and wrote a letter back to the adoptive parents letting them know she did not desire further communication as she didn't want to be a burden. It wasn't until later, when she became a parent to her daughter, that she realized all the events, large and small, she had missed. Ashley learned that she had been actively downplaying and rejecting her own role as her son's birth mother. She then wrote another letter to her son's family, stating her desires to reopen the adoption and get to know them once again. They obliged and have carried on an open adoption for the past eleven years. This has been beneficial in multiple ways, allowing Ashley to change her course and grow as an individual, giving the adoptive parents the opportunity to be receptive to change rather than punitive, and especially, giving an expanded experience of openness to her son.

Being an outsider is a persistent gut feeling for birth mothers. Nevertheless, we carry a responsibility to stick around through the awkward times. However, sometimes birth mothers don't have a rebuttal for the voices in their heads urging them to run. The remedy for this is not always simple, but a commitment is required by all: transparent and informative pre-adoption education, effective and continuing post-placement support, and an adoptive family that doesn't give up on them. Birth mothers must be told they are not a fleeting particle but, instead, an essential piece of the composition that is this child's opportunity to feel whole.

Giving Grace and Leaving Space

Birth parents can be difficult. Yes, I am talking about myself, as well. We are not always reliable and many times we aren't where we want to be in our lives, causing us to feel internal humiliation about showing up. Ashley says, "None of my trauma happened until after I placed. My life got significantly worse after adoption. I started drinking, then I ended up in jail. Trauma was really hitting me for the first time. I didn't have any of the skills or tools to be able to handle my major issues." When dealing with the worst life has to offer, sometimes birth parents must handle it on the main stage, and it can't be concealed. Ashley continues, "I wouldn't show up for a visit when I told them we could meet at the park. I didn't know how to function in this relationship."

When agreeing to open adoption, adoptive parents must recognize their own ignorance and fear surrounding birth parents.

Openness changes and people change. Further development for the constellation is certain and it may look different for everyone. Birth parents have lives that continue. They may relocate, marry, have other children, go to school, and experience the fullness of life. They may face additional struggles, make mistakes, and learn hard lessons. Regardless, they are deserving of love and support. The adoptive parents may experience change too and are deserving of the same, as they cannot be expected to be perfect people or parents. Most importantly, the adoptee grows into their individuality, finds their voice, and becomes a rightful governing party in their own adoption. We all must leave space for this to happen and give grace to the humans who occupy the roles in this incredibly challenging and lifelong arrangement.

Chapter 13

Downstream Effects of Our Decision

IN 1992, AT AGE TWENTY-SEVEN, MY FATHER REUNITED WITH HIS birth mother, whom I know as my Grandma Peggy. With the help of my mother, he jumped through hoops in Illinois to find her with only a surname to guide him. Through the reunion with his birth mother, who was an adoptee herself, he found he had half-siblings as well. In 1993, my parents welcomed a baby girl, who turned out to be me. When I was two months old, we all traveled from Chicago to Southern California so my father's maternal birth family could meet me and embrace me into their family—now and forever, our family. My grandmother bathed me, her long-lost son's daughter, in her bathroom sink and treasured that day for the remainder of her life, looking back on it with pride and radiant joy every chance we had to be together. When she passed away in 2021, she left me a scrapbook with photographs of her bathing me in the sink and so every time I open that page the moment lives on.

When people speak about the lacework of family, it's common to refer to the family tree. While the tree is suitable for intact families, I envision my family as a timeworn pair of blue jeans, with every ancestor and relative as a stitch. In my family, I am the fourth consecutive generation to relinquish a child for adoption; three infant adoptions and one stepparent adoption have frayed our stitches along a single bloodline in the last century. Some of the rips and tears have been sewn back together loosely, but the thread is weak and doesn't quite match. Between my stitch and the stitches of separated family members, there are lost years and memories that never were. From the time of my infancy, it appeared that the split seams of my family's history of separation were being patched back together. I never imagined that in my early twenties, I would continue the trend and find myself disjoining a new stitch.

For the first few years after placing my child for adoption, it was easy to live in ignorance that my child would stay little and adorable forever. It was effortless for me to believe that my experience of relinquishment and adoption was mine alone to lament because my child could not yet audibly sing the duet. I could reside in my own self-pity forever because this was something that happened to me and, to my knowledge at the time, no one else. However, when my child began to ask questions, it shocked me. It was heartening to know he thought about me, but this information also held an uncharted future that I had not yet reckoned. I racked my brain for all the possible questions my child might ask, with no inquiry being considered too dark, to prepare an answer for the future. I soon realized that so much of my story was tangled with my child's story. Where exactly was the line? Where did my story stop, and his story begin? I knew there was a separation somewhere. I felt it, I experienced it, I remembered it. But precisely where could I pencil it in?

The hard truth I had to accept was that I had a meager understanding of adoption and our stories. My family's story of separation and adoption did not end with me; it will continue to be written long after I'm gone, just as my late grandmother's adoption story is still echoing throughout our lives today. Adoption's life cycles have been impacting me throughout my entire life, but I had little grasp of the magnitude. Just as I had not yet met the reality of my little one as the adult he will become, I had also never paused to picture the adults in my life as the children they once were. My father was once a young adoptee with questions, and now he's an adult adoptee who still has questions. The stitches on our family's tattered blue jeans don't simply hold the denim together; they embroider our history with a rich and complicated story. Every stitch, attached or not, is intrinsic to the garment.

Watching our children grow up is difficult, whether they are the child we parent every day or the child we placed for adoption. There are questions our children may have that will absolutely be uncomfortable, even potentially retraumatizing, to answer. Our relinquishment, from a legal perspective, terminates our parental rights and responsibilities, giving us a false sense of security as though we don't have a duty to our children. On the contrary, we hold crucial duties to help them discover their origin stories and biological information. Additionally, we also have a moral obligation to show up as healthy as we can for our children, while also respecting boundaries and never causing divided loyalties. Legalities aside, our children grow up and become adults, whether or not we factor this into our initial decision. Our roles and responsibilities as birth parents never vanished with our signature upon consent forms.

REUNION AFTER CLOSED ADOPTION
The modern concept of open adoption in the United States, including visits, open communication, and exchanging identifying information began to be incorporated in the 1990s, but didn't reach the mainstream until well into the 2000s-2010s. Still, open adoption has not been fully realized for many, leaving a multitude of birth mothers behind the curtain of closed adoptions.

My Grandma Peggy gave birth to my father in the same hospital where she worked, where she experienced judgment and shame by her colleagues in addition to the notorious shame of the time. She never saw her baby and was only left to question if he was alive and all right. She would not receive an answer to that question for twenty-seven years. For birth mothers who have had their adoptions blown wide open after multiple decades with no information, being launched into reunion with their child can be challenging mostly because the intersection of two parallel stories that originated from the same event is anything but gentle. The infant a birth mother remembers has now become an adult with the ability to express feelings, opinions, experiences, and complexities. Because of this reality, birth mothers endure "mourning the loss of the baby they left behind while simultaneously accepting the presence of a distinct adult with an adoptive personal identity and an adoptive family history."[1] Leaving behind the long-held vision of their infant, and instead "accept[ing] the adopted adult who he or she had become"[2] is a common and necessary feat to have a successful adoption reunion. This now adult, whose first life event involved the separation from their mother, may possess strong feelings about their adoption, or they might not. Whatever a birth mother's anticipation of their child's disposition, there is potential for a letdown when the perspectives and expectations don't mirror one another.

Many birth mothers in closed adoptions count down the days until their child turns eighteen, hoping and dreaming that they will finally reach out to them and want to get to know their mother. When there is only empty space in the place of a relationship, there is that much capacity for optimistic fantasy. Some birth mothers enter the reunion with low expectations, having already been stung by the loss once, and feeling the need to protect themselves from being thrust back into tumultuous grief from separation once again. Amy E. relinquished her daughter in a closed adoption in 1995, as open adoption was never presented as an option to her. Just shy of eighteen years later, she was able to reunite with her daughter but kept her expectations low. "I always knew that I would welcome a reunion but had no idea how it would happen. I also did not want to walk unwelcomed into her life, and I am sure that came from the belief that my presence in her life would be a hindrance."[3]

Entering reunion generates an emotional upheaval. Karen March, an adoption researcher, describes it as the "process of mourning the loss of the baby they left behind while simultaneously accepting the presence of a distinct adult with an adoptive personal identity and an adoptive family history."[4] Reunion can involve so much emotional upheaval that some birth parents avoid it altogether. Unfortunately, this is experienced by adoptees as secondary rejection and can be incredibly painful. The good news is as birth parents we can choose not to inflict additional rejection upon our children. Katie M. has recently entered reunion with her adult daughter and stresses the importance of being available. "I'm here to engage and respond to her correspondence as quickly as I can, which has sometimes been a few weeks and I've felt terrible, but she's been gracious. I made it clear from the beginning that I am available. If she decides she wants to meet or deepen our relationship, we have created a solid base for the relationship to grow."[5]

OPEN ADOPTION: WATCHING FROM THE SIDELINES WHILE PLAYING ON A DIFFERENT FIELD

Contrary to marketing messages from the adoption industry, open adoption doesn't solve all the problems inherent with relinquishment. Open adoption lessens secrecy and solves a portion of issues rooted in the lack of information that was present in the era of closed adoption, but it does not offer respite from grief; it simply changes the scenery of grief. Open adoption gives birth parents a seat on the sidelines to their children's lives and creates new, unprecedented pain points. Another family raises their child, and they indefinitely observe this in silence.

Compared to the experiences of birth mothers in adoption reunions, birth mothers in open adoptions may also experience the loss of realizing their infant is at different stages. Instead of watching their child grow and develop every day as a more involved parent would, birth mothers capture the progression of their child in short instances, producing snapshots of each stage of the child's life. Amy S. relinquished her son in 2000 and had a consistent, open adoption. Still, Amy describes her loss in an ongoing open adoption as, "finding in our closeness the evidence of the time we lost."[6]

THE BIRTH MOTHER ROLE

Finding a role to play in the life of adult adopted children can be tricky. Not all adoptees desire the same things from their families of origin, so it's best to approach this new relationship with fluidity and let them lead. Kaedra connected with her son for the first time on his twentieth birthday through Facebook. She said, "We had a really precious conversation that just made me drop the weight I'd been carrying for so long. I still have the desire to have more of a relationship with him but now I *know* he knows that, and I'm leaving it up to him."[7] While navigating this new but often familiar relationship, it's crucial not to participate in a game of tug-of-war, causing the adoptee to feel as though they must declare allegiance with their adoptive family or birth family, as Sara mentioned in Part I. There is also the risk of placing too many expectations on the adoptee. Making forward assumptions about having a parent-child relationship or placing unwelcome labels on the adoptee can push them away or lead them to defensive detachment. In the 2014 study, *Birth Mother Grief and the Challenge of Adoption Reunion Contact*, researchers asked birth mothers to describe their reunion relationship with the adoptee as either: "disconnected," "sporadic contact," "regular contact," or "like my own child."[8] Researchers of this study concluded that a birth mother's chosen description of their relationship with the adoptee "was strongly associated with her ability to accept the contact role given to her by the adopted adult."[9]

The importance of letting the adoptee lead cannot be overstated, while still showing a commitment to the relationship and steady, unconditional love for the adoptee. Candace was able to have a relationship with her son for a short time before he passed away unexpectedly. She says, "I would reach out every three or four months, by email or text, just letting him know I was thinking about him, not putting expectations on him. I just didn't want it to go too long in between communication. Sometimes he would respond, sometimes not."[10] Eventually, when he was twenty years old, he reached back out to Candace and said he would like to meet. "We spent a full afternoon together; it was a beautiful, wonderful, amazing experience. When we got back, we went back to the sporadic texts and emails for the next couple years."

Just as in my own family, the birth mother role may extend into the role of birth grandmother. Shifting to a grandmother role can add additional complexities to the relationship. In the 2017 study, "Birth Mothers Now Birth Grandmothers: Intergenerational Relationships in Open Adoptions," researchers found that the loyalty divide can carry on to the next generation with potential competition for the role of grandparents.[11] However, we can rise above the friction to seek harmony. Janelle is both a birth mother and an adoptee. She expressed how she felt grateful to witness and participate in important milestones in her son's life, saying, "It was so rewarding to see how my bloodline, once a big mystery, was extending into the future. I had very mixed feelings about becoming a birth grandmother at thirty-something years old. However, I could see how important it was for my son to have me play the role of birth grandmother and that felt really good. We came up with a 'hip' grandma name and we get together as extended family as often as we can."[12]

It's possible that playing our assigned role will bring intense feelings of guilt. Sometimes, after listening to an adoptee's experience, it may be important to offer a sincere apology. Part of honoring the adoptee's experience is also recognizing that our choice of relinquishment, no matter how it felt to us at the time, may not have been the absolute best choice for the child, if only for the wounds of separation covered in Part I. Accepting the consequences and realities that this decision has affected more people than just the birth mother is a true parent's journey. When birth mothers honor their adoptee's story, they also honor their own.

BIRTH MOTHERS GROW UP, TOO

Birth mothers often have placed a child for adoption in a painful era of their lives. The age they were during that point in their life is forever associated with the loss of their child. It may feel conflicting for a birth mom to try and move forward with her life when grief continues to be experienced spontaneously and indefinitely. Kaedra reflects on the challenge of looking backward while addressing grief in the present, "The parts of my brain and heart that hold my son sort of stayed stuck as a nineteen-year-old girl. The times that my anxiety or grief gets the better of me, I feel myself turn into that nineteen-year-old worrier."

Many birth mothers express that later in life they realized they may have been able to parent the child they relinquished, proving to be a painful acceptance with added grief. Sarah describes her acceptance after a twenty-year journey in open adoption: "Growth is never without pain. What I have learned over the years about what I thought I had been empowered to choose has been very painful to uncover and come to terms with."[13] Similarly, some birth mothers, who later had other children that they chose to parent, have conflicting feelings about their losses and are often prompted to compare what they lost to what they have now. However, having other children and a limited relationship causes its own hardship, especially when siblings know of the adoptee's existence, but do not have access to a relationship of their own. Mellisa went on to have two children after the relinquishment of her son. As the adoption was closed when he was five years old, it was upsetting for her and her children that they could not have contact with their older brother. Mellisa says, "I always made sure that I talked to them about their big brother and to keep praying that we would get to meet him again one day."[14] To young children, the legalities of relinquishment and adoption do not matter. They can experience real pain and confusion surrounding the loss of a sibling they may have never known.

Chapter 13

A birth mother's reconciliation with what *was* and what *is* can propel her forward into a potentially successful relationship with the adoptee. Our kids get big. They grow up and then they have their own kids. Then those kids have kids, and the thread continues to weave. Birth mothers have a responsibility to their children, whether or not they live in our homes. Openness is a weight that birth parents carry as well.

Now that we've heard from birth parents sharing their unfiltered perspectives, next let's hear those of adoptive parents.

PART III

ADOPTIVE PARENTS UNFILTERED

WE HAVE FIRST HEARD FROM ADOPTEES AND BIRTH PARENTS—the lesser-heard voices of adoption. Now it's time to hear from adoptive parents. This section is written by adoptive parent Lori Holden. The adoptive parent perspective is better known and less mysterious, yet there are aspects of the adoptive parent experience that parents may try very hard to keep hidden, often from:

- Shame (*What's so fundamentally wrong with me that I can't have a baby?*)
- Grief *(Why am I still sad, even after becoming a parent?)*
- Insecurity (*What if everyone is right and I'm NOT the real mom/dad?*)
- Fear (*I'm going to be found out for the imposter that I am)*
- Feelings of inadequacy (*I presented myself as a stellar parent throughout the home study but here I am struggling with parenting*).

It's worth exploring the common challenges adoptive parents must confront and work through in order to navigate adoption most effectively. Why? Because adoptive parents provide the funding that drives the engine of the adoption industry as well as hold the power and privilege, as Kelsey shared in Chapter 11. We can and should use our power and privilege for good. By better understanding the impact of adoption on all involved and then "voting with our feet," we can aim our financial resources toward licensed adoption professionals who truly center adoptees and expectant parents, rather than professionals who center the transaction. This is how adopting and adoptive parents, by knowing better and doing better, must join their historically marginalized counterparts in reforming adoption.

Parenting, and even more so adoptive parenting, is often an invitation to a hero's journey. We may start with ignorance—a blind spot, which eventually and painfully becomes apparent to us. Next, we hear a call to rise to new challenges. We heed that call and emerge with new ways of seeing ourselves and the world, perhaps even ready to help others with our newfound wisdom. While we may start out naïve about the complexities of adoption, we begin the iterative and unending process of knowing and growing, seeing and slaying our own inner dragons, and eventually realizing what is required of us as the power-holders in adoption.

To know where we're going, let's first explore what true openness in adoption can look like for all adoptive families, both those that do have contact with birth family and those that don't.

CHAPTER 14

Getting to True Openness in Adoption

WHILE THE DYNAMICS OF OPEN ADOPTION HAVE YET TO BE understood by mainstream culture, for the last several decades more and more adopting and adoptive parents have been embracing open adoption. Though open adoption is by no means a panacea for the loss that comes with adoption, it has been an important step in centering adoptees' needs.

But what about intercountry and foster and closed adoptions, where open adoption may not be realistic? Or situations in which birth parents are unknown, on another continent, unsafe, incarcerated, unavailable, and even deceased?

I'm going to make a very bold statement that underlies everything this book is about: *Every adoption should be an open adoption.* Yes, you read that right. I repeat: *Every adoption should be an open adoption.*

How can I—and others involved in adoption reform—say this when I don't know all the things that can go upside down between adoptive parents and birth parents? How can I use an absolute such as "every" when every situation is different?

I can state this with confidence, if we examine what "open adoption" has historically meant and reconsider what it should mean instead. We've been measuring it all wrong, and I'll explain why.

Chapter 14

Contact Versus Openness

Historically, we have measured open adoption in terms of contact between the adoptive family and the birth family. We put open adoption on a spectrum, with "semi-open" and "semi-closed" somewhere between the extremes.

OPEN ADOPTION SPECTRUM

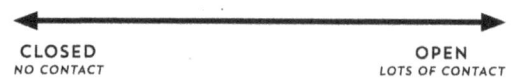

Figure 7

But there are two problems with using contact as the measure of an open adoption. First of all, it's imprecise; there is no consensus on what, exactly, we are measuring.

- Is it the *type* of contact? Is an open adoption based on periodic text messages equal to an open adoption based on periodic get-togethers? Is there a hierarchy among letters, texts, FaceTimes, in-person visits?
- Is it the *quantity* and *frequency* of contact: weekly, monthly, yearly, unscheduled?
- Is it the *quality* of contact—an unquantifiable but palpable way of how it feels to all those involved?

Contact as the measure may be a combination of all three aspects, but there is no precise and accepted definition of what constitutes an open adoption, other than the vague word "contact." If someone says they have an open adoption, you can't tell if there is a letter exchange to a P.O. box once a year, or if the families take vacations together.

The second problem with contact as the measure of an open adoption is its exclusivity. Parents who would otherwise *want* to have an open adoption but are faced with the unavailability of birth parents may feel unable to provide their child an open adoption.

And parents who are uncomfortable navigating relationships with birth parents, well, they may be glad to be excluded. But with a new measure of open adoption, they *must* get comfortable.

What is this new measure? It's not really new; it's been there all along. It's just been misunderstood and overshadowed by contact. This new measure sounds very familiar to what we're already used to, and it's much more integral to what serves the adoptee. The true measure of an open adoption should be—must be—openness.

For years, I mistakenly believed that open adoption was solely about my child's birth parents and me. As Kelsey stated in Chapter 12, I first thought open adoption was a favor for my children's birth moms (and, to a lesser extent, birth dads, as they were not present in our lives until years later), as well as an ongoing way to express gratitude for the opportunity to parent. Eventually, I came to understand that providing contact with my kids' birth parents turned out to be only part of our open adoptions. More importantly, open adoption was for my daughter and my son.

The real work came in learning to provide openness. How open and safe did I—*could* I—feel to them, to my children who

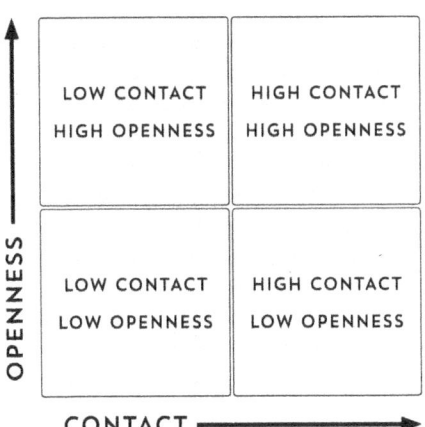

Figure 8
LORI HOLDEN, "OPEN ADOPTION GRID: ADDING A DIMENSION TO THE OPEN ADOPTION SPECTRUM," *LAVENDERLUZ.COM*, JANUARY 12, 2013, HTTPS://LAVENDERLUZ.COM/OPEN-ADOPTION-GRID/.

would, over time, have all their own thoughts and feelings about themselves, their adoptedness, their birth families?

This is when I added a vertical dimension to the horizontal spectrum to form the Open Adoption Grid (Figure 8), which includes both contact and openness in measuring the qualities of an adoption. *Every* adoption.

Some adoptees from the closed adoption era recognized this grid as representative of their experiences. After all, many of them grew up without contact in the decades before the movement toward open adoption, yet some still felt as though their parents provided for them a sense of openness. "This upper-left quadrant is how my parents raised me, what they gave to me," says interracial adoptee Angela Tucker. "While growing up, I had very little information about my birth parents, but my parents gave me the space to talk about my longing to know more about them, my desire to know more and more about my beginnings and my heritage."[1]

Angela, author of *You Should Be Grateful,* partnered with fellow adoptee and associate professor at the University of Washington Tacoma, Dr. JaeRan Kim, to further evolve the Open Adoption Grid into the Inclusive Family Support Model.

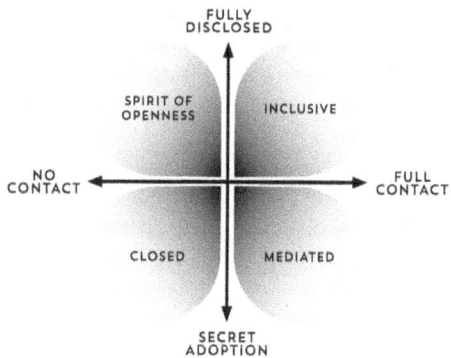

Figure 9

JAERAN KIM AND ANGELA TUCKER, "THE INCLUSIVE FAMILY SUPPORT MODEL: FACILITATING OPENNESS FOR POST-ADOPTIVE FAMILIES," *CHILD & FAMILY SOCIAL WORK* 25, NO. 1 (JULY 26, 2019), DOI:10.1111/CFS.12675.

Getting to True Openness in Adoption

Every adoptive family fits somewhere in this grid, even families that have no contact at all with birth parents. (To discover where your family is on the grid, please consult the IFSM assessment tool at https://bit.ly/AmaraOpennessAssessment.)

With a new, more precise, inclusive, and appropriate measure of what benefits adoptees most—openness—every adoption can and should be an open adoption. Regardless of contact, all adoptive parents should strive to be as open to dealing with and talking about adoption issues as they can be. Adoptive parents may not be able to fully control the horizontal aspect of their adoption arrangements, but we can always strive for elevation in the vertical component of them. When we focus on openness first, healthy decisions about contact will follow.

How to Elevate Your Openness

In reading this far, you have probably figured out that what everyone "knows" about adoption is incomplete at best and inaccurate at worst. We—adoptive parents, especially—may need to do some unlearning to make room for new information.

Myth: Closed adoption has always been the default setting.

Reality: I erroneously once believed that open adoption was something new, an anomaly to how adoption had always been practiced. I was surprised to later learn that confidentiality and sealing of records can be traced back only to 1917[2]—less than a century earlier—and that the practice of zealously inhibiting contact between birth and adoptive families began to decline in the 1990s. Adoptions became closed in a time when social pressures caused families to want to preserve the semblance of "as if born to."[3]

Open adoption wasn't the experiment; closed adoption was! And a failed one at that, as evidenced by all the adoptees and birth parents who "came out of the fog," found each other (pre-Internet!), raised their voices together, and began influencing social workers to do things differently in the latter part of the twentieth century. Our culture remains stuck in a closed adoption paradigm, with very few realizing all the ways it has failed people.

Myth: A "normal" family means exactly one mom and one dad.

Reality: In addition to the expectation that adoptive families appear as though they were biologically formed, there was also societal pressure in the mid-twentieth century for a rising White middle class to conform to the ideal standard of one mom and one dad. Now, decades later, complex families abound: one mom or one dad; two moms or two dads; or two households. Stepparents step in, as do grandparents and other kin. While we are no longer tied to the idea of the quintessential nuclear family, society's thinking around adoption has yet to catch up. Just look at the use of the word "real" around adoption. Pop culture is full of sensationalized stories that highlight an adoptee seeking, finding, and reuniting with their one and only "real" mom or "real" dad.

Even if adoptive parents were to scrub the word "real" from their vocabulary regarding parenting, an adoptee will still come home from second grade telling how another kid asked who their real mother is and why she didn't want them. "Real" splits our babies, and is just as cutting as the sword in the story of wise King Solomon and the two mothers.[4]

Once we unlearn that there can be more than one "real" mom or "real" dad in a child's life, we start to make a shift. We can recognize and honor that our child has the biology of one set of parents and the biography of another. When we shift from an Either/Or mindset—either *they* matter or *I* do—to a BothAnd[5] heartset— we signal that *all* are integral to the adoptee. It's a crucial step for parents to take for the sake of the adoptee and to set the stage for integration.

Evolving to a BothAnd heartset is not just about helping an adoptee incorporate all their parents into their sense of identity. It's also about us adoptive parents being able to accept the entire range of feelings we and our adoptee may have about adoption: love and loss, happiness and sorrow, contentment and anger, and all other emotions. Increasing our capacity to be that container for our child builds connection and provides space for our children to feel the gamut of their emotions and hopefully not get stuck in any of them.

Now let's shift from myth to math.

THE MATH OF OPENNESS

The closed adoption era demanded certain mathematical operations while the open adoption era requires something different from us. In the Either/Or mindset, we worked with subtraction (of birth parents), substitution (of adoptive parents), and division (of adoptee loyalties)—all of these taking away from the adoptee.

Consider instead a new math, that of addition and multiplication. When we include and honor our children's birth parents, whether present or not, we are adding to our children and not at all subtracting from ourselves. This new math comes easily with a BothAnd heartset.

If contact is possible, the benefits to the adoptee are many: connection with genetic family members and the genetic mirroring that goes with it; access to dynamic medical information of birth family (as opposed to the static records given at the time of an adoptee's birth, when birth parents are younger and presumably healthier than later in their lives); the ability to ask questions about the earliest chapters of an adoptee's life from those who were there, and hearing from the source why the adoptee was placed; with more details shared over time as the adoptee is able to understand more and more.

Even if contact isn't possible, openness always is—even if only in the ways we think and talk about our children's birth parents to honor their importance for our children.

Speaking of honoring, Sara ties together these themes of division, connection, and emotions in her essay "Moses and Me: A Biblical and Personal Case for Honoring Birth Mothers," which appeared in *Godspace*. An excerpt:

Chapter 14

My adoptive mother was uncomfortable talking about my first mother. And so I followed her lead. I hushed the questions that longed to spill from my heart. I did my best to make Mom happy. I had no choice—I couldn't risk losing another mother. It was a matter of survival.

It took me years to wake up to this, but I felt a divide. The significance of my first mother ignored, I felt I had to choose between mothers. One good. One bad. I don't think my mom minded much...until realizing she might not be the chosen one.[6]

As Sara reveals, the old math of subtraction created a divide. When our orientation is on addition and multiplication, there is more room in our adoptee's heart for *all* parents. Sharing our child doesn't mean we get half of them. It means we're setting the stage for our sons and daughters to move toward wholeness and healing. This summarizes the ultimate purpose of openness in adoption.

What keeps us adoptive parents from being able to take a stance of openness? Let's take a look at some untended wounds adoptive parents may carry.

Chapter 15
Unacknowledged Grief

JUST AS GRIEF IS A THREAD UNDERLYING MANY DYNAMICS FOR adoptees and birth parents, grief can also be an emotional undercurrent for adoptive parents. And in similar ways, grief for adoptive parents can often go unseen, unrecognized, and untended.

INFERTILITY-RELATED GRIEF
Often by the time a person or couple sets out to adopt a newborn, they have already endured a lengthy, expensive, and possibly fruitless journey of infertility, whether biological or situational.

Fairly common among moms who come to adoption through infertility (and possibly so, but less documented, for dads) are the emotional wounds that come from struggling with infertility. There is the pain of not being able to complete one of the most fundamental of biological processes—to procreate—as well as the indignities of fertility treatments themselves. There is high-level and high-stakes uncertainty along the way, often culminating in failure and, worse, unimaginable loss. Whether the issue is not being able to conceive, not being able to carry, or not being able to deliver a live baby, by the time a person/couple has arrived at the choice of adoption, chances are they have endured a lot of physical and emotional suffering.

There's usually immense grief and sadness that comes with infertility. For those of us who have spent what feels like a lifetime dreaming about having children, an inability to get pregnant or carry a pregnancy to term can feel utterly devastating. As children, we may have incorporated ideas about our future children into our play. Later, upon experiencing brand-new romantic love, we might have found ourselves gazing at a potential partner who'd captured our heart and fantasizing about what our children would look like. These are common experiences and daydreams. Like other mammals, humans are biologically wired to want to pass on our genetics, though not all individuals within our species feel this need acutely, if at all.

When hopes are thwarted for reasons outside our control, when dreams to bear children cannot be realized, there is loss. Will we find our way through it or not? We may feel distraught and unsettled, perhaps powerless and even hopeless. If others around us are becoming parents, and it seems so easy for them, we may feel isolated and alone. We *want* to celebrate our friends as they experience the joys of pregnancy, and at the same time, our loss remains a well of sadness within. We may feel brokenness and shame. While we've moved past loaded terms like "barren" that historically shamed women unable to reproduce, it can be embarrassing to talk publicly about infertility, leading to more isolation. Invitations to baby showers, though celebratory, can also leave us feeling the pain all over again. With thoughts of pregnancy weighing so heavily on our minds, it seems we see pregnant women all around us, looking robust and glorious and full of the promise of new life... more reminders of the ache inside us to experience that same creating-of-life energy.

Grieving is hard. As a culture and as individuals, we often go to great lengths to avoid it. Couples may be tempted to avoid approaching the well of grief by shifting the focus toward building a family another way. Adoption can seem to offer resolution—a way to regain a sense of control over uncontrollable circumstances—especially in a culture that paints adoption as win/win.

Even if it might be better for us to pause and grieve, our minds can play tricks on us. Why wallow endlessly in sadness when we can focus on the excitement of planning and preparing to adopt a baby? Rushing us along is a sense of the clock ticking on our attractiveness in the eyes of an expectant parent in a society that raises eyebrows at older parents.

BABY FEVER: WHEN UNPROCESSED GRIEF LEADS TO MYOPIA

While adoption is undoubtedly going to fill us with both sadness and excitement, along with many more emotions, the unconscious desire to get to the other side of the pain as quickly as possible can present as an intense case of Baby Fever. Not only can Baby Fever divert us from feeling our underlying grief but it can also blind us. Instead of proceeding with caution, care, and sensitivity, we might rush toward adoption focused primarily on surface-level questions like: how long will it take? And how much will it cost? This isn't because adoptive parents are heartless, but it's because we, like adoptees and birth parents, are living with a human brain that seeks protection from overwhelming pain.

"When an agency said it could get us a newborn in under a year, I was ready to sign up without digging in any deeper. Fast was important—everything was about becoming a mom during the time when I was blinded by Baby Fever,"[1] shares Rebecca, vulnerably sharing feelings she'd had as a prospective adoptive parent twenty-five years ago that she admits now make her cringe.

"On my end," says Beth, a mother through intercountry adoption, "there had been brutal fertility treatments culminating in a near nervous breakdown from grief and failure. I wasn't thinking of all the possible things that could go wrong in pursuing adoption; I was just hoping that a child would make things better. I got busy with adoption paperwork and getting our house and life ready for a baby."[2]

Chapter 15

The problem with trying to run from grief by looking for an easy fix is that infertility grief doesn't just magically disappear when we adopt a baby. As is grief's way it will catch up to us eventually. And like any big grief there may not be an end point. Sometimes we think we're through it but end up surprised that the loss remains, perhaps below our level of awareness. And it can affect both how we parent our adopted children and how we experience the parenting journey.

Rebecca shares, "I noticed something was wrong when I still felt insecure, despite finally being a mom to my sweet child. Sure, I'd made it into the mom club, which I'd longed to join for years, but even with my daughter in my arms, I still felt like an outsider."

Like Rebecca, Mallory, who is another adoptive mom through domestic infant adoption, felt similarly at first. "*Finally, I thought, I could be a part of those mom conversations and not someone on the outside looking in!* But what happened was that other moms were still talking about pregnancy, birth, and breastfeeding. Even though I had a baby in my arms, I couldn't take part in the conversations."[3]

Both Rebecca and Mallory had realized their dreams of starting a family and it fulfilled them in ways beyond any they could have anticipated. And yet their grief hadn't vanished. When other moms talked about their experiences of pregnancy, delivery, or nursing their infants the sadness showed up again, reminding them of experiences with their children that they had missed out on.

Another problem with experiencing Baby Fever is that it can end up hurting others. Adoptees can feel commodified, as though they were only a means to our end. Birth parents can feel this way as well, as if their losses don't matter and are just par for the course to grant adoptive parents' wishes. Getting stuck in a case of Baby Fever gets adoptive parents called names like adoptoraptor, meaning "a person who adopts a child for his/her own selfish needs."[4] Adoption in these cases can look a lot like narcissism.

For these reasons, it is crucial for us as adoptive parents to step outside ourselves to see and empathize with others' perspectives. I'll be getting to that more in later chapters.

SECOND-HAND GRIEF

When we grow a family through adoption there is likely to be grief to process beyond infertility grief, such as the grief we carry on behalf of our children. No caring parent wants to see their child suffer and it's a lot to hold the pain the child has experienced before coming to our families and because of adoption. It weighs heavily on a parent's heart. Even in what may from the outside seem like "ideal" circumstances—with a parent voluntarily placing a child, with a commitment to openness, with no substance use during pregnancy, no experiences of abuse—the trauma of family separation remains an incredibly difficult way for a baby to enter life, as Sara articulated in Part I.

When we parent a child through adoption there is no way to erase our child's suffering. It is simply not possible when adoption occurs because of and through loss. But again, that powerlessness over the cards dealt to our child can fill us with grief and it can be compounded by almost overwhelming guilt and shame, wondering if we had a role in creating pain for our children. Sometimes, in fact, we may have and there's mourning in this knowledge, too.

"Realizing that the adoption experience for my children was not the beautiful, happily ever after story I had believed in was very painful,"[5] says Karla, who adopted her two daughters from an orphanage in Haiti. "I had to take a hard look at my own misconceptions and biased perspectives that had contributed to their trauma. I wanted to defend my good intentions. I loved my children and would never knowingly do anything to harm them. But I had to face facts, regardless of my feelings. If I was going to change and grow to be a better support and ally for my children, I first needed to acknowledge my culpability."

Chapter 15

Those who are especially sensitive may also feel grief on behalf of our child's birth parents. If we think about their loss or have the opportunity to see it up close through an open adoption, we can be filled with more grief. Our gains have come at a price for another—even in situations where a parent voluntarily chooses adoption. Witnessing another's loss is sad as is knowing you get to watch and participate in milestones that another parent is missing out on.

Leslie, who with her husband adopted their daughter, five, and their son, three, as newborns, expresses the complexity of emotions she carries. "I worried about them [their birth mothers] when we brought both of our babies home because I knew their moms were thinking of those babies, too. I also felt guilt because I got to be there for the first scraped knee and the midnight cuddles. I knew how much I loved my children, so to not be with them? I couldn't imagine how devastating that was for their birth moms."[6]

The Temptation of Avoidance

Just like adoptees and birth parents can't look directly at their substantial grief, adoptive parents often have difficulty getting too closely acquainted with their grief. The temptation is to avoid the grief, not talk about it, not name it. Don't discuss it. Ignore it and maybe it will disappear. Like a baby hiding their face in a game of peekaboo and thinking they can't be seen, we might look away in hopes of making the pain of our children and their birth families disappear.

Trauma responses in our children might even seem to validate this approach. If our children themselves can't look at the pain of adoption until they're twenty, thirty, forty, or more years old, decades can pass where everyone is avoiding acknowledging the grief and loss, possibly cementing the idea that we've somehow made it vanish. But again, unresolved grief doesn't go away so easily. And these big griefs never seem to get fully checked off, though many find that the pain fades over time.

As this chapter shows, a common struggle of adoptive parents is the immense grief that exists in adoption. In the next chapter, we dive into the causes and impacts of another common dynamic, insecurity.

Chapter 16

Insecurity

At the root of much dysfunction in adoptive families is often a sense of insecurity that comes from not being the only mom or the only dad. There's no way around it: adoption includes more than one set of parents and recognizing this can be a painful reality. Sharing isn't always easy—especially when it comes to sharing a beloved child.

But that child's roots matter and it's crucial that adoptive parents move beyond their insecurity to become adoptee-centric. Attempts to dismiss—or worse, eradicate—the genetic and psychic attachment an adoptee has with their family-of-origin create an emotional divide within the adoptee where they feel they must choose to love either their adoptive parents or their birth parents. This is an unfair choice and sets everyone up for a lot of pain.

It is much healthier all-around to acknowledge and embrace reality: whether birth parents are around or not, we *are* sharing our child. Birth parents are there—in our child's DNA, in their implicit memories, in their wonderings, in their origin stories, and in their hearts. We can share with fear and resistance or we can share with grace and openness. One of these routes fosters connection with our child and support for healing. It's imperative to monitor the choices we make.

EITHER/OR MINDSET: WHO'S THE *REAL* PARENT?

Categorizing people and situations is something we humans do as a means of simplifying a complex and ever-changing world. Categorization isn't bad, but without checks and balances it can turn polarizing—such as when others seek to categorize our family dynamics. Throughout their lives adoptees are often asked, "Who is your *real* mother?" In similar ways, adoptive parents are asked this question, too. The implied message is that only one set of parents is legitimate—real. In a society that focuses on Either/Or, one parent (or set) must be a victor and one a loser. If our sense of insecurity remains unaddressed and unresolved, we may be unaware that we ourselves are feeling shaky about our own legitimacy, fearful that we aren't "real" enough in the eyes of society and perhaps even our child.

A subconscious case of imposter syndrome can cause us to go to great lengths to cover up our shameful fear. We may be unable or unwilling to enter conversations about adoption or feel the need to elevate ourselves while also putting down birth-family members in subtle or glaring ways. In open adoptions we may avoid or close off contact with birth family. None of these behaviors serve the child or the parent-child relationship.

Most new parents question their legitimacy and feel their confidence falter at different points in their parenting journeys. New adoptive parents have additional dynamics to maneuver, since there is another mom and another dad in the picture and it can take time and attention to get to the other side of feelings of insecurity.

Mallory and her husband are parenting E, seven, adopted at birth. Initially Mallory struggled over sharing "her" son: "I did not expect the emotional response I'd have to his birth parents claiming him as well, calling him 'their' son. My fears at that time were around E feeling angry at us for adopting him, or not feeling bonded to us. Looking back, I see that these feelings had very little to do with his birth parents and what they were doing, and everything to do with me trying to understand and create my identity as a mother."[1]

Rebecca shares about the early days in her adoptive parenting journey. "I had trouble accepting the truth that another woman also had a claim on my daughter, even more legitimate than mine. The fact that I wasn't the only mom was so hard to face that I went to great lengths to *not* face it."[2]

Mallory shares: "In the early days, E's birth mom already had her 'mine' experience because she grew him and birthed him, but I had not yet found my 'mine' experience, so it felt imbalanced. When she and her mom posted things on Facebook like, *We're going to raise him to like this sports team* or she would call him *my baby*, this felt very threatening to me."

My own initial experience of insecurity was an intense one. It happened the first time my husband and I visited our daughter's birth mom, Crystal, at her mom's home, where both she and her grandmother were staying, to introduce the newborn to the family matriarchs. Crystal's grandmother was thrilled to meet her great-granddaughter and within moments these three generations of mothers were checking to see if the new baby had the family toes, a wonky pinky toe.

She did.

I *don't* have a wonky pinky toe. Thoughts inside my head were yelling that I didn't belong in this picture. How could I ever be my daughter's real mom without the family toes? Who did I think I was fooling with the outlandish idea that I could be a mom—*her* mom?

To make matters worse, the baby started to cry, needing to be changed or fed—who could tell which!? In my inexperience as a brand-new parent, I had forgotten the diaper bag in the car. Now *everybody* else knew I was an impostor. I wanted to hide.

Crystal saved the day. Already a mother of a four-year-old son, she said, "Hey, Mama, you'd better go get that diaper bag. Looks like Little Missy here needs a change. I mean it *smells* like she needs a change!" My internal crisis was averted by Crystal's levity and grace.

And with that gift in that moment, I felt my insecurity long enough to name it. Crystal witnessed it, too, and offered not only compassion but also permission for me to be a real mom.

It's no surprise that many adoptive parents suffer from insecurity. But acknowledging its presence helps to grieve and heal it. Insecurity usually feels like contraction, like shutting down—perhaps explaining why so many open adoptions eventually close. Signals and sensations may include tightness in the chest or belly, an instinct to hide, a desire to overcompensate for the smallness by asserting power and becoming rigid. Noticing these signs can provide the opportunity to instead opt for expansion, making way for continual resolution and ongoing healing from insecurity. Sometimes simply being able to notice it and name it—*wow, when she called him her son, I felt a stab of insecurity*—begins to neutralize it so that we don't inadvertently hurt our children by parenting from our places of insecurity.

BothAnd Heartset: All Parents Are Real

A BothAnd heartset is a sign of maturity, so it can take time to evolve beyond an Either/Or mindset—it's rare to get there overnight and often it's specific situations that lead us on a path toward growth. Mallory recalls such a situation that helped her move into and beyond her insecurity. "One time I posted online about how I felt weird when birth family continued to claim 'my' son. Birth parents and adoptees in the group called me out for being so self-centered in my complaint, which came from my own insecurities starting to surface. While the response didn't feel great, it was really helpful. I needed to hear that I was being unreasonable, that he IS their child, that what the birth family were saying didn't have to take away from me, and that I could start to let it go."

Leslie, mom to two children via infant adoption, recalls being struck by a sense of shared humanity with her daughter's birth mom and how it helped her evolve. "We are both women. We are both mothers in different ways to this sweet child. Being able to show my child THAT can help make things better.[3] She adds, "It wasn't rational, like, *Hey I should really get over this. It's not good for my child.* It was more like a nurturing feeling toward our children's birth mothers as mothers, as fellow women no better and no worse than me. It was a wave of empathy that comes from a shared humanity."

Empathy, humanity, connection, gratitude; as Leslie came to understand, these are the ingredients necessary to any healthy, resilient, and well-functioning relationship.

Mallory says that another resource that helped her look at and begin resolving her insecurity was Amy Seek's memoir, *God and Jetfire: Confessions of a Birth Mother*.

"Amy Seek said she always felt watched with her son," says Mallory. "So we started leaving our son alone with his parents during visits. When he was about eight months old, we left him in their care while we ran an errand, and they reached out later to say how much it meant to them. I cannot stress how much connecting with birth parents online and reading Amy's book helped me. I'd been seeing everything only through my own lens and understanding what first parents go through was paramount."

When adoptive parents find a way to sense, acknowledge, and address insecurity that stems from not being the only mom or dad, from not giving birth to their child and sharing their DNA, from the existence of another legitimate family, they can begin to heal their wounds and better support the adoptee they love. Insecurity can resolve bit-by-bit as parents become more aware of others' perspectives, namely adoptees and birth parents—and their own deeper emotions around being parents by adoption. Ultimately, the goal is to see all parents as real, leading the way for adoptees to be able to comfortably feel this way, too.

WHEN CULTURAL UNDERSTANDING LAGS
Mallory and her husband were committed to having an ongoing

relationship with their son's birth parents. But she found an added complication: a lack of understanding on the part of friends and family. "I got understanding and education from our agency and from the cross-triad online group," she says, "but I found that I could not expect to get it from friends and family. Often they would reinforce negative and harmful ideas and practices around openness out of ignorance. My mom would have told me to cut off the birth family or demand they stop claiming our son, or something else unhelpful."

Though adoption professionals and adoptive families have been trending toward openness in adoption for decades, the general population has yet to understand that truth and transparency is healthier for all involved than is secrecy and the shame. We all understand the unspoken message that whatever we can't or won't talk about must mean there is something awful about it. As Sara shared in Part I, a young adoptee who has no one to talk with them about their adoptedness may end up personalizing that lack of talking as their own shame.

Further, the idea that an Either/Or mindset can make way for a BothAnd heartset has yet to become a mainstream idea. Society is still stuck in a closed adoption-era notion that there can be only one legitimate set of parents and the resulting zero-sum game decrees that any legitimacy granted to birth parents comes at the expense of the adoptive parents. As Mallory relayed this common experience, well-meaning friends, and family of adoptive parents often second-guess the presence of birth parents in an adoptee's life, perhaps out of ignorance of evolving practices as well as a desire to protect the adoptive parents.

Adoptees report that adoptive parents' ability to make space for birth parents, whether present in an adoptee's life or not, actually *strengthens* their bond with their adoptive parents rather than weakening it and research bears this out.[4] Much like "splitting the child" in a contentious divorce, we know that "splitting the child" in adoption, or expecting the adoptee to have loyalty to one side over the other, harms the adoptee and weakens a genuine and enduring connection between the adoptive parent and the adoptee.

Insecurity comes not only from within an adoptive parent but also from a culture that says there can be only one "real" set of parents. This is why so many adoptive parents have work to do to remedy their sense of insecurity within themselves and as a cultural narrative.

Mallory offers this advice: "Seek a community of people who understand and support openness in adoption. The sad truth is that most cannot understand why you are so committed to including birth family whenever possible. Friends and family have absorbed an insecurity and will advise you from that insecurity. Make sure you have people around you who know that being open comes from being secure in your role."

From Insecurity to Making Space for Birth Family

The ability and willingness for adoptive parents to make space for birth parents, physically and emotionally, is a critical component for the emotional health of the adoptee and the strength of the relationship between the adoptee and their parents. Adoptee and playwright Suzanne Bachner told me this during a podcast interview: "An adoptive parent can start carving that space from Day Zero, before the kid comes into their home, even. It needs to be a co-creation to keep space for those other people who are part of the kid."[5]

Carving out space offers an unexpected benefit for the adoptive parents. For when an adoptee feels like they do not have permission to think and wonder about their birth parents, they are apt to create fantasy birth parents and have fantasy attachments to them (recall Sara's discussion on fantasy attachment in Chapter 3). How can an actual, known parent who puts limits on behavior, bedtime, snacks, and activities compete with a fantasy birth parent? It's a paradox of adoptive parenting: if an adoptive parent wants their child's heart, they need to be willing to share it with whomever else the adoptee needs to invite in.

Healing from insecurity is something adoptive parents need to champion within themselves, between them and their adoptees, and radiate outward to help change society's ideas about what an adoptee-centered adoption looks like, one in which there is space for all. I'm making it sound simple, though it's not always so straightforward. Likely moving past insecurity is something each adoptive parent may have to address again and again over time.

Leslie realizes she is at the start of a very long journey, one that will continually bring new situations, emotions, and challenges. "While I would like to think I have it all figured out, I don't. I am still learning. Sometimes it will hurt. Sometimes it will make me feel overjoyed, but at the end of the day, I want to do right by my children and by the people who made it possible for me to be their mother. Our children should not have to sacrifice one family to gain another. We are all their family. I try to be secure in that."

Mallory, too, knows that being mindful of her own feelings of insecurity will continue to be important for her and her son. "I can't speak to the future, as each new life stage opens us up to discover new things about ourselves," says Mallory, "but at this time I feel very secure in my relationship with my son and his relationship with his birth parents. I worry more that he will *not* feel close and connected enough with his birth parents than I worry about him getting too close to them."

Mallory encourages prospective adoptive parents by saying, "Expectations are premeditated resentments. If you go into your adoption experience with set ideas about how it will feel and look, you will end up disappointed. Daydreaming is normal and fun but in the end you have to be ready to see where the path takes you and constantly adjust your expectations. You cannot control what you, your child, or their family will feel or do, so stop trying. Being rigid is one way insecurity expresses itself, so if you want to feel more secure in your role, stay flexible."

Working through issues of insecurity can transform an adoptive parent from someone who *avoids* contact to one who *creatively seeks* contact with birth-family members, thereby bringing a sprit of true openness to the adoptee. Healing from insecurity—or not—has effects that ripple through generations. Parents are wise to find their new path of feeling secure in their role as parents, trusting that the existence of birth parents is not a threat, but rather a pathway to extended family. To be able to metabolize insecurity about birth family and culture, and transform it into openness and curiosity, is one of the greatest gifts a parent can give their child.

Now that we've covered insecurity, in which dysfunctional defenses are up, let's start with an adoption trope that can cause adoptive parents to be unprepared for adoption's many complexities.

CHAPTER 17

Parenting through the Complexities of Adoption

ALL YOU NEED IS LOVE? (NOT SO FAST.)

Love is one of the most powerful forces in the universe. Just ask any spiritual teacher or The Beatles. All you need is love, and love is all you need. Love, said the poet Virgil, conquers all.[1]

It's no wonder that many people come into adoption believing so. Embedded in the expectation that love alone can prevent or resolve anything that needs conquering are several erroneous assumptions, such as:

- The baby is a blank slate whose script can be written by loving parents;
- Genetics and biology don't really matter compared to love;
- There is no trauma in being relinquished—especially at birth—and being adopted means a child is loved and lucky.

This book has been examining these cornerstones of the conventional wisdom of adoption. As you've seen throughout, the baby is *not* a blank slate, genetics and biology *do* matter, and there *is* trauma in being separated from one's mother and one's child.

On the long journey of parenting, these realities and others set in. Parenting is not poetry and love does not, in fact, conquer all when it comes to a child who has experienced separation trauma. Adoptive parents are parenting a child who has, at the very least, experienced the wounding of separation from a birth mother, who at one time had been the adoptee's entire universe (as Sara explained in Chapter 2). In the case of infant adoption the adoptee's brain may have been developing during a time when the mother was experiencing anguish, anxiety, uncertainty, and/or abuse, the forming brain swimming in cortisol due to maternal stress. The baby may have spent their entire gestation period being unacknowledged and psychologically unconnected. In the case of older-child adoption, there may also be postnatal trauma. In the case of intercountry adoption, there is usually cultural shock, as well.

Most adoptive parents eventually face the hard reality that it is not possible to love away an adoptee's struggles. Love *is* a powerful force. No healthy family can function without an abundance of it. But it's simplistic to think that love heals all. Sooner or later, families of all sorts, adoptive and otherwise, come to understand this. Family relationships, especially those with the not-insignificant component of adoption, are more complex than we can imagine, even when we commit to an ever-growing awareness and understanding of the vast spectrum of the adoptee experience. Love and optimism carry us further than we might go without it, but sooner or later it becomes clear that neither optimism nor love can dissolve all difficulties, of which there are many in adoption. This chapter covers some such challenges.

Early Life Experiences Matter

Karla, whom we met in Chapter 15, initially discounted the impact of the years her daughters lived in Haiti. "Even though I anticipated struggles along the way, I was optimistic. Children are flexible. Children adapt. My daughters would be so happy with all of the good things this new life brought them."[2] Mainstream information on adoption and parenting seemed to support such simplistic thinking, but Karla soon learned otherwise.

"Our first year together, the girls would occasionally start crying and not be able to stop," says Karla. "They would let me hold them, but they could not be consoled. They needed to cry out their pain, which I recognized as grief. My younger daughter was able to put words to her pain. When I asked, 'What is making you cry?' she would answer, 'I am thinking of Nanoush'—her name for her Haitian mother. I would tell her Nanoush is thinking about you. This went on into the second year but less often."

"I was astounded by the revelation that a baby knows their mother from the womb," says Karla. "Her smell, her voice, her heartbeat. Even a child adopted at birth has a subconscious realization that this is not my mother. Relinquishment can cause deep fear in their soul. Our children may struggle to believe that the world is safe and that they will not be abandoned again. Walls go up to protect their hearts. I began to see these things in my girls. I had no idea that so much is imprinted in the nine months they are developing in the womb."

"I had to face the hard truth," says Karla, "that giving my children a 'better' life was actually not better in many critical ways. It was heartbreaking and painful to finally get that."

Beth, also a mom via intercountry adoption, was confronted with the ways adoption and early history affected her son during his adolescence, when he began to seriously struggle. Reflecting on what she knew from the agency paperwork, Beth shares that her son's experiences after his birth were not ideal. For two weeks, he stayed with his birth mother and her family while they figured out what to do. "Those weeks must have been filled with angst and overwhelm,"[3] says Beth. "Then he was transferred to a maternity hospital, where he stayed until we met him seven months later. His caretakers changed every eight hours. I put myself in his shoes and realized how chaotic and scary that must have seemed for an infant, whose task at that age is to attach to a stable caretaker."

CHAPTER 17

The Complexities of Interracial Adoption

Karla knew that bringing a Haitian child home to her mostly White, rural town would present challenges for a child, so she decided to adopt two children who would share a common history, culture, and racial background.

"I considered myself colorblind," she says, reflecting on her initial naiveté. "My thinking was that color and nationality didn't matter. We are all God's children, and I believed having a multiracial family would give us a chance to show the world that it is all about love." She adds, "I was prepared to provide everything my children lacked, and every opportunity for them to grow to their potential. I knew my church community would embrace the girls and we would be surrounded by love, attention, and nurturing."

Karla eventually discovered how difficult the deep and hidden trauma of adoption and the complex dynamics of interracial adoption would be for her daughters. She began educating herself on issues at the core of her daughters' experiences and deepening her understanding of both adoption and racial issues. "I had unknowingly operated from the harmful belief that White values, culture, and aesthetics were preferable. I had looked at the children of Haiti and felt that I and my community could save them from this life of poverty. I assumed what I had to offer was inherently better. I learned that it is not. In not seeing color, I was actually not seeing my daughters."

Lisa, another White adoptive mom to an intercountry adoptee of color, has stepped up in this way. "It's imperative for me to educate myself on race and adoption so that my child doesn't need to do that. I'm the adult and the parent. Learning these things is my work; teaching them to me is not hers."[4]

Post-Visit Meltdowns in Open Adoptions

When there is contact between adoptive and birth families, there is also additional complexity. One aspect is what happens when meltdowns occur after a visit.

On the surface, it may seem like the visit causes the child to have a meltdown. That train of thought might lead parents to a seemingly logical solution: reduce the number of visits, or cease having them altogether because it's just too hard on the adoptee.

But by this point in reading, and from your own journey to deepen your understanding of the complexities of adoption, you may already know that the easy answer is often not the best answer.

"Last year, we visited our daughter's birth family at the start of our family vacation,"[5] says Sujata, a school psychologist and adoptive mom of a ten-year-old. "As we left their home to continue with our itinerary, our daughter asked if we would circle back around later in the trip. We explained that we would not be seeing her birth family again this time, but we would another time."

Near the last day of their vacation, Sujata's daughter started melting down. "We were in the most gorgeous setting at the end of a wonderful vacation, and she was more upset than we'd ever seen her. I worried for her, and I wondered, *what is she going through*? I realized I didn't need to know exactly. But I did understand that having just seen her birth family, she was probably feeling deep sadness seeing a life she doesn't get to have. How could she put words to all of that?"

I, too, have observed similar situations with families I coach through tricky open adoption situations. Rather than the visit itself being the *cause* of a meltdown, often instead it is the big emotions that arise at the *end* of the visit. In other words, the meltdowns result less from the hello and more from the goodbye. If this is the case, then the simplistic solution of reducing or eliminating visits does not address the core issue, which is sadness and grief that have no outlet (see Frustration Traffic Circle, Figure 6). In fact, such a solution can actually make things worse for the adoptee, and for the adoptee's relationship with their parents. What can adoptive parents do in response to a post-visit meltdown?

Sujata found an answer. "All we could do was to be there with her as she moved through her big emotions. We can just be in the muck and let it be messy, and validate her feelings by saying *I really miss your grandmother, too*, so that she doesn't have to hold it all by herself. We can acknowledge her BothAnd—that she loves her life with us, and also that she misses her birth family and longs for a life with them, too."

As is the case so often, feeling was not the problem, but rather the solution. "We let her have it all, feel it all," says Sujata. "We want her to know we can handle it."

POWER AND BOUNDARIES

A dynamic and structural aspect that undergirds relationships between birth and adoptive families is that of setting and patrolling boundaries.

Boundaries get a bad rap. We often think of boundaries as creating separation. But in truth, and in the words of Prentis Hemphill, "boundaries are the distance at which I can love you and me simultaneously."[6] In short, boundaries are necessary for connection. But for them to work as designed, they need to be set mindfully from our healthy selves and not from our fearful, insecure selves.

In Chapter 11, Kelsey laid out the power differential that exists between birth and adoptive parents. Before the ink is dry on the documents that reassign the parentage of a child, the power shifts like a playground see-saw when one kid hops off. Birth parents go from one-hundred percent to zero, and correspondingly, adoptive parents go from zero to one-hundred percent power. And we know what they say about absolute power: "power tends to corrupt, and absolute power corrupts absolutely."[7]

We owe it to our adoption counterparts to use our power wisely and compassionately.

Leah Campbell, adoptive mom and author of *The Story of My Open Adoption*, noted this: "I have more power than my daughter. I have more power than her mom. It's my responsibility to give power where I can."[8]

Does this mean Leah gives away her power and has no boundaries? Not at all. It means she is in tune with what does and doesn't work for her daughter at each decision point. It means she is making as much space as possible in her own heart for her daughter's birth family members. With awareness of these boundaries and an overarching desire to eventually empower her daughter to manage her relationships with birth family members, Leah discerns her boundaries with clarity and as much expansiveness as possible in each boundary-setting moment.

Kelsey reminded us that birth parents deserve to have boundaries, too. When we are on the receiving end of boundaries, we must try to be gracious, as well. We may not be privy to all that goes into a person's boundaries, but it costs nothing to assume best intent, that our child's other mom or other dad is doing the best they can with what they have to work with. Aren't we all?

It takes a high degree of emotional intelligence to monitor and manage the emotions that ebb and flow in one's self, one's child, and the adoptee's birth parents over time. Contrary to what some initially believe, open adoption does *not* mean a relationship without boundaries. Instead, healthy open adoptions—like all healthy relationships—require an ability to set boundaries of the Goldilocks sort: not too little and not too much. When we mess up on boundaries, which we inevitably will, we count the learning experience and do our best over and over.

CHALLENGES OF ADOLESCENCE

Adolescence can be challenging for many adoptees and their families. Since it's such an important time of identity formation and because separation is part of every adoptee's experience, this time of life can be additionally difficult. As Sara covered in Part I, feeling adoption's many losses is what leads to adaptation and maturation. But the wounds of adoption run so deep that many adoptees are unable to look at the pain too closely, making adolescence a time full of added turbulence.

Chapter 17

Karla says, "Around adolescence, the girls pushed me away and did not want to talk about their adoption. One daughter began acting out. She was defiant and I could see she was deeply unhappy with her life. The other was quieter and seemed, I thought, to be well-adjusted. She was artistic and did a lot of art, writing, dancing, and acting—her ways of escaping and coping. Our home was a war zone at times, as the girls argued and fought with me and each other."

What are the underlying dynamics between parent and adoptee during the tumultuous and often extended period of adolescence? During these push-away years an adoptee takes on the daunting task of identity formation (*who am I distinct from those around me and without genetic mirrors?*) and identity integration (of both birth and adoptive families and one's culture). Parents must remain one-hundred percent committed to the challenge of allowing separation while remaining connected. It's a tall order to recognize and make space for the BothAnd of separation and connection for years on end but it is possible, as other parents who've walked this journey reveal.

Lisa recalls when her adolescent daughter had had a rough day at school. "Some of her attachment issues were triggered by peers, so we connected by going to the mall and having boba tea together. I was actively listening to the details of her hard day, and she was responding and softening. It felt like a moment of deep connection, like I was able to be there for her and she knew she could depend on me."

But two hours later, Lisa reports, there was a snapback. "My daughter's behavior became uncharacteristically mean. *Why are you doing this?* I thought. It felt so close, and now this? I realized that the issues she has with attachment mean not only that she needs to feel secure, but also that she needs to test that security. When that happens, I must provide that space for her. I need to do whatever it takes to remain a constant for her."

Adoptees and Substance Use
"When he was about fifteen," says Beth, "my son, who had appeared to me to be a model child, began struggling in ways that were alarming. I never dreamed he would develop a major addiction or that he'd occasionally become violent toward himself and others. My original dreams for him have been dramatically revised in the last few years. Now my dream for him is that he stay alive and no longer need to numb or stop his pain."

Paul Sunderland is Clinical Director of Outcome Consulting in the UK, a psychotherapist who is oft-cited about the connection between adoption and addiction. He noticed that adoptees are overrepresented in treatment and suggests that the wound of relinquishment "can be seen as developmental post-traumatic stress disorder."[9] Sunderland explains:

> The legacy of this trauma for the relinquished child is a conflict between wanting to connect and fearing connection. This is often experienced as a hypervigilance that has an enormous impact on relationships and functioning which can disrupt the ability to be present, with feelings that one is both 'too much' and 'not enough'.

People, especially those who "do not have a pre-trauma personality," as Sunderland states, need ways to deal with the big emotions that come from big trauma. An even more extreme way an adoptee might try to resolve the urge to not feel is to consider, and maybe even attempt, suicide.

Suicide Attempts and Ideation
In spite of statistics that show adoptees are overrepresented in suicide attempts,[10] it's not uncommon for adoptive parents to never anticipate suicidal ideation as something that could affect their children, nor link such thinking to adoption. "Even at my son's

first suicide attempt," says Beth, "adoption wasn't on my radar as a possible factor."

What may look like a compliant adoptee may actually be a person who is desperately trying not to lose yet another mother or father and trying to keep signs of emotional struggle hidden. "A lot of adopted children and adults seem fine,"[11] says Amanda Woolston, adoptee and therapist.

Adoptee and memoirist Kevin Barhydt speaks of the agony and emptiness that solidified his low self-worth on a panel of adult adoptees presented by United Suicide Survivors International. "Suicidal ideation wasn't a definition to me; it was a companion, a friend. The sense of abandonment and relinquishment had echoed through every relationship I'd had. When you loved me, I knew you were going to leave me. When you hired me, I knew you were going to fire me. When you became my friend, I knew that was transactional and was going to end at some point."[12]

Not feeling big emotions is part of the issue when it comes to suicidal ideation, as Sara explained in Chapter 5. "We fundamentally disconnect from ourselves," says Lynelle Long, adoptee and founder of InterCountry Adoptee Voices."[13]

Feeling the sadness of adoption, as we learned in Part I, is what can start the healing. But *how*, when the emotions are so deep, so scary, so isolating? What can parents do to facilitate the feeling of these emotions?

Finding a support group, an adoption-fluent therapist, and/or an adoptee mentor (or more than one!) can ease the isolation, provide validation, and foster a sense of felt safety to brave the big, scary emotions around adoption—and tether adoptees through meaningful connections.

Lynelle explains how connection was healing for her. "The power of group connection, the validation, the empathy I received was so incredibly healing. There was finally some light, some examples of how to move through this pain and the fact that you can come out the other side. Some hope."

Amanda Woolston cautions adoptive parents not to delay getting help out of fear of judgment. "You almost need to remove yourself out of it and really focus on what your child needs, and getting them resources."

Adoptive mother and adoption educator Maureen McCauley reminds us: "We send our children to therapy. We should also be participating in therapy. It shouldn't be just the child; it has to be a family effort."[14]

Extended Adolescence

If an adoptee is slower to mature than their counterparts, there may be an extended adolescence and delayed launching of adult children. Should adoptive parents worry?

"While we parents may assume maturation in line with our children's age, it may end up being more asynchronous than we expect," says Elizabeth, mom via adoption to four now-adults. "Age and development may not always track in a typical way."[15]

If and when this happens, we parents may best help by not taking it as a personal affront but by becoming curious and attentive to where the adoptee actually is, developmentally, and what they need along the way.

"We might fear a failure to launch, that we will need to hold our adoptee's hands through everything forever," says Sujata. "But think of all that is necessary to achieve independence. If an adoptee needs an extended period to figure out their place in the world, I say why *not* continue holding their hand?"

Relationship Complexities with Adoptees Turned Adults

When our children grow up, it can be a challenge for any parent to switch from an active parenting role into a consultative one. After seventeen, eighteen, or more years seeing them as a child for whom we assume great responsibility, it can require a big shift for us to consider them as separate individuals with evolving ideas and thoughts that may not always be the same as what we've understood them to be, or that differ from ours.

This dynamic can be especially jarring to adoptive parents whose adult children begin thinking more critically about their adoption. Many adoptees, after living independently and with more room for their own ideas to flourish once outside their adoptive parents' home, can take what feels like a 180-degree turn in their thoughts around adoption and their identity as an adoptee. It's important for parents to make space for all of these emotions, recognizing that a shift may be an essential component of identity integration and maturation.

This isn't to suggest that it's always going to be easy. As part of the process, adoptees may express hurt or anger over the past. Our parenting and beliefs around adoption may feel like they're coming under attack. It's important to neither get defensive nor brush over the underlying heartache, as this can affect the adult child's sense of safety and closeness and sadly, can sometimes even lead to estrangement.

"There is an ebb and flow as our kids do independent things in their twenties and thirties," says Elizabeth. "I know a number of adoptive families in which the adoptee has separated for their own sanity. Sometimes the burden to educate parents on adoption issues, on race issues, and on not being seen for who they are is just too big to bear. Parents can get curious about what their adoptee is experiencing and why they chose estrangement. It's a big ask, to get out of their own hurt and viewpoint, but this is what can eventually open the door to reconnection."

A key component to help repair a rupture is to offer a true apology for not knowing what we didn't know. "Apologizing for some of the decisions we made when we didn't have the understanding of adoptee loss can go a long way toward healing," says Elizabeth. "It's also helpful for struggling parents to find a community of other parents who get it and can sit with you as you wonder how things got to the point of estrangement. If we can acknowledge our role in the situation and not be so defensive about it, we might be able to shift the dynamic."

Adoption Mosaic offers courses for parents that include a "Seasoned Parenting" course for adoptive parents of adult adoptees. Other possibilities for connection and education include various heritage camps and adoption networks like the National Association of Adoptees and Parents (NAAP), Adoption Knowledge Affiliates (AKA), Adoption Network Cleveland, and others.

OPENNESS AND ITS POWER TO BRING FORTH CLOSENESS

Certainly, love upholds any family structure—but as a starting point rather than an ending point. "Yes, all the love I poured into them for years was important," says Karla, "but it was the listening and learning that led to my daughter saying this: I know a lot of adoptees who cannot speak as freely as I do with my mom."

I am able to speak freely with my mom, my dad. What a universally gratifying sentiment for a parent to hear! What a treasure for us as adoptive parents to eventually know that the person we are raising thinks we feel safe enough for them to speak freely and show up authentically with us. How affirming, that during the long journey of parenting a toddler, a tween, a teenager, a young adult, that ultimately our grown child feels seen, validated, and accepted for who they are. That the love we cultivated along the way, supplemented with openness, curiosity, wisdom, and a willingness to keep learning, culminates in a person who feels whole and true—and chooses to remain connected to us out of love, rather than obligation or fear of abandonment.

Karla reports that even though she once felt like a failure as a parent, woefully ill-prepared to raise her interracial adoptees, her daughters never gave up on her and her capacity to grow. "They continued to extend their love and grace to me, which is both humbling and inspiring," says Karla. "It is not about blaming. It is about moving forward with new understandings. It is about learning and growing and then sharing with others so that my mistakes are not repeated by other adoptive parents."

The Beatles and Virgil were not wrong, Love *is* something you need, and love *does* conquer much. In stating their cases in the absolute of "all," these wise men simply missed an even more fundamental truth: that human beings and human relationships are nothing if not complex, especially with the added element of adoption.

CHAPTER 18

When Religion Hurts

Reexamining Religious Adoption Narratives

WE HAVE EXAMINED RELIGION AND ADOPTION TWICE, FIRST IN Chapter 7 on the impact religion can have on adoptees, and in Chapter 9 on how birth parents may struggle with religious beliefs and practices. Now we explore some of the religious issues around adoption for adoptive parents.

Religion and spirituality are more than just what one believes. Religion—or even the lack thereof—is a deep part of our identity. It is intertwined with the people we call ours and who call us theirs. Religion infuses and informs our worldview, what and how we think, and to a large extent, how we behave. Our traditions, our rituals, our language, our culture, and even who we mean by "we" and "us"—are all by-products of our fundamental beliefs about what life is and how one should live it. One's religion can be thoughtfully chosen but often it is passed down through cultures and families unquestioned. For all these reasons, religious practices and beliefs can be so deeply embedded within us we may not even think to question them. It's our circle, after all. It's who we *are*.

Narratives that stem from religious traditions can impact us in thousands of ways during a lifetime. One of those ways is in adopting to build a family. Sara covered well the issues that can arise from an unquestioned "call to adopt" and to "save" a child.

Kelsey covered the ways religion can harm or help a birth mother both in pre-relinquishment and post-placement. Now let's hear from adoptive parents who have taken a closer look at how religious beliefs guided them in the way they adopted and parented.

THE PROBLEMS WITH UNCHECKED ZEAL TO RESCUE ORPHANS

You first heard from Cynthia in Part I. She is a wife, lawyer, and mom to three children. She adopted her two sons, now nine and seven, from Korea when each of them was three-and-a-half. Her daughter, now a toddler, was born to Cynthia and her husband. Cynthia herself was adopted in the 1980s by a Jewish couple.

"My Jewish upbringing did not play any role in my choice to adopt, though the overarching Judeo-Christian mindset of adoption—saving a child, fulfilling a destiny or purpose, and obeying God's will in a general sense—certainly did,"[1] says Cynthia. "I believed that adoptive parents save adopted children and bring them to a better country and a better life. These are messages I received from my parents when I was adopted but also just through living in this culture. In the unexamined period of my life, I believed adoption should be a first choice, not a last choice. I absorbed the idea that adoption was an act of moral goodness."

Saving children is a common directive in religious communities. No one would argue that children in peril should be left in peril. As Kathryn Joyce points out in her book *The Child Catchers: Rescue, Trafficking, and the New Gospel of Adoption*, campaigns to save children imperiled by war, famine, natural disasters, disease, and other misfortunes always start with good intentions. But at some point, what tends to happen is that the noble rescue of finding homes for children morphs into commodification and a supply-demand scenario—in other words, finding children for homes. Along the way, new motives seep in: saving souls for some and making money for others. Corruption becomes part of the process as do-gooders do very well for themselves. After some time, a country—like those listed in Chapter 6—realizes that corruption has become rampant and that some "orphans" are not orphans at all, but trafficked children. The sending country then stops exporting its children, who now face a different kind of peril, having become the commodity in a booming business.[2] All because the line between saving children from legitimate and immediate peril, and building families and congregations, went unnoticed and unexamined.

Can you imagine discovering that your child was not, indeed, an orphan but instead a victim of human trafficking? Adoptive mom Lorelai faced just this situation. She adopted her daughter from the Democratic Republic of the Congo (DRC) in 2012. She'd been told that her daughter had been abandoned at less than a month old and her biological family could not be located.

After the adoption was finalized, Lorelai became suspicious about the veracity of the agency's version of events. Through an online group comprising parents who had also adopted from the DRC during the same time period, Lorelai realized that it was quite possible, even probable, that very little of the agency's narrative was true. "Although I hired an investigator years later, after I became suspicious, none of the key information in my daughter's paperwork could be verified—or disproven,"[3] says Lorelai. "Common stories from other adoptive parents who searched for and found their child's birth families revealed that so many of our children were taken from their original families to enter a profitable pipeline through deceit or bribery. And all this happened alongside cases of actually abandoned children who needed a family to care for them. It's difficult to tease out the likelihood of the legitimacy of any one particular adoption, but we know that way too many of them weren't what they seemed."

Lorelai did not shy away from the horror of this revelation and the lasting impact it has on her and her daughter. "It dawned on me so slowly, so there was a lot of time to process. I feel terribly guilty that I may have unwittingly contributed to child-trafficking.

I'm angry that my agency didn't do more to follow up on what, in hindsight, seemed like obvious red flags—that's something that should not have been left to their clients who lacked the expertise and access to in-country personnel that agencies advertise. Now many of us parents are scrambling to piece together what happened and help our children navigate the information we've learned—or the fact that we may never know how they came to be declared orphans."

We can be certain that what Lorelai discovered in the DRC has happened—and continues to happen—in other countries where there is unchecked zeal to rescue orphans. The question is, how might we check that zeal and become more cognizant of the line between necessary child-rescue and predatory child-trafficking?

There's an age-old drama, memorialized in vaudeville times, in which there is a villain, a victim, and a hero, and it has to do with rent. "You must pay the rent," says the dastardly villain. "I can't pay the rent!" says the virtuous victim. "I'll pay the rent!" says the noble hero when he finally enters the scene and saves the day. Not only does every victim need to be saved, but every hero also needs someone to save. A hierarchy emerges in which the hero and the victim are locked in their roles, in a dynamic that was not meant to be permanent. If left unaddressed, the "victim" ends up meeting the need of the hero to be a hero. Can we agree that if we, as adoptive parents, feel the need to be a hero or a savior, we should address that need within ourselves or with a trusted professional and not lay it at the feet of our child, keeping them perpetually in need of being saved? Like all distinctions between the unexamined and the examined, it's a fine line.

QUESTIONING ADOPTION NARRATIVES

Cynthia was raised by parents who loved her and whom she loved in return. Adoption seemed unquestioningly wonderful during her childhood and early adulthood. But when Cynthia set out to adopt her first son, a situation prompted her to take a deeper look at the original and simplistic view she had inherited.

"As part of the adoption process, we attended a pre-adoption education class," recalls Cynthia. "The presenter was an adoptive mother of Asian children, and I sat there listening to her talk about her mistakes. My ears perked up. What were these mistakes? I didn't want to make them if I could help it."

The presenter at Cynthia's adoption class went on to say she was mistaken to raise her children to believe in a colorblind world, mistaken to think that love was enough, and mistaken to use the story that God chose them for her. "I listened to her not only question the things I learned from my parents and society but also say these things were wrong. Then I began the long, slow, and painful process of re-looking at my own adoption and, of course, my own beliefs and motivations about the adoption of my son," says Cynthia. "It sounds strange and unbelievable that I, an adoptee, would not understand that these things were true, but I needed someone else to give me permission to see it. That adoptive mother did."

Questioning the narrative is an essential step for adoptive parents to take to avoid remaining locked in a dysfunctional dynamic. Joanna Ivey, also an adoptee and adoptive parent, said this when I interviewed her on my podcast, *Adoption: The Long View*: "It's tempting for adoptive parents to package our grief, loss, and anger into a narrative that makes us the hero of the story, to say that our journey was 'meant to be,' or God's plan. It's okay to start there but not to stay there."[4]

Sara said previously, "Looking at the ills of adoption requires rethinking long-held beliefs." We are called to examine adoption and adoptive parenting with a critical eye to make sure we truly are in position to meet our child's needs as well as our own.

Parenting with Healthier Narratives

With that aha moment in her adoption class, Cynthia began to settle on a new adoption narrative that would best serve her son. Suddenly, adoption did not seem simply wonderful. There was much more going on that did not fit into the framework she'd always accepted. In parenting her son, she had the opportunity to see her own adopted baby-self through her grown-up eyes.

"When our son joined our family, he was obviously having a hard time attaching and adjusting to such a monumental change," says Cynthia. "He struggled with emotional management, tantrums, and externalizing behaviors. We had read all the books and done all the courses, and thought we were prepared to manage these things. But in crisis, old patterns slipped in—authoritarian parenting, frustration, and helplessness."

Stemming from the shame of not seeming to be enough for him (otherwise, she surmised, he wouldn't be struggling so), for being unable to take away his pain and for being unable to control her child, Cynthia's instinct was to react the way she'd learned powerful beings act, whether a parent, teacher, or a deity. "I wanted to yell, demand, and make my approval conditional on compliance," says Cynthia. "However, I knew my son needed something much different. He needed me to sit with him, bear witness to his pain, and proactively help him feel safe attaching to me. And I figured out that I needed help in learning a different way to parent and to love."

Cynthia had crossed the line into examining all that she "knew" about authority, God, and parenting. She needed to figure out her own path because the one she'd inherited was not going to serve her son, and later, her other children.

Cynthia soon figured out two things *not* to do in parenting her son: emphasize obedience over connection and lead her son to believe that God had willed the loss and trauma that caused her to become his mom. Next, she needed to figure out what *to* do. If her old beliefs would not serve him—or her, for that matter—what new beliefs and approaches would? And how would she and her husband figure it out?

Like many of us, Cynthia heard the continual call to be morally good. But dividing the world into "good" and "bad" can confound an adoptive family in many ways. If adoption itself is "good," as is obedience to authority and the resulting well-behaved children, parents will be stymied when faced with anything different. Lost are nuances and complexities, and added is the shame of not being good enough to deliver on the expectation of good.

"Everyone said how great we were for adopting and how our son was so lucky. Yet we could not admit how hard it was and how unlucky he obviously and rightfully felt," Cynthia recollects. "We did not have any friends or family we felt we could talk to, mostly because of the shame. It felt shameful that we didn't look like 'good' parents raising well-behaved children. My husband and I relied heavily on each other but even then we floundered and eventually we had to seek therapy. We found an adoption-competent therapist to work with all of us, and she became our hero."

Cynthia also began meditating and finding other avenues into spirituality that felt welcoming in ways that Judaism did not. "By this time we had also completed the adoption of our second son, and we began to make significant changes in our lives. These changes were driven more by what our children needed and less by what our community expected us to do."

These internally driven changes involved making the kids the center of their world, maintaining schedules and balance in their lives that also kept their children balanced, and choosing to homeschool. "This allowed for more attachment time, child-directed learning, and the time/energy to attend the therapy we all needed. We opted not to move homes despite it being a bit cramped, in order to avoid additional changes for our boys."

A New Path: No Need for a Hero

Cynthia was prompted by circumstances and her love for her sons to question the religious tenets she had inherited. She has remained connected to her Jewish upbringing but now she also consciously chooses practices that serve her and her family and modifies those that evoke shame or minimize grief and loss in her children.

CHAPTER 18

"I am a completely different person from who I was when we decided to adopt years ago. I went from being completely 'in the fog' as an adoptee (and therefore as an adoptive parent) to being entirely open to the realities of adoption in myself, my kids, and other adoptees. I write about adoption, I read about adoption, and mostly, I live the experience as an adoptee and adoptive parent to model positive care for my kids. I now do this more consciously and with more intention around religious beliefs and other influences."

Her sons were open and big about their pain and loss, which made it impossible for Cynthia to ignore, and for that she is thankful. "I am also appreciative of my husband, who is not adopted and not Korean, and works every day to challenge his own ingrained parenting expectations and patterns. And we owe so much to our adoption-competent therapist, who guided us as we changed our lives."

When we start to pay attention to—examine mindfully—the beliefs behind an adoption narrative and a parenting approach, we can meld a religious or spiritual tradition with what works within our own families, in situations in which our child has experienced a fundamental loss, that of their original mother and often so much more.

Cynthia's inner journey in questioning authority broke the hero/victim dynamic in her family, and even within herself. As Joanna stated so well in our podcast interview, "If your narrative has you as the hero and the child as being saved, your community will see you as a gift to your child, and your child will always carry the burden of being 'saved.'"[5]

Not all people who face the overwhelming desire to build a family and explore adoption as a means of achieving parenthood end up adopting. Let's look at some of the driving forces behind the quest for parenthood, and another way of resolving that quest.

CHAPTER 19

NOT Adopting Amid the Cultural Backdrop of Pronatalism

THERE ARE TWO TYPES OF INFERTILITY THAT LEAD PEOPLE TO domestic infant adoption. One is biological, in which the necessary parts (egg, sperm, uterus, for example) do not work in concert to conceive, carry, and deliver a live baby. The other is that of circumstance, "the inability to have children because one doesn't have a partner with whom to conceive."[1] Not everyone comes to domestic infant adoption because of infertility, but for a large majority, adoption is considered after first trying to have a baby through fertility treatments and/or attempts at donor conception.

Domestic infant adoption is a multi-billion-dollar industry.[2] Every year, at least a million[3] prospective parents pay a licensed agency, a private attorney, and/or an unlicensed "facilitator" or "consultant" more than a billion dollars[4] in hopes of finding and adopting a baby.

To understand the odds of success for adopting a newborn, let's do some easy math. We need to know (1) how many people want to adopt and (2) how many babies are available to adopt.

The number of people wanting to adopt an infant is impossible to pin down because there is no central clearinghouse to track this data. However, the Executive Director of the National Council for Adoption stated in 2017 that there were "1 million families trying to adopt at any given time"[5] (that is not an annualized figure; an annualized figure would be even higher). As for the number of babies to adopt each year, Creating A Family, an adoption education and support nonprofit, estimated in 2022 that 0.5 percent of all live births in the United States become infants available for adoption, meaning just under twenty-thousand babies were placed in 2020.[6] This number is corroborated by the National Council for Adoption's 2022 report *Adoption by the Numbers*.[7]

The 2022 Supreme Court decision to overturn *Roe v. Wade* may have an impact on the number of available babies in the coming years, but not as much as many expect. Research from sociologist Dr. Gretchen Sisson shows that "birth mothers were most often choosing between adoption and parenting, not adoption and abortion,"[8] and that ninety-one percent of those seeking abortion and denied one will parent instead of relinquish.[9] We can predict that a majority of additional adoptions from the *Dobbs v. Jackson Women's Health Organization* Supreme Court decision may be through foster care (which is subsidized by government entities) rather than the more highly competitive arena of domestic infant adoptions (in which prospective parents are willing to pay large sums of money).

This raw math means that there are *at least fifty or more* prospective adopters waiting to adopt each available baby at any given time. Why are we willing to pay vast sums of money to adopt a newborn and wait indeterminately long periods of time for the mere *chance* of becoming parents?

The answer is partially internal: an innate desire to parent. But a portion of the answer may be external, stemming from cultural forces. Pronatalism, perhaps the very first -ism that arose in humans, is the deeply ingrained belief that parenting is prized over nonparenting, and the consequence that those who parent are elevated in countless ways over those who don't. Linda Rooney, a writer in New Zealand who lives Childfree Not By Choice (CNBC),[10] describes pronatalism as "the promotion of childbearing and parenthood as desirable for society, meaning parents are deemed to have more value than non-parents."[11]

Unspoken, yet well communicated, is the idea that parents are more important in our culture than nonparents. We dedicate holidays to parents, we accommodate their needs with tax breaks and parental leave, we elevate those who start sentences with *As a parent*—because "parent" is an exalted credential.

No exploration of adoptive parents' viewpoints and decisions would be complete without an examination of the undercurrent of pronatalism in our culture and its effects. Here are stories of two couples who became Childfree Not By Choice after considering adoption as a way to build their families, and how they've come to terms with both pronatalism and childlessness.

The Pressure to "Just Adopt"

Jess and her husband were married in their early thirties and spent years trying to conceive. After a series of expensive and painful treatments and resulting losses, they consulted an adoption agency. After all, friends, family, and the public are quick to offer the advice that if you can't conceive and deliver a baby, you can always "just adopt."

The agency she and her husband selected prided itself on its track record with relatively fast matching, so Jess and her husband figured it was only a matter of time before they would have a baby in their arms. But coming close and repeatedly not getting chosen exacted a heavy toll. Toward the end of the second year of waiting and with a couple of months left on their home study, they were turned away again. At this point, Jess experienced several severe and sudden stress-related symptoms that caused her to examine the ongoing cost of being in limbo.

"The crisis was both physical and mental,"[12] Jess explains. "My well-being was at risk, all the signs telling me I'd had all I could take. While I was pulling myself back together, my husband called the agency to deactivate our profile. They pressured him to keep us active so we didn't 'lose out' on opportunities. To 'give up' seemed outlandish to the agency. *Who does that??*—they seemed to be saying to us."

Jess and her husband received pushback from friends and family after sharing that they would never become parents. "We waited to tell until things were irreversible. We told no one outside a very small circle until a couple of months after the decision was made, after we'd ended our home study with the agency, and after we'd donated the nursery. Why? Because, as we predicted, when we announced our decision we were flooded with, *WHY? How could you? What about [insert every possible way to adopt a baby here]?*"

Despite the fact that "in one-third of infertile couples, the problem is with the man," one-third is with the woman, and one-third is unexplained,[13] people in our culture tend to assume that infertility is a female issue. Such was the case with another couple, Greg and his wife, who declined fertility treatments after Greg found out in his early thirties that he lacked the ability to contribute sperm. Contemplating the path to "just adopt," Greg engaged with online communities that included adoptees, birth parents, and adoptive parents. After learning all he could about adopting, adoptive parenting, and the experience of being adopted, Greg and his wife decided not to get on the adoption roller coaster. This decision shocked and disappointed friends and family.

"We received pushback from family members as to why we didn't at least try fertility treatments or adoption,"[14] says Greg. "Not pursuing parenthood was something people couldn't wrap their minds around. One person compared the adoption process to when we adopted our dog. It took a lot of patience on my end to explain how adopting a human isn't the same as adopting a pet."

Greg noticed how pronatalism showed up in others' reactions to their decision. "It hurts to hear people say, *But you don't know what love really is until you become a parent,* or, *you won't be as busy as people with kids.* Ideas like that can make you question your own self-worth, especially when it's not your choice to be childless. This societal pronatalism puts a stigma on nonparents that they aren't as valuable to society as parents are. I internalized those kinds of conversations, and it affected my self-esteem."

Accepting and Integrating an Unexpected Identity

Jess and Greg, along with their spouses, began to grieve two wounds: being childfree and disappointing the expectations others had for them.

"Before we could attempt to get others to understand, first *we* needed to fully trust that our decision to accept a childless existence—gut-wrenching as it felt at the time—would eventually be liberating," says Jess. "That acceptance finally allowed us to live in our *actual* life, not a vaguely possible future that never materialized and haunted us. The most difficult times were when others were successful in adopting around the same time we ended. It was hard for people to understand that just because those people had gotten matched and placed didn't mean that it would have ended that way for us."

Then Jess had to learn to navigate the typical get-to-know-you conversations that often revolve around whether you have children and how many. "It was incomprehensible to so many that I would say, *My husband and I are a family of two and our cats. And that's fine. That's great. We can still contribute to all of the things.*"

These conversations were a struggle for Greg, too. "I had to come to terms with the subtle ways people devalue those who didn't have children. Even now, years later, I notice it, though not as much as in the beginning." Some conversations caused Greg to question his value to society. "I had thoughts like, *What if something was to happen to me and I get hit by a bus?* Like it would be no big deal if I was gone. What's the point of my existence? And yes, I *do* want to leave something behind. I want the future to be better for the next generation, one way or another. And I want to contribute in some way."

Acceptance of an unexpected reality is a gradual process. Jess and Greg and their respective spouses needed to discard their original wished-for identity—that of a parent—and integrate the choice to walk away from adopting into a new and revised identity.

Much of the integration was around purpose and legacy. "Parenting is supposed to be your life's work or whatever," says Jess. "Without that, we had to reconfigure. In a weird way, there's an Oprah syndrome kind of thing. Like, *What am I going to do now that I won't have kids? I better be something spectacular!* It's hard to get around that societal message that your worth is in producing a baby."

Greg was faced with the legacy issue as well. "If I'm not careful, I could obsess over it every day: what's my legacy going to be? I'm not a parent, so in some people's eyes I have to work that much harder to make a contribution. Therapy has been helpful in discovering where my hurt came from and how to heal."

People are capable of doing their own inner work but for such deep grief work, a therapist can be a good option. An effective therapist can help a client feel and name their emotions and express them appropriately. It's important for those grieving the loss of parenthood to find a therapist who is aware of the possible existence of their own pronatalism bias.

Having the courage and support to feel the grief and sadness is key. As Dr. Gordon Neufeld says, "Sadness is extremely important because sadness brings an end to the emotional work. Sadness is the end of the sentence. It puts a period on it."[15]

This is one way healing can begin, by feeling sadness and futility, getting to the turnaround point, and rising from there.

FINDING FULFILLMENT OUTSIDE OF PARENTING

Jess and Greg and their spouses were ultimately able to find purpose in their lives, pour their energy into meaningful endeavors, and consider ways to leave their mark on humanity.

"We didn't have a proper honeymoon when we married. I was already near that dreaded Advanced Maternal Age and needed to jump right into fertility treatments," says Jess. "When not successful, we moved to considering adoption. By the time we ended that quest, we realized we could have the honeymoon we didn't have time or resources for eight years earlier. We took a two-week trip to California that felt insanely decadent, but we thought, *Know what? We can do this now. This is how we can mark the start of our new life together.*"

Five years since the decision to walk away from adopting, Jess is proud of the way she and her husband continue to honor and celebrate their life together. Their relationship is strong, in part, because of what they have survived, and they continue to build a life they love. "We deliberately listed things we can spend more time doing with our new life, like going for long hikes and going on vacations that are not child-friendly. I channel my nurturing energy with a passion for gardening. I like to say that 'mother' can also be a verb. I'm not a mother, but I get *to mother* in various ways. For example, as a middle-school teacher I get to make a difference in kids' lives all the time. I didn't get to raise one myself, but I do have that impact, which addresses the legacy issue."

Jess also credits community with helping her heal. "I have a very strong online community, people who helped me see others living childfree, either by choice or not. That also gives me purpose to be that light for someone else, as other people were for me. There are more and more voices showing that childfree/childless living is a viable and valuable alternative path. And people like me who wanted to parent but didn't get to, we can still make for ourselves a glorious life."

Greg shares how he began to fill up his life, seven years into living childfree. "There was no one thing that would replace the hole left behind. I knew I would need to come up with a number of different things. I ran cross country in high school and college and had an injury that caused me to stop. After deciding not

Chapter 19

to pursue parenting, I got back into running, and it became my therapy. I could go out for an hour or two and be just with myself and my thoughts."

"I wouldn't say I've focused on my career," continues Greg, "but I don't need to put quite so much energy trying to figure out *how can I make enough money to support and raise a child?* Now, it's more like *I need to be in a position where I'm not miserable.* Also, I love dogs. My wife and I have rescued two greyhounds. Our first helped us get through as we poured our love into her. We lost her a few years later, unexpectedly, and we rescued another, who's just as wonderful and makes us laugh. Giving the love we would have given to a child to our dogs—that's been wonderful. And we don't have to worry about spoiling them rotten."

Like Jess, Greg and his wife have traveled and take trips they wouldn't have been able to with children. "We are able to be more spontaneous. It's one of the perks, and all in all, we have built a fulfilling and meaningful life together."

The choice *not* to adopt a baby as a way to build a family comes with much loss and heartache and requires a huge readjustment of the vision for one's life path. Part of the loss is from letting go of the dream to parent, the dreams of raising a family. And some of the loss is from going against the grain of society's expectations, of living out one's life in a culture of pronatalism. Parents are lauded and elevated while nonparents are in the margins, sometimes misunderstood, often ignored, rarely centered. Understanding what it is like for people who make this choice and construct their own adoption off-ramp is important for anyone wanting to grasp the adoptive parent perspective.

CHAPTER 20

Adoptive Parents and the Dance of Attachment

WITH FIFTY OR MORE APPLICANTS WAITING TO ADOPT EACH available newborn, you might think that the standards for who get to become parents to an infant are high. What does it take to pass a home study? Who passes and who doesn't? Though a home study causes much angst for would-be parents going through it, the bar is, in fact, fairly low. "More often than not, agencies are looking for ways to rule families in rather than rule them out."[1]

The caseworker conducting a home study is looking for stability and safety. Is the prospective adoptive parent in good health? Do they have adequate income to meet the needs of a child placed into the home? Is there a history of stable residency? Is the prospective parent able to pass a background check?[2] The idea is to place the baby in a home that has low risk for more loss—a proactive attempt to prevent additional Adverse Childhood Experiences (ACEs).[3]

Such criteria are adequate for tending to the most basic needs of a human when it comes to physiological and basic safety. In the state of Colorado, for example, adopting parents need to show that they have fire extinguishers, that they will prevent foreseeable electrical, water, and stair hazards, and that they have a refrigerator to adequately store perishable foods; all necessary but not exactly a high bar. If you look at Maslow's Hierarchy of Needs, as illustrated in Figure 10, this covers only the lowest levels of human needs.

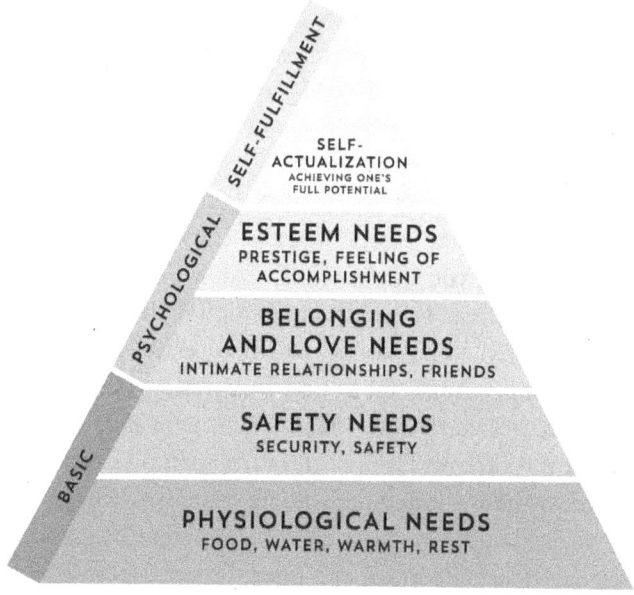

Figure 10
ABRAHAM MASLOW, *HIERARCHY OF NEEDS*, VISUAL REPRESENTATION OF MASLOW'S HIERARCHY, 1943.

Not addressed in a home study is a willingness and ability to meet an adoptee's higher-level needs of belonging and self-esteem and to support them in reaching their full developmental potential. To do so requires an openness and curiosity to reflect on what we bring from our own journey of connection, attachment, and belonging. In short, for us to more effectively cross the threshold into adoptive parenting, we need a simple *willingness* to do our own healing work and grow our capacity as parents.

No matter how wonderful our own parents were, no matter how idyllic our childhood seems in memory, we all carry wounds, some small and some large. On top of all that, many come to adoption through heartbreaking loss, which requires grieving so that we don't unconsciously expect an adoptee to resolve our heartache. Unaddressed wounds can affect the ways we respond in our parenting. All humans have basic emotional needs of seeking togetherness, which means that our child's emotional responses to separation, which Sara covered in Part I, can easily activate our own emotional responses to it. Signing up to be a parent means signing up to be the adult in the room—an ongoing balancing act of becoming the parent your child needs, no matter what, while tending to our own unhealed parts.

Dr. Brad Reedy makes a point about a parent's capacity to provide secure attachment to a child: "The basis of all relationships is the relationship that we have with our self, the awareness that we have with our self."[4]

The Roots of Attachment

Dr. Reedy also says this: "Children will expose your unfinished work."[5] How is it that my two toddlers could bring out toddler behavior in *me*? It happened over and over again when my children were young. Turns out that Lori the Parent had some unfinished business with Lori the Child.

The template we instinctively parent from stems, in large part, from how we ourselves were parented, the soil we grew in. We tend to follow the general values and methods of those who parented us and those who parented them, without giving it much thought. Many of us did not grow up with parents who were capable of honoring our full and authentic selves. Through mindfulness, intention, and feeling our own losses, we can take ourselves off auto-pilot and aim to provide our child what they need to feel seen, known, and wholly loved by us.

Being familiar with one's authentic self and connecting with others from that authentic self requires a commitment to a practice of self-reflection because experiencing the parent-child dynamic as a parent will almost certainly bring up emotions left over from when we were in that same dynamic as a child. When that happens during a stressful parenting moment, we may feel overwhelmed by big emotions that seemingly make no sense. Without awareness, we may be triggered by painful times from childhood when we felt scared, alone, not enough, unable to control our world. To counter that flash of powerlessness, we now seek control—but it comes out as out-of-control. We overreact to the present situation with our child and don't even know why.

Consider the first time a child yells, "You can't make me! You're not even my real mom/dad!" Out of past hurt, from not feeling good-enough, comes a current reaction of a wounded and maybe even angry child: *I am TOO! I AM your real parent and don't you forget it!* The parent is showing up *as* a child *with* the child, not knowing exactly why that declaration hurt so badly and caused such an eruption from deep within.

When we parent from our wounds, we risk wounding our child. Conversely, to the degree that we are able to parent with an awareness of attachment dynamics, we can better attune to our child and offer a sense of being seen, known, safe, and connected. In the "not my real parent" example, rather than pushing away remnant memories of powerlessness when they arise we can take it as an opportunity to grieve our now-identified loss—and heal.

Must we be "perfect" parents, to expect to get everything right every time? That expectation would actually harm our child, as it would compromise our ability to be present with and attune to them, being overly focused on our own ego's needs. We were all wounded by our parents and we will all wound our children—that's a given. To the degree we can own and feel our hurt parts, we are in a better position to be there for our child and not expect them to take on the burden of our healing.

Who Is Responsible for Attachment?

Since the Baby Scoop Era, adoptive parents have heard messages like, "Just love 'em like your own," or, "Adoption doesn't matter. Parenting is parenting."

Such messages didn't lead adopting parents to understand we would have our own work to do to become securely attachable *to*. Those messages left the entire burden of secure attachment on a baby! But when a child struggles, the whole family struggles. Parents might think: if we fix the child and alleviate their struggle that will fix the family. Parents who are less familiar and facile with the dance of attachment can end up believing that the child is solely responsible for a negative impact on the whole family system, and then the child is at risk of being scapegoated.

Because both parties come to this relationship with wounds—adopting parents through infertility, for example, as well as our own unexamined childhood hurts—and a baby through a primal wound of separation through adoption, it makes sense that a deeper understanding of attachment might be necessary.

Support, Blueprints, and Architecture

To pass a home study, adoptive parents must put on our "I've got this!" game face even before we've actually got it. All parenting requires a certain amount of bravado for our children to have confidence and trust in our leadership. But at some point, prompted by a parenting challenge or an ongoing issue between us and our child, adoptive parents may need to seek professional support. What finally gets people to come to an attachment therapist? "Pain," says Jen Winkelmann, an attachment-based, adoption-fluent therapist. "Pain and frustration. Adoptive families don't often seek help or support until their suffering has been intense and prolonged, five to ten years post-placement."[6]

"After placement," Jen explains, "many adoptive parents are afraid to share challenges because they have just spent the previous months (and sometimes years!) proving to an agency that they are equipped for adoptive parenting. After all that vulnerability and upon finally becoming parents, they are eager to move on to a new normal. Bringing a concern to an agency or social worker can make families fear judgment. They have put a lot into communicating, *I've got it.* It can be really uncomfortable—or terrifying!—to have to say, *I actually don't think I've got it.*"

Attachment therapists don't focus merely on the child. Instead, they help parents explore their inner landscape and the spaces between. "Healing the space between a parent and child means looking at the 'architecture' of the relationship," says Jen. "This includes an unfolding of the blueprint each person brings to the way they navigate connections with others. It's not just about how your child's blueprint for relationship has been formed and impacted—but also how *yours* has."

"Many parents and children could be spared significant pain and heartache if it was a standard expectation to access adoption support early on," says Jen.

This is not to assert that passing a parenting assessment should be required to pass a home study. Rather, that one component of a home study could be an assessment of openness to understanding attachment dynamics and seeking adoption-fluent support. If parents are unwilling to look at their own role in the attachment dance, they could end up trying to "fix" or blame the child when difficulties arise.[7]

INCORPORATING ATTACHMENT AWARENESS EARLIER IN THE PROCESS

What if we were to move upstream from the attachment issues we know are coming? What if all prospective adoptive parents started off understanding attachment dynamics early in the process, and what if families connected early with an attachment therapist or with adoption-fluent educators (not affiliated with adoption agencies) as a matter of course?

"Such a connection would support the family through the placement and early stages of the adoption," says Jen. "That person might also be available as the child grows and enters new developmental stages. When life gets tricky, families wouldn't need to orient a counselor or parent educator to the situation at a point in time when they are discouraged and exhausted; the relationship would already be established. Families would both launch better and have ongoing access to support."

Jen advises that by doing their own reflection and healing, parents can "recalibrate their approach to the relationships with themselves, their partners, daughters, and sons."

Lori the Parent eventually reconnected with Lori the Child. And when we met, I found sore spots from my own childhood that, left unhealed, had come out sideways on occasion with my children. I had too many knee-jerk reactions, blurted too many words that couldn't be reeled back in, and too often set up consequences that undermined my ability to connect. And I had a "good" childhood with wonderful and loving parents!

We can surmise from Part I that the last thing adoptees need is more separation as an unintentional response from their parents. Too often to count, I found myself needing to (1) be more connectable, (2) increase my own distress tolerance, and (3) release some of the expectations I had put on my daughter and son to make *me* feel okay. It would have been better for all if I'd sought attachment education and/or professional help sooner.

We need to find ways to help hold our child's big feelings while staying strong and authentic. It's not up to our children to attach to us; it's up to us to help make it safe for them to attach to us. How? By starting from our own inner connection and radiating from there. Dr. Gordon Neufeld says that "as caregivers, we don't need directions. We need to understand our children so the answer comes from within us."[8] Similarly, the better we understand ourselves, the more we can trust ourselves. And when we practice tuning in to ourselves, we can be better at both *self-regulation* (our ability to manage our own behavior and reactions) and *co-regulation* (our ability to foster self-regulation in another with our own self-regulation). Much as a car battery can "jump" another car's electrical system by sharing power, a self-regulated caregiver can "soothe" another person's nervous system by briefly syncing with the other and then intentionally bringing down one's own intensity. This is by no means easy, and for me, it required the support of a trusted adoption-fluent therapist and a lot of practice.

TENDING THE SOIL AS PART OF THE ADOPTION PROCESS

If you were to transplant a treasured plant from one place to another, wouldn't you want to do everything you could to increase the likelihood of that plant thriving? Depending on just how badly you want it to thrive, you might even invest time and energy to assess the soil—to see what has gone into it and how well primed it is to nourish whatever is planted there.

"When I offer our training," says Jen, "I tell attendees, *If Adoption World ran according to Jen, I would insist that a willingness to understand attachment and one's own patterns be a requirement of the adoption process.* Some folks sigh. There are already so many hurdles to clear it feels unfair to propose that states and agencies would require more of adoptive parents."

Jen continues: "But there are always some who smile, nod, and wish the same along with me. These folks know. They have already walked that early part of the journey and their hindsight is 20/20. They nod and smile, with clear vision around how beneficial an assessment of their own attachment history could have been on their lifelong adoption journeys."

Let's tend the soil well, for everyone's sake. Let's proactively and deliberately seek to understand the roots of attachment. Let's cultivate openness and curiosity in the gardens we grow in so we can best meet the needs of our youngest saplings.

PART IV

HEALING AND HOPE

THE FIRST THREE PARTS OF *ADOPTION UNFILTERED* HAVE FOCUSED on common struggles experienced by adoptees, birth parents, and adoptive parents. If reading about our struggles has left you feeling sad, imagine us reaching through this book to give you a hug (or if hugs aren't for you, a gentle nod of camaraderie and a steaming mug of chamomile tea).

At the same time, if you *are* feeling sad, we have done our job well. Adoption *is* sad, which isn't to say that it's *only* sad. Adoption is not possible without great loss, and we've been pretending for too long that that isn't true. Whether it's adoptees needing to push down on the pain of adoption in the name of survival, or birth parents turning away from adoption to keep their losses and guilt from getting the best of them, or adoptive parents looking only at the sparkly side of adoption—until now we've been remiss in attending to the answer that will lead us toward healing and transformation: *feeling* our many losses in order to begin healing from them.

We're not saying that elation and joy isn't feeling, too—nor that they are not valid! But our culture as a whole tends to place a skewed emphasis on positivity. As Dr. Stephen L. Salter writes in "The Culture of Positivity and the Mistreatment of Trauma," "The pressure to think positive pervades our everyday language and practices: It's the reflexive response, 'Put on a happy face,' if we are not smiling. 'Think cheerful thoughts and good things will happen.' We feel pressure to display a pleasant countenance even if it is insincere. And we often feel guilty if we're not quite able to don that cloak. The underlying belief, it seems, is that hurt and discontent can be done away with simply by acting as though it isn't there."[1]

Allowing ourselves to feel grief also allows us to feel joy. The two are interconnected. When we try to squeeze out our hearts' aches, it's harder to feel our hearts' highs, just as we don't know what it's like to be full until we've felt hunger.

In *The Wild Edge of Sorrow*, psychotherapist Francis Weller says, "It feels somewhat daunting to step off into the depths of grief and suffering, yet I don't know of any more appropriate way to undertake the journey of reclaiming soul than by spending time at the grief shrine. Without some measure of intimacy with grief, our capacity to be with any other emotion or experience in our life is greatly compromised."[2]

Sad does not mean there's no hope. Grief doesn't mean we're guilty. It's not darkness, even when it seems so. It's simply what's needed to step into the brightest light.

With this in mind, supporting adoptees is more straightforward than you might think. As humans, we are built with a capacity for and inner essence that seeks healing. Perhaps this is why you're already yearning to head in that direction now.

Recognizing that multiple audiences are reading this book, we'll share ideas for distinct groups of readers: (1) parents and other caregivers in Chapter 21; (2) adult adoptees in Chapter 22; (3) adoptive parents, agencies, and adoption professionals in Chapter 23.

CHAPTER 21

Supporting Adoptee Maturation

Advice for Parents and Other Caregivers

(From Sara)

Supporting adoptees distills to this big-picture essential: we need parents to provide us with the conditions for our emotional growth to naturally and spontaneously unfold. This may sound overly simple. That doesn't mean it is always easy ... or that it won't require a hefty amount of patience and time—perhaps even decades. But the adoptee in your life is more than worth it!

Six Ways to Meet Adoptees' Needs and Support Our Maturation

1. Provide us with space and opportunities to feel our sadness.
First and foremost, are you willing to sit with us in our grief? If you've made it this far in the book, all signs point to yes, because you're already doing so as you listen to adoptees' truths.

Your willingness to come alongside us in our sadness, or gently help draw it out when it's missing, is perhaps what adoptees need the most. We have so much to pour out of our hearts.

"Adoptees aren't given time to grieve," says Lanise. "We're not given the appropriate space to grieve our past life. Parents get so wrapped up in the excitement for themselves, and say, 'Oh, now our family is complete.' They do not consider that for many of us, our families were already complete, and now they're broken because of adoption."[1]

Making space for adoptees' grief often means accepting our sadness however it comes out. In our younger years, we often don't recognize that the sadness we sometimes feel for no apparent reason is related to adoption. But those deeper wounds can get stirred up in big ways over other losses, such as when we misplace an item we've become attached to, when facing the long separation of nighttime, when friendships or romantic relationships fail, when a beloved pet dies. For me, playing hospice nurse to a butterfly as a seven-year-old brought forth colossal waves of grief, much to the bafflement of my mother.

Even if you don't relate to what may seem like outsized sadness, all that's needed is that you relate to your child. In the wise words of Mister Rogers, "People have said, 'Don't cry' to other people for years and years, and all it has ever meant is, 'I'm too uncomfortable when you show your feelings. Don't cry.' I'd rather have them say, 'Go ahead and cry. I'm here to be with you.'"[2]

It's a parent's job to attune to their child and effect change as needed. But the bigger wounds of adoption cannot be changed. Making space for us to grieve means discerning the difference between the two.

In his book *Embers: One Ojibway's Meditations*, adoptee Richard Wagamese writes: "Sometimes people just need to talk. They need to be heard. They need the validation of my time, my silence, my unspoken compassion. They don't need advice, sympathy, or counseling. They need to hear the sound of their own voices speaking their own truths, articulating their own feelings, as those may be at a particular moment. Then, when they're finished, they simply need a nod of the head, a pat on the shoulder or a hug."[3]

Adoptees may not know ourselves that we need to make space for grief. That's why it's important for the adults in our lives to know better. It's not a parents' job to tell a child how they are feeling or should feel, which can quickly lead to shutting down—but attuned caregivers can seek opportunities to bring down the defenses that exist, for good reason, and gently walk adoptees toward tender feelings. Here are some ideas:

- Read young children books that touch on loss—and they don't have to be about adoption. In fact, it's often best if they're indirect, so that you're not shoving their faces in loss but rather "touching the bruises" one step removed. "Through the guise of another character's story, a child can be introduced to similar emotions as their own. Looking through the lens of a character, emotions that would otherwise feel too vulnerable may not feel so emotionally threatening to the child. Over time, touching the bruises in this way helps to melt the defenses from the inside out."[4]
- Supply older children with journals or sketchbooks for them to pour their hearts onto the page or simply engage in quiet reflection.
- Listen to a lot of heart-felt music. Encourage us to make our own music. Dr. Gordon Neufeld has said, "If you think of sadness as being the most important thing, what is the thing that will make you sad when you don't know why you are sad? And what has the power to actually find that sadness in us? It's music."[5]
- Show us what it looks like to express your own vulnerable emotions while ensuring that you're not making the adoptee responsible for your feelings.

These are just a handful of ideas. The ultimate goal is to help adoptees *feel*. Keep our hearts soft. According to child psychoanalyst Alice Miller, "It is not the traumas we suffer that make us emotionally ill, but the inability to express the trauma."[6]

Chapter 21

When we have an outlet for the big emotions of trauma, we have space to begin healing.

2. Welcome our full range of emotions.
Sadness isn't the only emotion adoptees need to feel. We also need compassionate support for our alarm, defensive detachment, and frustrations that can take time to drain from mad to sad. Humans are emotionally driven beings, and as Chapters 3, 4, and 5 described, adoptees are brimming with primal separation-related emotions. For maturation to take place, *all* of our emotions need to be welcomed and supported by adults ready to guide their healthy expression.

Many of these emotions don't come out at opportune times or in the ways parents wish they would. When loud emotions come out in public, it can lead parents to feel embarrassed or full of shame. Should adoptees' emotions erupt when parents are full of their own frustrations, suddenly caregivers can be full of attacking energy, too. How much simpler it would be to have all the "messy" emotions always harnessed and under everyone's complete control!

Tammy's foster parents may have felt this way, too. "I was a detached kid, and at times my family didn't really know how to draw me out. In some ways they were probably relieved that I was detached because it made me easier to handle."[7] Of course, short-term "easier" gains aren't the answer when we're playing a longer game of helping children reach their full developmental potential.

This isn't to suggest that caregivers let children's emotions rule but that they recognize that adoptees' emotions offer a roadmap to what is going on underneath their behaviors. Tammy says, "Nobody thought to see what was going on. Nobody asked, 'What are the emotions that are leading to this behavior? Why is Tammy so impulsive? Could it be anxiety that's making her super impulsive? Is she feeling unsafe?'"

The emotional responses to separation offer insight into how to dig deeper and respond accordingly. Alarm and defensive detachment need an answer: an increase in connection and a reduction in separation to make it safer to depend. If you recognize dynamics of pursuit, that lends insight: the adoptee has likely been making themselves small in some or many ways, and needs an ongoing invitation and felt sense of safety to bring their full and whole selves to the relationship. Frustrations and attacking energy signal that change is required, or if it can't be changed, drained. (See #1.)

Welcoming a full range of emotions will ultimately lead adoptees to develop the capacity for holding more than one emotion at a time. This is important when it comes to the mixing bowl of big emotions at play for adoptees and being able to make sense of adoption's many dualities—crucial to identity development. Astrid Castro says, "I meet adoptee after adoptee who say, 'I have these beliefs about adoption, but these beliefs don't coincide with loving my parents. And I'm torn between these two.' But you get to have both. You get to say, 'I love my parents *and* adoption sucks.' I think the hardest part about my job is watching adoptees not know how to hold space for these both/ands."[8]

3. Reduce additional separation and instead add connection.

While the separation created by and through adoption cannot magically disappear or go away, great care should be given to reducing additional separation for adoptees and adding connection whenever possible. This is not to be confused with attachment parenting for infants, such as baby-wearing or co-sleeping. Ideas for reducing separation and adding connection in several different situations follow.

Open or Closed Adoptions

Whether it's an open or closed adoption, parents should not make adoptees feel as though they have to choose one set over the other—adoptive parents or birth parents. It's a lose-lose situation for adoptees, facing us into additional separation no matter which "side" we pick. Just as parents of multiple children can love them all, adoptees should be able to freely love all their parents and extended family members without pressure or responsibility for adults' feelings about it. As a culture, we now understand the importance of this for children of divorce. Adoption should be treated in a similar manner to preserve connections for the adoptee—even if it's only space for connection in a closed adoption.

In open adoptions, a wholehearted commitment to uphold connections between birth and adoptive parents is important to reduce separation and serve the best interests of adoptees. This should include a pledge to find a way through the awkwardness of what often begins as a manufactured relationship that's immensely complicated and comes without any sort of cultural script as well as a commitment to resolve differences between adults—no matter how arduous it may seem at times.

When contact isn't possible, Tony offers this advice for birth parents, which is just as applicable for extended birth family members who yearn for contact that's not allowed or feasible: "It's really important to continue thinking about—maybe even being active in writing letters—to your adopted children that you never send, or just thinking actively about questions that you have for them, about how their lives were and things that you'd like to tell them."[9] This is an example of bridging separation, trusting that later the adoptee recipients of these letters will one day see that you were holding on to the connection all along.

In closed adoptions, reducing separation still requires honoring our first families and cultures. That means introducing children to their communities. It also means speaking kindly and respectfully of adoptees' birth parents and families—and finding ways to talk about them often, because omitting one set of parents from the conversation can be as harmful as speaking negatively of them. Again, the goal is to reduce separation, not create more, to help adoptees feel connected to all of the adults in their lives, including those from whom they originate.

Discipline

When it comes to discipline, it's important *not* to employ separation-based approaches such as timeouts, sending adoptees to their rooms for misbehaving, or harsh authoritarian punishments, all of which add to adoptees' separation and frustration and can create a rift in the relationship. Lily shares, "Having a very gentle approach to children, especially children who are adopted, is necessary for our healthy development and healthy attachment and greater understanding of belonging."[10]

Separation- or fear-based discipline is wounding to all children, so it makes sense that it is especially problematic for adoptees—where separation is foundational and constant, and identity development already so challenged. Dr. Deborah McNamara explains, "When a young child is preoccupied with being good to avoid separation from what they care about, there is less energy left to focus on becoming their own person."[11]

Problem behavior in childhood is often unavoidable, of course. When it needs to be addressed, wait until emotions have diffused, and always hold on to the connection with reminders that your love is constant, no matter what. This way, Dr. McNamara writes, "A child's shortcomings do not become a source of shame or disconnection. Their failures do not set them up for losing a parent's belief that they are lovable just as they are."[12] By now, you are well aware of how crucial this is for adoptees.

When adoptees' frustrations come out as attack or behavioral issues, as they inevitably will, Dr. McNamara suggests these responses to come alongside a child's emotions, rather than shutting them down:

- Acknowledge their frustration
- Control the environment, not the child
- Lead through the impasse
- Convey that the relationship is okay

- Don't identify the child with their attack
- Talk to them when emotions are down
- Solicit good intentions for when they are next upset[13]

For the long-term, the alternative to separation-based discipline is adding in connection and focusing on the underlying emotional work needed to lead adoptees toward maturation (back to #1 above).

Nighttime, School, Visit Goodbyes, and Other Inevitable Separations
It is impossible to shelter adoptees from all additional separation. Separation is inescapable. Even going to sleep at night—closing one's eyes and entering the dream world—is experienced by young children as a separation from their loved ones. Then there's daycare, school, or other separations that young children experience, adopted or not. Other inevitabilities occur for adoptees in open adoptions: facing separation from their adoptive parents at the start of a visit and from their birth parents as the visit ends.

In unavoidable cases such as these, it may not be feasible to reduce separation. Rather, the caregiver's role is to reassure adoptees that the connection between you is strong enough to make it through time apart, while conveying a sense of warmth and delight in the child. Placing an emphasis on plans for reconnecting goes a long way, too—this applies to both adoptive parents and birth parents, and anyone to whom the adoptee has become attached and has difficulty holding on to when apart. Adoptees are sensitive to goodbyes and defenses can make it a challenge to hold on to loved ones when apart. It's the role of the adult to assume responsibility for holding on to the adoptee and communicating so.

4. Approach adoption with a spirit of openness.
As stated in the Introduction and Chapters 12 and 14, openness is not merely about whether an adoption is open or closed. Tony says, "Just because you have an open adoption doesn't mean there's

open communication, necessarily, about the intersectionality of your child's experience as an adoptee." Openness is a leadership style and general approach to adoption. For adoptees, openness is:

Open, Heart-led Communication

To lead adoptees to their vulnerable feelings, open communication and a willingness to speak from the heart and invite the heart, are key. This means tapping into your own soft feelings first because this kind of openness needs genuine warmth, smiles, and a twinkle in the adult's eyes. It requires that parents have their own tender feelings accessible to be able to offer authentic empathy.

Reflecting on racial isolation experienced at her synagogue, Cynthia shares, "I just wish there was an opening to talk about it, that I knew it was okay to talk. That would have made a difference, because my parents would have been with me on my side going into that situation, rather than me by myself."[14]

Amanda says, "My adoptive parents never asked me, 'How are you?' Or, 'How do you feel about that? Is there anything you want to talk about? You have questions, and I'm always here for any conversation you need to have.' Much of the adoptee anger is because we feel like we haven't had that space."[15]

Cynthia shares words she wishes she'd heard from her parents: "'Sometimes, I wonder if it's strange or if it feels different when you look around and don't see people who look like you.'"

Openly Honoring Adoptees' Complete Experiences

Adoptive parents are typically the ones who convey a child's adoption story to them. Repeated over time, this story can become rather firm—a part of family history and folklore that's the baseline for all kinds of thoughts and fantasies, which matter deeply to adoptees and take on great significance.

In this process, though, an adoptee's first and full experiences are often disregarded, making it challenging to claim their own story—something that's vital to developing a solid sense of self. In the book *Fingerpainting on the Moon: Writing and Creativity as a Path to Freedom*, author Peter Levitt writes, "People have always sought the story of their beginning. It is a primordial yearning at the root of all creation myths."[16]

From a storytelling perspective, it's clear how this can be problematic. Dr. Joyce Pavao so often says, "Adoption is about finding families for children, not about finding children for families."[17] If this is true, then the hero, or main character, in every adoption story should be the adoptee. The adoptive parent can't be a reliable narrator because they haven't been in the shoes of the hero from the start. They don't know the child's complete point of view. They don't offer an omniscient perspective.

Amanda explains the dynamic with a different analogy: "I envision a canvas. The adoptive parents come in with their happy colors and rainbows, painting this beautiful picture but leaving no space for the adoptee. The canvas is completely filled with happiness and beauty. And then if the adoptee doesn't agree with that, it's like they're splattering gray paint all over it."

Leading with openness is recognizing how important our full stories are and offering a generous acceptance of the complete story from the adoptee's point of view.

"You have the right to be happy. You have the right to share the happy news. You have a right to share your happy adoption story," Amanda says, adding, "But leave room for the adoptee to tell their story in their own way. We have a different story to tell, and we should have as much right to tell it as you do."

Open to Different Perspectives

I won't linger on this one, because you wouldn't be reading this book if you weren't already open to different perspectives. As you know, listening to many voices—especially those of adult adoptees, since we're most profoundly impacted by adoption and understand it from the inside—means resisting the temptation to seek confirmation bias. While not everything adoptees share will resonate, truly listening results in a flexibility and willingness to adjust previously held beliefs and practices about and around adoption—better equipping everyone to find emotionally sound ways of supporting adoptees and discovering an individual and collective wisdom that guides how we proceed.

5. Assume a leadership role.
You're already assuming a leadership position if you're welcoming our emotions, reducing separation, and adding in connection. Here are additional ways to lead that honor adoptees and their emotional well-being:

Normalize Adoptees' Emotions
As previously mentioned, adoptees often live with a core belief that something is inherently wrong with them explaining their experience of relinquishment. Add to that the confusing and sometimes larger-than-life emotional responses to separation, and many of us spend a good deal of time quietly pondering whether we're crazy.

On the contrary, our responses are completely rational when looked at through a lens of attachment and the primal emotional responses to separation. How reassuring this information should be to both parents and adoptees!

Leading requires discerning age-appropriate ways to explain and normalize common emotional dynamics experienced by adoptees to help them better navigate the world. Holly insightfully says, "Having an understanding of abandonment issues and how they can manifest can be really helpful to a family who is raising an adoptee, so when certain emotions come up, they can help normalize the experiences for the child so that they don't feel like they're going out of their minds or that there's something wrong with them."[18]

Introduce Adoptees to Themselves
Similarly, making sense of adoption and our identities is colossal—something many adoptees spend their entire lives—and often a lot of high-priced therapy, trying to do. Young children cannot do this alone, and adoptees shouldn't have to wait until

reaching adulthood to find support. Adoptees need adults to take responsibility for helping them understand themselves.

Holly says, "I wish that I'd had someone to navigate me, to say, 'Hey, you may be feeling this, and this is what it could look like. Here are some ways that you can manage that.'"

In her younger years, Holly struggled in school, largely due to adoption. "When I came to the United States, I was malnourished, underweight, and delayed in lots of ways. I started kindergarten at the regular age, and then I ended up going into second grade twice because I wasn't ready to be in school. That really had an impact on me, because I felt like I was stupid." Looking back, Holly wishes her parents had introduced her to herself by saying something like: " 'Yes, things may be harder for you because you have to start out at two-and-a-half, when all the other kids learn from a baby. It's not that you're stupid. It's just that you're learning something new while they've had more time to practice.'"

Create a Wide Support "Village"

Understand that both parenting and adoption are undeniably hard at times. It's not feasible to go it alone. You will need a community of support. Maneuvering through adoption's complexities alone is no longer acceptable. A wide attachment "village" can help all involved in adoption feel less alone. For adoptees, it can offer other hierarchical relationships, where caring and understanding can flourish—often in less charged relationships than with parents (helpful during the turbulent time of adolescence, when identity matters can be especially complex).

For parents, community can offer an "adults-only" outlet for valid emotions and frustrations—important, too.

Lily shares, "Whether it's an online community, whether it's an in-person community, a church community, you need community."

Your support village may include extended family members and close friends/chosen family—a wide, loving circle to wrap up you and your child in unwavering support. It goes without saying that it's important that they're committed to staying in your family's lives for the long haul, and that they're aware of adoptees' sensitivities to separation.

While it's not necessary for everyone in the support village to be completely adoption savvy, boundaries and pruning may be needed to protect adoptees. Shelise expounds on this: "For families and parents and allies of transracial adoptees, it's one thing to learn about race, which is great, but it needs to be paired with protection. Ultimately, your job is to protect your kids. I don't think my parents did a good job of protecting me—partly out of their own ignorance, partly because of their own participation in white supremacy and racism." She adds, "Parents of interracial adoptees need to be willing to make some hard choices. Like, are you willing to forgo your own relationship with your own mother? If she's terribly racist and you have Brown kids, how are you going to protect them? That responsibility often falls on the adoptee, who has to tolerate the racism, the poor treatment, and the microaggressions—so their mom can still see her mom. It's important we start putting that responsibility onto parents."[19]

A support village can also come through teachers, parenting coaches, guidance counselors, other professionals, and adult adoptees that you include in your circles—to support both you and the adoptee.

Donna says, "Before you even consider adopting, my first and best advice is to build your own resources, learn on your own, and get your own therapy. For your child, find competent post-adoption services and some form of an adoptee community, if that is resonating for the adoptee."[20]

Diego says, "If you can find a therapist who will do family therapy, as well, that's important."[21] This is necessary because treating adoptees as if they are a problem or that they have problems may reinforce any shame that's already present. What's more, it misses the fact that attachment issues are relationship issues. As Dr. Pavao says, "It's very popular to diagnose children with reactive attachment disorder. I'm opposed to that. You cannot have attachment *anything* without another. The child doesn't have attachment disorder. The child and *whoever* have attachment disorder."²²

"An adoption-competent therapist will be aware of potential issues and will be able to educate and support the family in avoiding or at least learning how to manage those issues," David says, adding, "I believe it's crucial for families to have such professionals in place before they bring the child home."²³

The Adoptee Mentoring Society, The Adoptive and Foster Family Coalition of New York (AFFCNY), Adoption Knowledge Affiliates (AKA), Adoption Mosaic, Adoption Network Cleveland, Center for Adoption Support and Education (C.A.S.E.), Celia Center Inc., and the National Association of Adoptees and Parents (NAAP) are a few support organizations that have been led and/or informed by adult adoptees. There are also many adoption-fluent therapists now in practice, many of whom can be found in the adoptee-led *Grow Beyond Words* directory.

Don't Make Everything about You

This one might hurt a tad, but bears including because it's a common frustration shared by adoptees. Adoptive parents: please do not make everything about you. Birth parents and others in a caregiving role, this can apply to you at times, too.

1. Don't take our natural instincts personally, even when you're the target.
2. Don't make us responsible for your emotions.
3. Do not ask the adoptee to take care of your emotional needs.
4. Do not allow the adoptee to take care of your emotional needs if they instinctively try to do so to keep you close. Just as you wouldn't let them gorge on junk food all night because it's not good for them, gently redirect any signs that your child is attempting to reverse the caregiving role.
5. Do not overshare your adoption story and in the process overshadow the adoptee's adoption story.

Trust Your Inner Knowing

Historically, adoptive parents were instructed and believed that "love is all adoptees need." We wouldn't have written this book if raising children with deep separation wounding boils down to such a simple quip, as Lori shared in Chapter 17. And yet, you can quickly drive yourself bonkers trying to absorb all the information about raising adoptees and working hard to get every little thing "right."

Diego says, "I want to get away from the notion that there's a perfect way to raise an adoptee. Adoptive parents are always asking questions like, 'How can I do it better? How can I be better than your parents?' And the reality is I don't think you can." Chasing an ideal of becoming a perfect parent is an illusion. While continuing to learn and grow is important, it needs to be balanced with an inner peace that comes with recognizing when you've acquired enough information and integrated it to the point that it's become a part of your being—your guide, rather than your answer.

Solid leadership requires discerning when and how to respond in thousands of unique and specific interactions each day—and doing so from your own inner wisdom. Nobody knows your child and family circumstances in the intimate ways you do. Nobody can provide you with scripts suited to all the scenarios. No single person or book (even ours!) can equip you with solutions to every potential problem. The answers you and your family need will have to come from within.

Guilt as a Guide

Most parents feel guilt, which is a natural response to feeling the weight of such a significant responsibility and so desperately wanting to be a good parent. All parents recognize a gap between what their kids need and what they are able to deliver. We all have human limitations and blind spots, and we all make mistakes.

Find ways to express your natural guilt (and grief, losses, and frustrations)—best done with other adults, such as a partner, close friend, or therapist. But try not to let these feelings get in the way of seeing what's needed to fully support your adoptee. Spending too much time focusing on your guilt will distract you from meeting the needs of the adoptee.

Guilt can be a guide, though. Guilt is a signal that you care in the ways of a good leader. Guilt can also signal when it's time for a heartfelt apology with an aim to do better, both of which can go a long way.

6. Remain one-hundred percent committed to the challenge of meeting our attachment needs, remembering it's a marathon.
Melting an adoptee's defenses and bringing their primal emotions to a place of rest may not always be easy. Don't fret—perfect parenting is not a prerequisite, nor is it possible. More than anything, separation-sensitive adoptees need to see that you are showing up for us again and again. We need you to remain committed to us—no matter how long it takes. Even if we don't appreciate this in the bumpy seasons, hindsight can help us recognize your commitment and deep caring.

Maturity can take time—sometimes, a lot of time. As Dr. Neufeld often says, "Everyone gets older, but not everyone grows up." Adolescence is the bridge between childhood and adulthood. Many adoptees get delayed in crossing to the other side, since adoption complicates important tasks of adolescence when it comes to identity and belonging, and as previously covered, feeling adoption's many losses to adapt and fully mature. Leading up to turning forty, I felt as if I was going through adolescence all over again as I finally faced many of adoption's futilities that until then I'd successfully evaded. Many adoptees go through a stalled or second adolescence later in life, too.

Diego says, "We often think that adoptees are like any other adult and get to 21 and they're going to be fine. Well, research shows that we struggle in adulthood to actually land jobs and to maintain intimate relationships. Maturity for us really doesn't start to happen until we get into our thirties."

Supporting Adoptee Maturation

Diego recommends parents "Set aside funds to be able to get us to maturity. Therapy is not cheap." He adds, "And then you have open communication, too, through saying, 'This is for you to travel to your country. This is for you to relearn your language. This is for whatever will make you feel connected to your culture throughout the years.'"

In her case, Kayla says such financial support from her adoptive parents would be used "to pay for private Mandarin lessons, cultural cooking classes, therapy, birth family search, medical stuff."[24]

Astrid agrees with these sentiments, saying, "If you're going to be involved in separating a child from their first connections through adoption, understand that you should be available to offer resources to this individual for the rest of their lives. I know that sounds absurd. It sounds absolutely absurd. But we have statistics that show adoptees are overrepresented in the prison system and with mental health issues and with suicide attempts. How is it that we know that, yet we're not doing serious work around providing long-term support?"

That doesn't mean adoptees won't become capable, functioning adults, of course, but our mental health needs don't disappear when we reach legal voting age or move out of the home. Pitching in with mental health costs acknowledges that separation wounding runs deep and shows that our parents stand by us.

Diego says, "What a better message for the adoptee to feel, 'Oh, my adoptive parents are supporting me. They are not turning a blind eye to the fact that I have this reality that I'm just coming into awareness of, and it's not being shoved off as if it's not a big deal.'"

Because of our deep and ongoing separation wounding, adoptees can struggle to believe in the authenticity and longevity of close relationships. Adoptive parents—usually mothers—can feel like the most psychologically dangerous. As I wrote in *Searching for Mom*: "Hadn't I already experienced first-hand how tricky mothers could be, how they vanish when you least expect it?"[25]

Chapter 21

It can take time for adoptees to develop trust, to feel safe enough to depend on our parents, and ultimately, to give our hearts to them. Stick with us through the magical times and the challenging times. Don't let our defenses, alarm, and frustration convince you that you can't handle us, or that we don't need you. We do need you! We need you to see us and know us—the full us. We need you to have the confidence that shows us we're not too much for you and our emotional responses to separation aren't, either. We need to know that nothing we could ever say or do has the power to break your connection to us. This is true whether you're an adoptive parent or a birth parent. We need to know that in spite of the act of adoption and all of the heartache that can come with it, you'll always remain attached to us.

Persevere and keep the faith. Parenting is a marathon, as is adoption. While you will likely experience bumps along the way, you are more than equipped to see us to the finish line of meeting our developmental potential. I'm cheering for you!

CHAPTER 22

Journeying Home

Words of Encouragement for Adult Adoptees

(From Sara)

I LOVE THE CONCEPT OF THE HERO'S JOURNEY, A NARRATIVE PATtern articulated by Joseph Campbell, in which a hero is called to venture out of the ordinary world into a journey through the unknown. Along the way, there are mentors, challenges, and temptations. There's revelation, death, and rebirth, which lead to the hero's transformation and return "home"—literal or within oneself. Many well-known films and stories follow this structure, including one of my all-time favorites, *The Wizard of Oz*, which, interestingly, many adoptees say resonates for them, too.

Perhaps this is because every adoptee is on a hero's journey. Through the act of adoption, we've already been placed into the Great Unknown. It is up to us to decide if and when and how we venture further into the wilderness. Like Dorothy, our hearts long for transformation, to return home anew—in whatever ways that looks like for each of us. It might involve seeking clues about our roots to learn more about where we come from, to inform who we are, and to understand how our birth parents and cultures influence us. It may be coming to a place of rest in our adoptive families, discovering that there we have found a sense of true belonging

CHAPTER 22

that comes not through the act of adoption but through years of lived experiences together and the trials and triumphs of family life. It may be discovering confidence and a true sense of identity after years of its elusiveness. It could be each of these things or all of these things and any number of other possibilities. Each journey is unique and deeply personal, and we often don't realize we're on a journey until looking back and seeing how far we've come. Sometimes, it's only clear after we've arrived at a destination or as we pass mile markers along the way.

No matter where you are in your journey you will need mentors. That's what this chapter is about: offering support and guidance from fellow adoptees who've been journeying in the wilds of adoption, too. While it may seem lonely at times, rest assured you aren't alone. Many others have trail-blazed these paths and countless others will, too. Our routes and any obstructions along the way may be individual but as our paths meander and wind we'll criss-cross and intersect. Let's help each other out, waving hello from atop the hills, reaching a hand down into the steep valleys, and refilling each other's water bottles when we're thirsty. The journey can be formidable at times, but the sweeping views from the mountaintops are breathtaking—and best enjoyed in each other's good company.

VENTURING INTO THE REALM OF FEELINGS

One of the most important things we can do to begin healing from adoption is to access our sad feelings. Referring to the traffic circle from Chapter 5, giving ourselves permission to feel our heartaches and disappointments leads to adaptation.

Dr. Gordon Neufeld says, "What adoption does is fill the brain with all kinds of unfinished business, full of all these emotional solutions that need to be resolved. There is a deep sense in the psyche that you've got to make something better, or somebody has to make something better." Lori shared Dr. Neufeld's explanation earlier, and it bears repeating: "But the brain has to *feel* its way through. That's where sadness comes in. Sadness is extremely important because sadness brings an end to the emotional work. Sadness is the end of the sentence. It puts a period on it."[1]

Writes psychotherapist Francis Weller: "We are called back, not so much to make things right, but to acknowledge what happened to us. Grief asks that we honor the loss and, in so doing, deepen our capacity for compassion. When grief remains unexpressed, however, it hardens, becomes as solid as stone. We, in turn, become rigid and stop moving in rhythm with the soul. When we are in touch with all of our emotions, on the other hand, we are more verb than noun, more a movement than a thing."[2]

I spent years as a noun: *Busy Person*. I worked hard pretending that I'd had no losses from adoption—only gains. I bypassed my more vulnerable, sad feelings by staying distracted. Deep down, I feared that if I truly felt my grief, I would drown in sorrow. It was terrifying to begin—I won't pretend otherwise—but the payoff has been worth it and continues to be. While I still have to catch myself, I'm more willing to welcome my sad feelings now and am given hope through the many other adoptees I see relaxing into their feelings, too.

Amanda shares, "I'm still a victim of certain things, but I don't live in victimhood. Sometimes that means I've got to lock myself in the bathroom for five minutes and just cry for a little bit—not to hide but just to get it out."[3]

It's not possible to always stay so attuned to our feelings or recognize when it's time to trust our tears. Feelings are matters of the heart, rather than cognitive issues. We can't simply decide to feel, but we can cultivate spaces and opportunities to allow sadness to enter. One such way is through writing, which is one of the reasons, I believe, that so many adoptees pen memoirs and join writing groups.

"I've written my entire life—poems, song lyrics, diaries, journals—that's how I process. That's how I make sense of everything," Amanda says. "My feelings come out in writing that I don't even know I have in there." Damon says, "Storytelling and sharing our personal truths is a powerful form of healing because it allows the adopted person to acknowledge and own their story."[4]

Other ways might include creating art, reading sad-tinged books, spending time in nature. Music is another way of accessing our feelings, since so many of our emotions don't have words that go with them. Daniel J. Levitin writes, "Your brain on music is a way to understand the deepest mysteries of human nature."[5]

Sometimes sadness can be felt through absorbing others' experiences. Rich shares, "Watching movies and listening to songs with lyrics that touch relinquishment and adoption-related emotions have given me access to untapped feelings."[6]

Professional Guides

Many adoptees turn to professionals for therapeutic support to guide us in our journeys. As Rich says, "Certain wounds can be so serious and debilitating that self-healing cannot begin without outside help." There are many adoption-fluent forms of therapies available, as more adoptees become therapists themselves, and more professionals with insight into attachment, separation, and neuroscience focus on adoption. Talk therapies can offer a safe conduit to draw out tears. Somatic therapies can help release emotions stored in the body for which there are no words. Eye Movement Desensitization and Reprocessing (EMDR) can help with forging new associations in the brain. Internal Family Systems (IFS) is a useful framework for many adoptees to recognize and feel compassion for ways their younger parts learned to cope that may no longer be necessary in adulthood.

Peer support groups and adoptee-led coaching can offer much-needed understanding and a normalization that can bring down alarm and frustration to make way for feeling. Sharing about how this has happened in the Adoptee Voices writing groups, Julian says, "I'm writing about adoption, and people who may not have had my same experiences are saying, 'Yeah, me too.' I think that's where the real healing is coming from: actually feeling mirrored."[7]

These are just some of the supports adoptees have found helpful as they journey toward healing. As Kathy says, "My recommendation is for everyone to discover what works for them, as long as they are actually healing from their wounds rather than just managing them."[8]

Donna offers words of caution: "There are a lot of therapists who do not have an understanding of adoption trauma and can say and do things that are damaging to adoptees. It's a common experience for adoptees to express ourselves to therapists and find that they, like others in society, can be uncomfortable with us going against the packaged story of adoption that we get from the industry, that adoption is a blessing and beautiful. They can say things like, 'Well, aren't you lucky that she gave you away?' Or, 'She loved you enough to give you away.' Or, 'Aren't you glad that you weren't aborted?' All of those things are really damaging to us, and for which we have really complex answers for."[9]

Sadly, there are also therapists and other helping professionals who can take advantage of adoptee vulnerabilities. It's okay to be discerning. It's okay to inquire about a professional's experience with adoption. While being an adoptee does not necessarily equate to being an adept therapist, being adoption-fluent and attachment-informed is important.

Religious and Spiritual Support

Many adoptees discover inner peace and comfort through a religious or spiritual practice. This is true for me, too, though it's complicated because of the wounding that can take place in Christian spaces. I empathize with adoptees who have experienced too much religious trauma to feel safe entering these spaces. Sometimes I, too, question whether the hurtful comments, attitudes, and practices around adoption are worth the rewards of attending church. As I shared in Chapter 7, adoption also led me to believe that God didn't want or care about me. If it weren't for experiencing God's love in a deeply personal way when I faced the great separation of my adoptive mother's death, I would probably still be clinging to that belief. My faith helps me see the goodness in everyone, though, and try to forgive.

Rich has embraced a similar religious framework in his healing journey. "Rather than blame God," he says, "I am learning to look to Him rather than people for unconditional love and a fundamental understanding of relationship. I am learning to define my identity as someone who bears the *imago Dei* (image of God)."

Lily, also a practicing Christian, describes a comfort in being able to give her pain to God. "I could barely open my Bible, but I began to write. And it was this invitation to be honest, to tell God how angry I was at Him, to tell Him how upset I was, to grieve everything that I had been through, to grieve all of my choices, to blame Him, to blame my parents, to blame everyone under the sun besides myself." She adds, "Slowly but surely, He continued the invitation of, 'Okay, so you've said this. Now give it to me.'"[10]

Mar shared their complex relationship with both Judaism and Catholicism in Chapter 7, and how they have found healing through both religious traditions. They share, "I had an affirmation ceremony to make the proactive choice to join my adoptive family's lineage. Since adoption is so passive, I wanted to bring myself into the relationship in a way where I was saying, 'I choose you' to these people, rather than just sort of waffling between I'm sort of Catholic and I'm sort of Jewish, but I'm not really sure how God and I speak to each other. Since Hebrew is the sacred language of the Jews, I wanted to be able to talk to God in the language of my adopted people."[11]

Mar has found healing in other spiritual ways. "Mary has been a placeholder for the pain of missing my mother," they share. In their youth, Mar received therapy from a humanistic Jewish doctor and spent a week at a Zen center. "I was brought into a way of looking at meditation as a way to connect to that world inside. And what I was finding inside was a lot of pain," they share. "With God's help, it's like God is helping me heal that pain."

Other adoptees find a regular meditation practice useful. Carmen says, "Meditation allows me to stay focused in the moment, listening only to the sound of my breath, the inhale and exhale, and to pay close attention to my body and how it feels. Meditation feels like a mental shower and gives me permission to engage in self-care, relaxation, and peace for a few minutes."[12]

Moving Toward Acceptance

Taking a close look at our grief and feeling our sadness isn't about endless wallowing, ongoing victimhood, or getting stuck in the abyss—nor does it mean overshadowing our joys. The point of sadness is to lead us to a place of acceptance. While many believe a bold fight to survive through tightly clenched fists is "grit," or misinterpret fierce independence as resilience, true resilience is about coming out the other side of our pain and adapting. Sadness is the transformation that occurs and helps deliver us victoriously home on our Hero's Journey.

David carries this perspective for his story, evident as he shares, "The very foundation of my conflict, healing, and recovery lies in the fact that I've acknowledged that I was relinquished, that that is a part of my story, and that I've lived the life I lived and I came out triumphant despite my circumstances."[13]

Acceptance doesn't equate to a judgment of good or bad. Many of our adoptions are the result of unethical adoption practices, or result in additional pain such as abuse—sadly, often common for adoptees. *Acceptance* on our part does not mean any such atrocities are *acceptable*.

Accepting our losses is also not a betrayal to our adoptive parents. We are still absolutely free to love them and appreciate any privileges we have received through adoption. We're allowed to mix conflicting thoughts and emotions. In fact, it's par for the course as we grow and mature. Susan says this so well: "I live in this gray area. I live in this place in between. I claim it. I have set up housekeeping here. Because this is where I've been all my life. I don't mind it here."

Adoption as a Lifelong Journey

One of the gifts of transformation is finding or returning to a sense of "home" within yourself—perhaps seeing yourself or your situation in new ways or having a better understanding of how to move forward as the journey continues. And it will most likely continue—or one journey will lead you to the next... and the next.

The wounds from adoption may fade to the background, or come and go, but as far as I can tell from this vantage point and from those who've journeyed before me, don't completely disappear. Many of us find separation is ongoing and shows up differently through our life experiences, relationships, and as we age. As Kathy articulates, "Rarely, if ever, do you feel completely done, as you do when you reach the top of a mountain or finish a project." She adds, "I have experienced healing and continue to heal from relinquishment/adoption, but I haven't healed from relinquishment/adoption."

Echoing Kathy's sentiments, Holly says, "I'm definitely feeling better, but I think it's going to be a lifelong process."[14]

It's also important to remember that our needs and supports evolve over time. Says Kathy, "What I find healing at one point, I may not find healing at another. It depends on where I am at the time, where I'm coming from inside me." Damon agrees: "What an adoptee needs changes over time as milestones are reached, doors are opened or closed, and our collection of facts or sense of self evolves throughout the journey."

Rest assured that each passage gets a little easier, as our practice and comfort with emotions accumulate and teach us to trust in the process.

Healing Together

No matter how deep and dark the abyss in your journey may seem at times, my wish is that you are able to hold on to this basic tenet: *you are not alone.* Lanise says, "The biggest myth that adoptees face every day is that they're the only person on the planet this week who felt that."[15]

Isolation is a liar. Isolation whispers that something is wrong with us. Isolation tries to tell us we don't belong. Isolation tells us to keep quiet, stay small, pretend to be someone we're not. Isolation tells us we're a problem and there's no hope for us. Isolation says we deserve bad things and everything is our fault, and nobody has ever really loved us, anyway, and never will.

Isolation is dead wrong.

Isolation doesn't want you to know that you're not alone, or to have the truth exposed: that we desperately need each other. This is why community can be so meaningful. Community and connection are the antidote to separation and isolation.

Rich advises, "Find a community in which to heal. This is not the same thing as finding people with similar experiences who are stuck in the same state of confusion, pain, and anger as I was. We need others who have walked the path ahead of us to help us navigate."

As a young adult, Mar found community through what was at the time an adoption triad group. "That was really wonderful because it felt like I was in good company with other people who were like us adopted people, but also other people whose family members were making every effort to come to terms with adoption." Through Adoption Mosaic's "Better Together" group made up of adoptees, adoptive parents, and birth parents, I have found a similar sense of healing.

Damon, too, knows the power of company and camaraderie. "The adoptee community offers strength to one another, healing, and support that's awe-inspiring to me. We are people from different walks of life, from all around the world, who share the lived experiences of being adopted. Our adoption experiences are vastly different, but in many ways very similar. Gathering in a supportive community unifies us toward healing each other and healing together." Additionally, community provides us with ongoing opportunities to practice—perhaps a re-do of skills we may not have been ready for before, such as establishing necessary and healthy boundaries, communicating our needs, learning to depend on others and ask for help, trusting in the permanency of love, working through inevitable conflicts. As Rich says, "Developing healthy emotional intimacy with a small circle of trusted individuals is reframing what trust in another person looks like. Healing comes in relationship." Often through these less charged relationships where the stakes aren't as high we can form new neural pathways and tools that will serve other relationships.

Returning Home

I want to trust in the permanency of love. I want to feel each and every one of my highs and my lows. I want to believe in myself and love myself and stand up for myself while still being able to hold on to my softness, my compassion for others, my abilities to walk around all angles and perspectives. I want to look back to realize how far I've come and feel proud. I want my victories to show me I have the strength and courage to keep going and the vision for all that can be. I want to wholeheartedly love others and love myself with innocent abandon, too. I'm ready to feel completely at home.

I have proof that I can do this because I'm already doing it in so many ways. Each of us has the capacity for all these things—and more! We are never beyond hope. We are meant to live into our full developmental potential. We're built for survival. We're wired to heal. Look around, others are holding the doors wide open and welcoming us with open arms.

Amanda shares, "I'm in a place of self-love, accepting myself for who I am and building the safety I needed as a child from within for myself. And it's made a world of difference." Diego says, "I'm finally now, at my age here at forty-seven-ish, coming into the comfort of trying to own my identity."[16]

We will find our way home. I can't wait to meet you there. In the words of adoptee Dorothy as she clicks her ruby slippers together, "There's no place like home."

CHAPTER 23

What Now?

How Adoption Must Evolve

(From Sara, Kelsey, and Lori)

ADOPTION PRACTICES IN THE TWENTIETH CENTURY WERE rooted in secrecy and shame. To be conceived out-of-wedlock was so shameful that we falsified records and locked them away. To have evidence of sex outside of marriage was so scandalous that parents sent their daughters away to protect the family's reputation. To be unable to conceive and carry a baby to term was so humiliating that we went to great lengths *not* to talk about how we created our families, even with adoptees themselves.

Everyone was to pretend that something significant had not happened. The birth parent was expected to "move on" from one of the most significant losses of all—the loss of a child—to never talk about it, never process it. The adoptee was expected to be interchangeable between families, unaffected by separation from the one who had been their entire universe, from the two whose DNA would forever exist in every cell in their body. The adoptive parent was to pretend that the family tree had not been branched by graft. Why bother learning how to deal with, talk about, and heal from all this when nothing was significant enough to acknowledge in the first place?

Chapter 23

We'd like to think we've arrived at enlightenment in adoption, hoping that "open adoption" has cured all. Yet in so many ways, we have focused on surface-level change rather than rolling up our sleeves to truly figure out better ways, both in our homes and in the wider world. We still have remnants of the closed era. People continue to hold outdated Either/Or ideas of adoption that pit birth and adoptive families as opposites. Adult adoptees cannot access their own complete birth records in a majority of states—not to mention the fact that amended birth certificates perpetuate the myth that only one set of parents matters at a time. Most intercountry adoptions remain closed (both in terms of records and connections) and are rife with unethical practices, in spite of protections in place with the Hague Convention. Too often, adoptees still aren't able to talk openly with their adoptive parents about adoption or their struggles, carrying their heartache in isolation. Still unrecognized are the many ways separation trauma ripples through generations.

Adopting a child in or into the United States is a minefield, and adoptees, birth parents, and adoptive parents remain vulnerable to those who know the terrain better and profit from others' naïveté. High prices, and little to no regulation of adoption practices, is a prescription for corruption, evidence that what is allowed to happen in the shadows for profit ends up hurting the rest of us.

Each of us has long been immersed in immeasurable, dysfunctional shame. It's no wonder we experience the difficulties we collectively do. But when we listen to and understand each other and align our efforts we can dare to transform adoption with true consideration for and honoring of *all* impacted. We do not have to perpetuate dysfunction just because "we've always done it this way."

After hearing from courageous voices sharing unfiltered views on their struggles, these revelations can positively impact how adoption is done in our homes and in our society—even if it means fewer adoptions. While one book cannot solve the massive systemic problems of adoption, we hope to spark hope and inspiration in those who wish to work toward reform. Pennies make dollars make change.

What Adoptive Parents Can Do Individually

Curiosity, compassion, openness, and self-reflection are ingredients that help adoptive parents use their power in adoption relationships wisely and attune with those who do not yet hold power.

Curiosity: When conflict or discomfort arises, as it inevitably will, adoptee-centered parents explore context and get creative about ways of relating that honor everyone. They strive to respond to situations mindfully rather than react mindlessly. Adoptive parents become curious to understand a wide range of adoptee voices. When they find themselves triggered, they wonder why. *What may be behind my intense reaction? What may need to be attended to within?*

Compassion: Parents aim to be less judgmental and more compassionate with their child, their child's birth family (whether present or not), and with themselves. Judgment breeds shame, while empathy breeds connection.

Openness: Adoptive parents signal that there is room for the adoptee to wonder about their birth parents and culture and that their origins are valued. By attending to their own "stuff," adoptive parents provide space for the adoptee to feel a full range of emotions, thus indicating that they are willing and able to "go there" with their adoptee, wherever that may be. They commit to avoid further splitting the adoptee's heart, mind, and loyalties.

Self-reflection: When discovering trigger points or sore spots, like insecurity about not being the Only, envy over another person's special connection to the child, grief over their own losses, or anything else adoption-related, adoptive parents self-reflect and endeavor to release big emotions with a trusted adult. It's not bad or shameful to have these "negative" emotions—we're human, after all (self-compassion). These emotions are not the child's to navigate or resolve. As a point of self-responsibility, parents consciously cultivate a vibe that lets the adoptee know they in no way need the adoptee to validate them.

These are some qualities parents can cultivate within their homes and hearts to help remain truly adoptee-centered and maintain respect for all. These qualities sound simple—but recalibrating our mindset in parenting is a steady process that requires emotional intelligence and humility, and is by no means easy.

WHAT WE CAN DO ON A BROADER LEVEL

Beyond the walls of our homes, there is need for evolution on a macro level, through adoption policies, practices, and laws, starting with adoptive parents as allies. While not all people have the time, energy, resources, or desire to take part in broader change, for those who do, here are some ideas.

Leverage Adoptive Parent Privilege

Adoptive parents are the ones who insert money into the adoption machine. They have a moral obligation to their counterparts to prioritize ethics and advocate for better policies and laws in the midst of their participation in a faulty system. Adoptee Astrid Castro, Founder of Adoption Mosaic, says, "Every adoptive parent should be asked: 'When you hear the phrase ethical adoption, what does that mean to you?' Every person who is even considering adopting should be able to answer that question without getting defensive."[1]

Some adoptive parents end up appalled by all they didn't know and the hurt caused by their ignorance, and may wish to widen their circle of influence and help others who come after them. Consider what adoptee and adoptive mom Joanna Ivey suggests of adoptive parents in an interview for *Adoption: The Long View*:

> We talk a lot about privilege these days, usually in terms of racial and economic privilege. There's also a privilege that we have as hopeful adoptive parents and adoptive parents. You might think of all the ways we're not privileged as

adoptive parents. We come to adoption with years of loss. We're financially vulnerable. We're holding our hearts in our hands, wanting to be parents. And all that is true.

But our privilege comes from the one thing it often comes from, and that's money. We are the consumer and agencies cater to us in their marketing, in their services, and in the words agencies use. Media sees our privilege. Stories and movies and TV are framed with adoptive parents as heroes. Our churches and our communities see us as benevolent gifters of stable homes. We have privilege.

With privilege comes power. Because *we* can have discussions within our communities. *We* can talk to our adoption agencies. *We* can write to media companies who get adoption wrong or incomplete in their storylines. And *we* can ensure that adoptee voices and birth parent voices are heard and that they are valued in the same way that our voices are valued. Because *we* have the privilege, the power to change that narrative is on us as adoptive parents.[2]

What Aspects of Change Are Adoption Professionals Responsible For?

While adoptive parents hold privilege and power in adoption and are necessary to effect change, responsibility does not land solely on the shoulders of adoptive parents. Astrid says, "I struggle holding parents accountable in isolation without the social workers and the agencies and the systems."

In any professional space, it's difficult to encourage change on a deeper level. But we must work toward change regardless of how hard it may be. Adoption has not been truly child-centered, despite altruistic goals and intentions. Astrid says, "If you look at the history of adoption practices, you'll see repeated use of the phrases 'child-centered' and 'in the best interests of the child.' Historically, the people who've said that are not adoptees, but rather others who have determined what is in the best interest of the child when we weren't old enough to give our opinions. But now as adults, we are saying, 'Wait a second... I get that *back then* you thought that was child-centered. But here are all the reasons why it wasn't.'"

For child-centered adoptions to truly be the norm, professionals must take substantial steps toward meaningful change of internal policies, and be open and supportive of policy change legislatively. Internally speaking, here are a few changes that should be made:

Reasonable and Justifiable Fees: Charging reasonable fees for the services provided. Adoption fees have such an extensive range, with a high end that is unjustifiable. With some agencies charging as little as $7,500 and others climbing above $75,000, there is no valid accounting for such extreme fees. The adoption industry must turn away from the commodification of children in all areas. Where is the line when charging for expectant birth parent expenses and advertising fees? The highest bidders should not be establishing higher thresholds for adoption fees and raising the cost. Do away with fees that encourage coercion and the brokering of children.

Comprehensive Support for Adoptees: Adoption comes with lifelong effects for adoptees (Part I). Professionals need to recognize this and find ways to support adoptees and their families for the long-term. Astrid speaks directly to social workers and adoption professionals in saying: "It's time to demand that better resources are in the hands of these adoptive families." Offering some ideas, adoptee Diego Vitelli suggests, "We need to have proper protocols in place where these systems are accountable to funding adoptee therapy, homeland visits, cultural camps—all the things we ask adoptive parents to do—they should be paying for."[3]

Counseling for One, Counseling for All: Counseling for adoptees, expectant mothers, birth mothers, and adoptive families is an essential piece of adoption work. The fact that this is a line item that some professionals think is expendable is regrettable. It's critical that professionals provide clients with multiple options of third-party adoption-fluent therapists. When there are no options, encourage local therapists to become adoption-fluent through training initiatives.

Separate Legal Representation: Providing a separate attorney for birth parents is simply the right thing to do (Chapter 8). Social workers cannot give legal advice and the adoptive parents' attorney is under no obligation to provide an expectant mother with a thorough explanation of her legal rights. The responsible and ethical thing to do is to provide an attorney with whom she can consult.

Post-Adoption Contact and Facilitating Openness: Talk about openness with clients early and often, educating all parties to take contact seriously for the sake of the adoptee. Drafting a post-adoption contract agreement (PACA) together can be part of a larger conversation surrounding openness, clarity, and collaboration and may offer legal comfort to birth parents, who may otherwise feel powerless. PACAs are not an end all, be all and should *always* be coupled with education in openness. They're not enforceable in many states, and there are nuances. Grace, understanding, and empathy support a healthy long-term relationship better than legal action, which has potential to ultimately hurt the adoptee more than anyone. Nevertheless, adoption professionals should be drafting a PACA to help bring parents from both families together to set intentions with the adoptee's emotional well-being as the central focus.

Third-Party Adoption Education: Social workers and agencies need to provide adoptive families with better pre- and post-adoption education, best delivered through reputable third-party organizations without a conflict of interest. As Astrid says, "The same organization placing children shouldn't be the organization that educates them."

Diego explains why: "I don't want to call adoptive parents victims by any means, because many of them just don't do their due diligence. But they're part of a system designed to keep them without information they need. The system gives them what they want to hear."

Many agencies are already doing this important work and can share best practices. Forward-thinking agencies are already bringing in adoptee educators and requiring online interactive adoption education, with follow-up discussions to foster a safe environment for learning and asking questions. Expectant parents need pre- and post-adoption education, as well (Chapter 12).

Cross-Cultural Evaluation and Anti-Racism Education: Just as an openness to learning about attachment dynamics should be part of a home study, as Lori suggested in Chapter 20, parents wishing to adopt across racial lines should show a commitment to honoring, exposing, and understanding the culture and race of a potential adoptee. Anti-racist education should be mandated.

Support Policy Initiatives Happening Now: All over the country, adoptees and birth parents are fighting for open records. Licensed professionals are advocating to eliminate unlicensed adoption intermediaries and require adoption entities to only advertise in states where they hold licensure. Advocates and professionals are gathering to ask their states' attorneys general and licensing boards to enforce already-existing laws to protect adoptees, birth mothers, and adoptive families from exploitation.

Adoption professionals could, after taking a critical look at all we've outlined, choose to stand behind reformers in solidarity and give their support. Listening to clients' experiences and hearing about the needs that have not been addressed is a critical first step in change.

Committing to some of these monumental changes is necessary and will take courage. Adoptee Marci is an advocate for adoptee rights. "I'm not an adoption abolitionist. But I would like to abolish the way adoption is currently handled in America and all of the trappings that we have."[4]

As we've seen with other seismic cultural shifts in the twenty-first century, an evolution in who tells the story inevitably leads to changes in perspectives, practices, and policies. Adoptees who have thought critically about adoption—both the "good" and the "needs improvement" parts—are telling their stories, and we need to listen. Birth parents, too, are adding their stories to the multi-faceted narrative that is adoption. It's not a stretch to believe that with the benefit of information from such voices, we can re-envision healthier and ethical ways of doing adoption when it's truly necessary—ways that leave less anguish in its wake, offer more resources to deal with inherent separation trauma, and spread the word that adoption is not as simple as win/win.

For the betterment of 100 million families affected by adoption, let's join efforts to finally bring adoption practices out of the twentieth century. Let's leave closedness behind once and for all and aim instead for true openness in all aspects of adoption.

Acknowledgments

WE ARE GRATEFUL TO LINDA KONNER, OUR AGENT WHO FOUND us a home with Rowman & Littlefield. Thanks to Suzanne Staszak-Silva, Joanna Wattenberg, and Elaine McGarraugh for ushering this book into the world. In addition, we are thankful to Dr. Joyce Maguire Pavao not only for her longtime work and education in the adoption space but for believing in this project enough to write its foreword.

To each other, we say: Who knew a book's three-year gestation could be so much fun, and yield such a safe and supportive circle of safety, respect, and trust? Thank you for your dedication to this project and our friendship that has grown from it.

Sara

Anytime I write about adoption, I am taking a turn with the baton, handed to me from other adoptees who've run this relay first. I thank each adoptee who has shared their perspectives and inspired me to do the same and look forward to passing the baton to adoptees yet to share their stories. Collectively, we're making headway in shifting adoption narratives, education, support, and laws. It's an honor for me to play a part.

To the adoptees or fosterees interviewed for this book—Amanda, Astrid, Bonita, Carmen, Cynthia, Damon, David, Diego, Donna, Holly, Julian, Kathy, Katie, Kayla, Lanise, Lily, Mar, Marci, Rich, Shelise, Susan, Tammy, and Tony—Thanks for trusting me with your vulnerable stories and for your belief in and support of this book.

I'm also thankful for adoptee first readers Alice Stephens and Donna Turner, along with Astrid Castro, Tamara Strijack, Susan Harness, and Marci Purcell—friends and super smart people who spent time talking about this project with me, offering insights, responding to questions, and cheering me along to its completion.

Likewise, I'm eternally thankful for Dr. Gordon Neufeld, for the many insights and contributions you have made in the science of attachment and field of child-developmental psychology. Thank you for reading drafts of my chapters, and for the ways you and Joy have mentored me over the last decade, welcoming me as part of the Neufeld staff and family.

I'm lucky to be part of many communities that provide support, mirroring, learning, laughter, and friendship. Thanks to my Adoptee Voices co-facilitators—Jennifer Dyan Ghoston, Susan Harness, Kate Murphy, and Alice Stephens—along with our talented, courageous Adoptee Voices writers. Likewise, a call out to Adoption Mosaic's special "Better Together" community and lifelong friends found through Adoption Savvy.

To my family members, friends, and mentors: thank you for being such an important part of my life and for reminding me to live, play, and love outside adoption spaces, too.

Dad, thank you for your encouragement and unconditional love, even when reading my words can at times be challenging. Diane, I appreciate you in this way, too. It's not lost on me that sharing publicly about adoption impacts my parents, both by birth and adoption. I share without blame, full of love for you and how you've shaped the woman I have become.

Finally, I owe immense gratitude to my husband Jeff. Your practical and emotional support of me in writing this book has been immeasurable. Thanks for standing by me, always. To Violet and Olive, I love you so much and am so proud to be your mom. Your interest in and awareness of adoption takes my breath away, as does seeing you grow into the amazing, bright young women you are becoming.

Kelsey

I am so grateful to the women I share a sisterhood with, those who have been a sounding board for my darkest thoughts, and lifted me up when I needed to see light. To the women who contributed to this book with vulnerability and strength: Ashley Mitchell, Allana Jackson-Wade, Amy Erickson, Amy Seek, Candace Cahill, Emily Rodriguez, Erica Shaw, Erika Gonzales, Erin Mason, Janelle Ison, Jessie Mattos, Kaedra Blue, Katie Monroe, Mellisa Lathion, Muthoni Gaciku Kittredge, Raquel McCloud, Sarah Schmidth, and Shonda Larson.

To my colleagues who fight for change alongside me every day: Celeste Liversidge, Rebecca Vahle, Alli Mohler, and so many others who have mentored me and stuck with me through every hill and valley of my advocacy and professional journey.

To my child's adoptive parents, I love you. Thank you for your patience, humility, and grace in this open adoption. You are incredible parents and I hope you don't forget that.

To some of my friends who have stood by me in crisis and continue to be someone to lean on, Samantha Henley and Rachel Kohn.

To my family members, my parents, my siblings, and my Grandma Peggy, thank you for giving the best you could give with what you had. I am here because you nurtured my growth and independence to forge my own path.

To my husband, the one who signed up to do the long haul with me, thank you for your patience as I say yes to several-year-long projects. Thank you for walking through grief with me so I no longer have to go it alone.

To my kids, you are bright lights in this world. I am proud of you always.

ACKNOWLEDGMENTS

Lori

So many are represented on these pages, people who have supported me and infused *Adoption Unfiltered* with their gifts. First, I thank contributors Beth, Cynthia, Elizabeth, Greg, Jen, Jess, Karla, Leslie, Lisa, Lorelai, Mallory, Rebecca, and Sujata, plus Kim and Linda.

Next, my cheerleaders: VSG, Adoption Book Club, Thursday Nighters, and ALI bloggers. You have enriched me beyond measure in all the important ways.

For my adoption teachers: Lesli, Jim, Rebecca, Janelle, Debbie, Barbara, Dawn, Anne, and every guest, past and future, on *Adoption: The Long View*. Thank you for generously pouring your wisdom into the world.

For my life teachers: Ethel and Tim. Thank you for the how-to of expansion.

To my yoga, etc. people, David, Kristen, Vickie, Cheryl, and Lucy, thanks for the yin and the yang of it all.

Dad, thanks for showing me how to put words into the world with courage, and Mom, for the loving heart-heart-base to write from. Sheri, thank you for loving my horrible rotten parts. Tami, I honor you for embodying both sunshine and strength (what strength!).

Deni, I love you. Debora, I feel you. Susan, I see you.

To my extended family, we now truly know the necessity and power of connection, and I'm so grateful for mine with you.

Lastly, for my amazingly supportive husband Roger, who cooked many suppers and walked Dexter on the days I was glued to my desk: WATYAI and I love you. Tessa and Reed: you continue to love me through my bumbling. You have my eternal love and gratitude. I am so excited to watch you flourish. Love, Mimo/Mama.

Resources

Because the adoption landscape is ever-changing, we encourage you to visit AdoptionUnfiltered.com/resources for a dynamic list of books, podcasts, films and videos, research, advocacy organizations, and legislative efforts.

Books
Human Development and Trauma
Accessing the Healing Power of the Vagus Nerve by Stanley Rosenberg
The Body Keeps the Score by Bessel van der Kolk, MD
Complex PTSD: From Surviving to Thriving by Pete Walker
The Developing Mind by Daniel J. Siegel, MD
Healing Developmental Trauma by Laurence Heller PhD and Aline LaPierre PsyD
Journey of the Heroic Parent by Brad Reedy, PhD
My Grandmother's Hands by Resmaa Menakem
The Myth of Normal by Gabor Maté MD
Nurturing Resilience by Kathy L. Kain, Stephen J. Terrell, and Peter A. Levine PhD
What Happened to You? by Bruce D. Perry, MD, PhD and Oprah Winfrey
When the Body Says No by Gabor Maté, MD

Adoption
Adoption in America, edited by E. Wayne Carp
Adoption in a Color-Blind Society by Pamela Anne Quiroz
American Baby by Gabrielle Glaser
The Family of Adoption by Joyce Maguire Pavao, EdD
The Girls Who Went Away by Ann Fessler
Parenting in the Eye of the Storm by Katie Naftzger
The Primal Wound by Nancy Newton Verrier

RESOURCES

The Open-Hearted Way to Open Adoption by Lori Holden
Seven Core Issues in Adoption and Permanency by Sharon Kaplan Roszia and Allison Davis Maxon
Wake Up Little Susie by Rickie Solinger
What White Parents Should Know about Transracial Adoption by Melissa Guida-Richards
You Should Be Grateful: Stories of Race, Identity, and Transracial Adoption by Angela Tucker

Adoptee and Birth Parent Memoirs

After decades of adoptee and birth parent voices being left out of the adoption publishing scene, it's wonderful that more and more adoptees and birth parents are penning memoirs. Any printed list will be outdated immediately, leaving out many important books. Following are just some of the books we recommend reading.

All You Can Ever Know by Nicole Chung
Bitterroot: A Salish Memoir of Transracial Adoption by Susan Devan Harness
The Girl I Am, Was, and Never Will Be: A Speculative Memoir of Transracial Adoption by Shannon Gibney
God and Jetfire: Confessions of a Birth Mother by Amy Seek
Goodbye Again by Candace Cahill
Growing Up Black in White by Kevin D. Hoffman
Hole in My Heart by Lorraine Dusky
Invisible Boy by Harrison Mooney
Junkyard Girl by Carlyn Montes de Oca
Lions Roaring Far From Home: An Anthology by Ethiopian Adoptees edited by Aselefech Evans
Parallel Universes: The Story of Rebirth by David Bohl
Searching for Mom by Sara Easterly
The Shoebox Effect by Marcie Keithley
Somebody's Daughter by Zara Phillips
The Son With Two Moms by Tony Hynes
Surviving the White Gaze by Rebecca Carroll
Who Am I Really? by Damon Davis
You Don't Look Adopted by Anne Heffron

See AdoptionUnfiltered.com for a broader list and visit Adoptee Reading.com for a comprehensive directory of adoptee-written memoirs and books.

VIDEO AND FILM
Neufeld's Traffic Circle Model of Frustration
    https://youtu.be/cLYaQ4WX4xw
The Wisdom of Trauma featuring Dr Gabor Maté
    https://thewisdomoftrauma.com
Inclusive Family Support Model assessment tool: https://amarafamily.org/programs-resources/post-adoption-program/openness-assessment/

ORGANIZATIONS
AdoptChange.org
The Adoptee Mentoring Society
Adoptee Rights Coalition
Adoptee Rights Law Center
Adoptee Voices
Adoptees Connect
Adoptees for Justice
Adoption Knowledge Affiliates (AKA)
Adoption Mosaic
Adoption Network Cleveland
Adoption Savvy
Adoption Search Resource Connection (ASRC)
The Adoptive and Foster Family Coalition of New York (AFFCNY)
Alliance for the Study of Adoption and Culture (ASAC)
Celia Center Inc.
Center for Adoption Support and Education (C.A.S.E.)
Coalition for Truth and Transparency in Adoption (CTTA)
Concerned United Birthparents (CUB)
The Family Preservation Project
Heritage Camps for Adoptive Families
InterCountry Adoptee Voices
KAAN (the Korean American Adoptee Adoptive Family Network)
Lifetime Healing Foundation
National Association of Adoptees and Parents (NAAP)
Neufeld Institute
On Your Feet Foundation
PACT, an Adoption Alliance
Rudd Adoption Research Program

THERAPISTS
Adoption Savvy, birth parent and adoptee therapists: adoptionsavvy.com
Grow Beyond Words, directory of adoptee therapists: growbeyondwords.com/adoptee-therapist-directory/

RESOURCES

Training for Adoption Competency Mental Health Professionals directory: adoptionsupport.org/member-types/directory-of-tac-trained-mental-health-professionals/

Notes

INTRODUCTION

1. Jo Jones, PhD and Paul Placek, PhD, "Adoption: By the Numbers," ed. Chuck Johnson and Megan Lestino (National Council for Adoption, 2017).

2. Gabor Maté, MD, *When the Body Says No: The Cost of Hidden Stress* (Toronto: Vintage Canada, 2004), 244.

3. Paul Sunderland, "Relinquishment and Adoption: Understanding the Impact of an Early Psychological Wound," *YouTube.com* (International Conference on Addiction and Associated Disorders, May 2019), https://youtu.be/PX2Vm18TYwg.

4. Remarkably common occurrences, to hear the stories of adult adoptees seeking their birth records via their adoption agencies, the hospitals they were born in, and offices of vital records.

5. Tony Hynes, Adoption in Interracial & LGBTQ+ Families, interview by Lori Holden, *Adoption: The Long View Podcast*, September 2, 2022, https://www.adopting.com/adoption-podcasts/adoption-the-long-view/adoption-in-interracial-lgbtq-families.

PART I

1. Gordon Neufeld, PhD, *Hold on to Your Kids*. (2004; repr., Toronto: Vintage Canada, 2013.)

2. "Dr. Gordon Neufeld," *Neufeld Institute*, accessed October 5, 2022, https://neufeldinstitute.org/about-us/dr-gordon-neufeld/.

3. Joyce Maguire Pavao, EdD, LCSW, LMFT, "About," *Pavao Consulting*, accessed October 5, 2022, http://www.pavaoconsulting.com/about.

4. Joyce Maguire Pavao, *The Family of Adoption* (1998; repr., Boston: Beacon Press, 2005).

5. Nancy Newton Verrier, *The Primal Wound: Understanding the Adopted Child* (Baltimore: Gateway Press, Inc., 1993), 14.

6. Nancy Newton Verrier, *Coming Home to Self: The Adopted Child Grows Up*. (Baltimore: Gateway Press, Inc., 2003).

7. Nancy Newton Verrier, "The Primal Wound," June 5, 2020, https://www.youtube.com/watch?v=bsEgDHkLhzg.

8. Gordon Neufeld, PhD, "Session One: Becoming Attached," Recorded Class Lecture (The Art & Science of Transplanting Children Course, 2011).

9. Nancy Newton Verrier, *The Primal Wound: Understanding the Adopted Child* (Baltimore: Gateway Press, Inc., 1993), 14.

10. Karen Wilson-Buterbaugh, *The Baby Scoop Era: Unwed Mothers, Infant Adoption, and Forced Surrender* (Karen Wilson-Buterbaugh, 2017).

11. Ann Fessler, *The Girls Who Went Away: The Hidden History of Women Who Surrendered Children for Adoption in the Decades before Roe v. Wade* (New York: Penguin Group, 2006), 8.

CHAPTER 1

1. Adam Chau and Kevin Ost-Vollmers, eds., *Parenting as Adoptees*. (CQT Media And Publishing, 2012).

2. Cynthia Landesberg. "Adoption Is Not a Fairy-Tale Answer to Abortion," *The Washington Post*, June 20, 2022: https://www.washingtonpost.com/opinions/2022/06/20/adoption-not-fairy-tale-alternative-to-abortion/.

3. Damon Davis, *Who Am I Really?* Self-published, 2019.

4. David B. Bohl, *Parallel Universes: The Story of Rebirth*. (Milwaukee: HenschelHAUS Publishing, 2018).

5. David B. Bohl, MA and Jamie Marich, PhD, *Relinquishment and Addiction: What Trauma Has to Do with It*. (Milwaukee: HenschelHAUS Publishing, 2021).

6. Katie Naftzger, *Parenting in the Eye of the Storm: The Adoptive Parent's Guide to Navigating the Teen Years*. (Philadelphia: Jessica Kingsley Publishers, 2017).

7. Lily P. McLaughlin, *Love Letters by LilyPearl*. Self-published, 2022.

8. Sara Easterly and Linda Easterly, *Searching for Mom: A Memoir*. (Seattle: Heart Voices, 2019).

9. Susan Devan Harness, *Bitterroot: A Salish Memoir of Transracial Adoption*. (Lincoln: University of Nebraska Press, 2018).

10. Tony Hynes, *The Son with Two Moms*. Self-published, 2014.

CHAPTER 2

1. Gordon Neufeld, PhD, "Separation, Trauma, and Healing in Adoption with Dr. Gordon Neufeld," interview by Sara Easterly, Kelsey Vander Vliet Ranyard, and Lori Holden, *Adoption Unfiltered Video Podcast*, May 31, 2022, https://youtu.be/WeHLnrhPkaQ.

2. David Bohl, MA, CASC, MAC, interview by Sara Easterly, July 29, 2021. All quotations in this chapter from David Bohl result from this interview.

3. Rich Uhrlaub, MEd, interview by Sara Easterly, July 28, 2021.

4. Donna Turner, interview by Sara Easterly, August 7, 2022.

5. Holly, interview by Sara Easterly, August 10, 2022. All quotations in this chapter from Holly result from this interview.
6. Diego Vitelli, LMFT, interview by Sara Easterly, July 20, 2022. All quotations in this chapter from Diego Vitelli result from this interview.
7. Tony Hynes, "Problematic Behaviors of Birth Parents with Tony Hynes," interview by Sara Easterly, Kelsey Vander Vliet Ranyard, and Lori Holden, *Adoption Unfiltered Video Podcast*, May 17, 2022, https://youtu.be/ENzs7fdEClM. All quotations in this chapter from Tony Hynes result from this interview.
8. Mar Meislin, interview by Sara Easterly, July 29, 2022.
9. Lanise Antoine Shelley, interview by Sara Easterly, July 27, 2022. All quotations in this chapter from Lanise Antoine Shelley result from this interview.
10. Kayla Zheng, interview by Sara Easterly, August 6, 2022. All quotations in this chapter from Kayla Zheng result from this interview.
11. Astrid Castro, interview by Sara Easterly, August 15, 2022.
12. Shelise Gieseke, interview by Sara Easterly, July 27, 2022.

CHAPTER 3

1. Gordon Neufeld, PhD, "Session Three: Problems Rooted in Separation-Triggered Pursuit," Recorded Class Lecture (Neufeld Intensive II: The Separation Complex Course, 2016).
2. Pete Walker, MA, *Complex PTSD : From Surviving to Thriving* (New York: Azure Coyote, 2013), 12.
3. Katie Naftzger, LICSW, interview by Sara Easterly, July 8, 2021.
4. Shelise Gieseke, interview by Sara Easterly, July 27, 2022. All quotations in this chapter from Shelise Gieseke result from this interview.
5. Amanda Medina, interview by Sara Easterly, June 22, 2021. All quotations in this chapter from Amanda Medina result from this interview.
6. Donna Turner, interview by Sara Easterly, August 7, 2022. All quotations in this chapter from Donna Turner result from this interview.
7. Tammy Perlmutter, interview by Sara Easterly, November 18, 2022. All quotations in this chapter from Tammy Perlmutter result from this interview.
8. Lanise Antoine Shelley, interview by Sara Easterly, July 27, 2022. All quotations in this chapter from Lanise Antoine Shelley result from this interview.
9. Gordon Neufeld, PhD, "Session Three: Problems Rooted in Separation-Triggered Pursuit," Recorded Class Lecture (Neufeld Intensive II: The Separation Complex Course, 2016).
10. Gordon Neufeld, PhD, "Session Twelve: Problems Rooted in Defensive Detachment," Recorded Class Lecture (Neufeld Intensive II: The Separation Complex Course, 2016).
11. Julian Washio-Collette, interview by Sara Easterly, July 30, 2022.
12. Holly, interview by Sara Easterly, August 10, 2022.
13. Gordon Neufeld, PhD, "Session Twelve: Problems Rooted in Defensive Detachment," Recorded Class Lecture (Neufeld Intensive II: The Separation Complex Course, 2016).

14. Lily McLaughlin, interview by Sara Easterly, November 21, 2022. All quotations in this chapter from Lily McLaughlin result from this interview.

CHAPTER 4

1. Gordon Neufeld, PhD, "Session Four: Making Sense of Alarm," Recorded Class Lecture (Neufeld Intensive II: The Separation Complex Course, 2016).
2. Donna Turner, interview by Sara Easterly, August 7, 2022. All quotations in this chapter from Donna Turner result from this interview.
3. Amanda Medina, interview by Sara Easterly, June 22, 2021.
4. Katie Naftzger, LICSW, interview by Sara Easterly, July 8, 2021. All quotations in this chapter from Katie Naftzger result from this interview.
5. Gordon Neufeld, PhD, "Session Four: Making Sense of Alarm," Recorded Class Lecture (Neufeld Intensive II: The Separation Complex Course, 2016).
6. Gordon Neufeld, PhD, "Session Five: Making Sense of Alarm Problems," Recorded Class Lecture (Neufeld Intensive II: The Separation Complex Course, 2016).
7. Carol A. Wingfield, MA, "The Role of Shame in Infant Development," *Journal of Prenatal and Perinatal Psychology and Health* 26, no. 2 (December 2011): 122–23.
8. Bessel Van der Kolk, MD, *The Body Keeps the Score: Mind, Brain, and Body in the Transformation of Trauma* (London: Penguin Books, 2014).
9. Bruce D. Perry, MD, PhD and Oprah Winfrey, *What Happened to You?: Conversations on Trauma, Resilience and Healing* (New York: Flatiron Books, 2021), 80.
10. Veronique P. Mead, MD, MA, "Adverse Babyhood Experiences (ABEs) Increase Risk for Infant and Maternal Morbidity and Mortality and Chronic Illness," *Journal of Prenatal and Perinatal Psychology and Health* 34, no. 4 (2020): 15.
11. Kimberly A. Tremblay and Elizabeth Soliday, "Effect of Planning, Wantedness, and Attachment on Prenatal Anxiety," *Journal of Prenatal and Perinatal Psychology and Health* 27, no. 2 (December 2012): 109.
12. Arthur Janov, PhD "Life before Birth: How Experience in the Womb Can Affect Our Lives Forever," *Journal of Prenatal and Perinatal Psychology and Health* 23, no. 3 (March 2009): 159, https://birthpsychology.com/wp-content/uploads/journal/published_paper/volume-23/issue-3/4O02a7Ng.pdf.
13. Arthur Janov, PhD "Life before Birth: How Experience in the Womb Can Affect Our Lives Forever," *Journal of Prenatal and Perinatal Psychology and Health* 23, no. 3 (March 2009): 148, https://birthpsychology.com/wp-content/uploads/journal/published_paper/volume-23/issue-3/4O02a7Ng.pdf.
14. Gordon Neufeld, PhD, "Session Four: Making Sense of Alarm," Recorded Class Lecture (Neufeld Intensive II: The Separation Complex Course, 2016).
15. Veronique P. Mead, MD, MA, "Adverse Babyhood Experiences (ABEs) Increase Risk for Infant and Maternal Morbidity and Mortality and Chronic Illness," *Journal of Prenatal and Perinatal Psychology and Health* 34, no. 4 (2020): 14.

Notes

16. Veronique P. Mead, MD, MA, "Adverse Babyhood Experiences (ABEs) Increase Risk for Infant and Maternal Morbidity and Mortality and Chronic Illness," *Journal of Prenatal and Perinatal Psychology and Health* 34, no. 4 (2020): 13.

17. Veronique P. Mead, MD, MA, *Adverse Babyhood Experiences (ABEs)*, The Chronic Illness & Trauma Connection Series, Book 4 (Chronic Illness Trauma Studies, 2018).

18. David Bohl, MA, CASC, MAC, interview by Sara Easterly, July 29, 2021.

19. Gordon Neufeld, PhD, "Session Four: Making Sense of Alarm," Recorded Class Lecture (Neufeld Intensive II: The Separation Complex Course, 2016).

20. Tammy Perlmutter, interview by Sara Easterly, November 18, 2022. All quotations in this chapter from Tammy Perlmutter result from this interview.

21. Nancy Newton Verrier, "The Primal Wound," June 5, 2020, https://www.youtube.com/watch?v=bsEgDHkLhzg.

22. Gordon Neufeld, PhD, "Session Four: Making Sense of Alarm," Recorded Class Lecture (Neufeld Intensive II: The Separation Complex Course, 2016).

23. Gabor Maté, MD, *When the Body Says No: The Cost of Hidden Stress* (Toronto: Vintage Canada, 2004), 245.

24. Shelise Gieseke, interview by Sara Easterly, July 27, 2022.

25. Bruce D. Perry, MD, PhD and Oprah Winfrey, *What Happened to You?: Conversations on Trauma, Resilience and Healing* (New York: Flatiron Books, 2021), 78.

26. Gordon Neufeld, PhD, "Session Four: Making Sense of Alarm," Recorded Class Lecture (Neufeld Intensive II: The Separation Complex Course, 2016).

27. Arthur Janov, PhD, "Life before Birth: How Experience in the Womb Can Affect Our Lives Forever," *Journal of Prenatal and Perinatal Psychology and Health* 23, no. 3 (March 2009): 162, https://birthpsychology.com/wp-content/uploads/journal/published_paper/volume-23/issue-3/4O02a7Ng.pdf.

28. Nadine Burke Harris, MD, "How Childhood Trauma Affects Health across a Lifetime," 2014, https://tedmed.com/talks/show?id=293066.

29. Gordon Neufeld, PhD, "Session Four: Making Sense of Alarm," Recorded Class Lecture (Neufeld Intensive II: The Separation Complex Course, 2016).

30. Thomas R. Verny, MD, "What Cells Remember: Toward a Unified Field Theory of Memory," *Journal of Prenatal and Perinatal Psychology and Health* 29, no. 1 (September 2014).

31. Veronique P. Mead, MD, MA, *The Science of How Trauma & Adverse Life Experiences Interact with Genes to Shape Health, Why It's Not in Your Head, and How Healing Trauma Offers Hope for Reducing Symptoms of Chronic Illness*, The Chronic Illness & Trauma Connection Series, Book 1: An Overview (Chronic Illness Trauma Studies, 2020), 49.

32. Joyce Maguire Pavao, EdD, LCSW, LMFT, "Thoughts of an Adoptee By-The-Sea," *Pavao Consulting*, July 1996, http://site-4sgcknkk.dotezcdn.com/uploads/4A253959B094F655.pdf?v=0.

Chapter 5

1. Gordon Neufeld, PhD, "Neufeld's Traffic Circle Model of Frustration," *Neufeld Institute*, September 22, 2022, https://www.youtube.com/watch?v=cLYaQ4WX4xw.
2. Gordon Neufeld, PhD, "Neufeld's Traffic Circle Model of Frustration," *Neufeld Institute*, September 22, 2022, https://www.youtube.com/watch?v=cLYaQ4WX4xw.
3. Gordon Neufeld, PhD, "Neufeld's Traffic Circle Model of Frustration," *Neufeld Institute*, September 22, 2022, https://www.youtube.com/watch?v=cLYaQ4WX4xw.
4. Shelise Gieseke, interview by Sara Easterly, July 27, 2022. All quotations in this chapter from Shelise Gieseke result from this interview.
5. Amanda Medina, interview by Sara Easterly, June 22, 2021. All quotations in this chapter from Amanda Medina result from this interview.
6. Julian Washio-Collette, interview by Sara Easterly, July 30, 2022. Unless otherwise notes, all quotations in this chapter from Julian Washio-Collette result from this interview.
7. Julian Washio-Collette, "Gift," *Anne Heffron's Blog*, November 29, 2021, https://www.anneheffron.com/blog/2021/11/29/gift-guest-blog-post-by-julian-washio-collette.
8. Tony Hynes, Problematic Behaviors of Birth Parents with Tony Hynes, interview by Sara Easterly, Kelsey Vander Vliet Ranyard, and Lori Holden, *Adoption Unfiltered Video Podcast*, May 17, 2022, https://youtu.be/ENzs7fdEClM.
9. Kayla Zheng, interview by Sara Easterly, August 6, 2022. All quotations in this chapter from Kayla Zheng result from this interview.
10. Margaret A. Keyes et al., "Risk of Suicide Attempt in Adopted and Nonadopted Offspring," *Pediatrics* 132, no. 4 (September 9, 2013), https://publications.aap.org/pediatrics/article-abstract/132/4/639/64833/Risk-of-Suicide-Attempt-in-Adopted-and-Nonadopted.
11. Gordon Neufeld, PhD, "Neufeld's Traffic Circle Model of Frustration," *Neufeld Institute*, September 22, 2022, https://www.youtube.com/watch?v=cLYaQ4WX4xw.
12. Donna Turner, interview by Sara Easterly, August 7, 2022. All quotations in this chapter from Donna Turner result from this interview.
13. Holly, interview by Sara Easterly, August 10, 2022. All quotations in this chapter from Holly result from this interview.
14. Tammy Perlmutter, interview by Sara Easterly, November 18, 2022.
15. Katie Naftzger, LICSW, interview by Sara Easterly, July 8, 2021.
16. Gihyun Yoon et al., "Substance Use Disorders and Adoption: Findings from a National Sample," ed. Antonio Verdejo García, *PloS One* 7, no. 11 (November 2012): 1, https://www.ncbi.nlm.nih.gov/pmc/articles/PMC3499473/.
17. David Bohl, MA, CASC, MAC, interview by Sara Easterly, July 29, 2021. All quotations in this chapter from David Bohl result from this interview.
18. Mar Meislin, interview by Sara Easterly, July 29, 2022.

CHAPTER 6

1. Bonita Rockingham, interview by Sara Easterly, July 9, 2021.
2. Dawn Peterson, *Indians in the Family: Adoption and Politics of the Antebellum Expansion* (Cambridge, Mass: Harvard University Press, 2017), 12–13.
3. Carol J. Singley, "Building a Nation, Building a Family: Adoption in Nineteenth-Century American Children's Literature," in *Adoption in America: Historical Perspectives* (Ann Arbor: The University of Michigan Press, 2002), 53.
4. Carol J. Singley, "Building a Nation, Building a Family: Adoption in Nineteenth-Century American Children's Literature," in *Adoption in America: Historical Perspectives* (Ann Arbor: The University of Michigan Press, 2002), 55.
5. Julie Berebitsky, "Rescue a Child and Save the Nation: The Social Construction of Adoption in the Delineator, 1907-1911," in *Adoption in America: Historical Perspectives* (Ann Arbor: The University of Michigan Press, 2002), 136.
6. Judy Pace Christie and Lisa Wingate, *Before and After: The Incredible Real-Life Stories of Orphans Who Survived the Tennessee Children's Home Society* (New York: Ballantine Books, 2019).
7. *Stolen Childhoods*, Audio Documentary (SoundCloud: KFAI's MinneCulture, 2017).
8. Kathryn Joyce, "How Ethiopia's Adoption Industry Dupes Families and Bullies Activists," *The Atlantic*, December 21, 2011, https://www.theatlantic.com/international/archive/2011/12/how-ethiopias-adoption-industry-dupes-families-and-bullies-activists/250296/.
9. Nicole Acevedo, "A Painful Truth: Guatemalan Adoptees Learn They Were Fraudulently Given Away," *NBC News*, December 8, 2019, https://www.nbcnews.com/news/latino/painful-truth-guatemalan-adoptees-learn-they-were-fraudulently-given-away-n1095066.
10. Alice McCool, "'I Want My Kids Back': How Overseas Adoptions Splinter Uganda's Families," *The Guardian*, May 29, 2020, https://www.theguardian.com/global-development/2020/may/29/i-want-my-kids-back-how-overseas-adoptions-splinter-ugandas-families.
11. Anastasia Maloney, "Haiti Orphanages Hotspot of Child Trafficking, Abuse, Says Charity," *Reuters*, June 22, 2017, https://www.reuters.com/article/us-haiti-children-trafficking/haiti-orphanages-hotspot-of-child-trafficking-abuse-says-charity-idUSKBN19D2PO.
12. Hilary Mosia, "The Baby-Selling Scheme: Poor Pregnant Marshall Islands Women Lured to the US," *The Guardian*, January 7, 2021, https://www.theguardian.com/world/2021/jan/08/the-baby-selling-scheme-poor-pregnant-marshall-islands-women-lured-to-the-us.
13. Ernesto Londoño, "Stolen at Birth, Chilean Adoptees Uncover Their Past," *The New York Times*, December 17, 2017, https://www.nytimes.com/2021/12/17/world/americas/chile-adoption-pinochet.html.
14. John Leland, "For Adoptive Parents, Questions without Answers," *The New York Times*, September 16, 2011, https://www.nytimes.com/2011/09/18/

nyregion/chinas-adoption-scandal-sends-chills-through-families-in-united-states.html.

15. "More South Korean Adoptees Who Were Sent Overseas Demand Probes into Their Cases," *National Public Radio*, December 9, 2022, https://www.npr.org/2022/12/09/1141912093/south-korea-adoptees-fraud-investigation-western-families.

16. Meghan Collins Sullivan, "For Romania's Orphans, Adoption Is Still a Rarity," *National Public Radio*, August 19, 2012, https://www.npr.org/2012/08/19/158924764/for-romanias-orphans-adoption-is-still-a-rarity.

17. Joanna Heywood, "The Children Sent to a DR Congo 'Holiday Camp' Never to Come Back," *BBC News*, August 14, 2019, https://www.bbc.com/news/world-europe-48948774.

18. Marion Scott, "Forced Adoption Scandal: How Many Women Were Given These Tablets? We Have No Idea," *The Sunday Post*, August 1, 2021, https://www.sundaypost.com/fp/forced-adoption-scandal/.

19. James Pheby, "Campaigners Say U.K. 'Forced Adoption' Scandal far from Over," *The Japan Times*, July 17, 2022, https://www.japantimes.co.jp/news/2022/07/17/world/crime-legal-world/uk-forced-adoption-scandal/.

20. Tik Root, "The Baby Brokers: Inside America's Murky Private-Adoption Industry," *TIME Magazine*, June 3, 2021, https://time.com/6051811/private-adoption-america/.

21. "Six Words: 'Black Babies Cost Less to Adopt,'" *National Public Radio*, June 27, 2013, https://www.npr.org/2013/06/27/195967886/six-words-black-babies-cost-less-to-adopt.

22. Joyce Pavao, EdD, LCSW, LMFT and Maureen McCauley, "Joyce Maguire Pavao Speaks out against CHIFF," *Light of Day Stories*, April 2, 2014, https://lightofdaystories.com/category/joyce-maguire-pavao/.

23. Kayla Zheng, interview by Sara Easterly, August 6, 2022. All quotations in this chapter from Kayla Zheng result from this interview.

24. Holly, interview by Sara Easterly, August 10, 2022. All quotations in this chapter from Holly result from this interview.

25. Lanise Antoine Shelley, interview by Sara Easterly, July 27, 2022. All quotations in this chapter from Lanise Antoine Shelley result from this interview.

26. Susan Devan Harness, interview by Sara Easterly, July 16, 2021. All quotations in this chapter from Susan Devan Harness result from this interview.

27. Shelise Gieseke, interview by Sara Easterly, July 27, 2022. All quotations in this chapter from Shelise Gieseke result from this interview.

28. Diego Vitelli, LMFT, interview by Sara Easterly, July 20, 2022.

29. Tony Hynes, Problematic Behaviors of Birth Parents with Tony Hynes, interview by Sara Easterly, Kelsey Vander Vliet Ranyard, and Lori Holden, *Adoption Unfiltered Video Podcast*, May 17, 2022, https://youtu.be/ENzs7fdEClM.

30. Lily McLaughlin, interview by Sara Easterly, November 21, 2022.

31. Katie Naftzger, LICSW, interview by Sara Easterly, July 8, 2021.

32. Marci Purcell, interview by Sara Easterly, November 21, 2022.

33. Astrid Castro, interview by Sara Easterly, August 15, 2022.

34. Carmen Hinckley, interview by Sara Easterly, January 17, 2023. All quotations in this chapter from Carmen Hinckley result from this interview.

CHAPTER 7

1. Kathryn Joyce, *The Child Catchers: Rescue, Trafficking, and the New Gospel of Adoption* (New York: PublicAffairs, 2013).

2. Erin M. Heim, *Adoption in Galatians and Romans* (BRILL, 2017).

3. Sara Easterly and Linda Easterly, *Searching for Mom: A Memoir* (Seattle: Heart Voices, 2019).

4. Bonita Rockingham, interview by Sara Easterly, *Personal*, July 9, 2021. All quotations in this chapter from Bonita Rockingham result from this interview.

5. Cynthia Landesberg, interview by Sara Easterly, *Personal*, July 20, 2022. Unless otherwise noted, all quotations in this chapter from Cynthia Landesberg result from this interview.

6. Cynthia Landesberg, "Passover: An Adoptee's Story," *Adoption Squared*, April 7, 2022, https://www.adoptionsquared.com/post/passover-an-adoptee-s-story.

7. Rich Uhrlaub, MEd, interview by Sara Easterly, *Personal*, July 28, 2021.

8. Kayla Zheng, interview by Sara Easterly, *Personal*, August 6, 2022. All quotations in this chapter from Kayla Zheng result from this interview.

9. Mar Meislin, interview by Sara Easterly, *Personal*, July 29, 2022. All quotations in this chapter from Mar Meislin result from this interview.

10. Diego Vitelli, LMFT, interview by Sara Easterly, *Personal*, July 20, 2022.

11. *Geographies of Kinship* (Mu Films, 2019).

12. Alice Stephens and Sara Easterly, review of *Adopting for God*, by Soojin Chung, *Englewood Review of Books*, May 19, 2022, https://englewoodreview.org/soojin-chung-adopting-for-god-feature-review/.

CHAPTER 8

1. Rebecca Wiechhand and Kathleen Strottman, "2014 Adoption Attitudes & Awareness Survey" (The Congressional Coalition on Adoption Institute, April 15, 2014).

2. Kelsey Vander Vliet Ranyard and Celeste Liversidge, "How to Choose an Adoption Professional," Podcast, *Thinking about Adoption*, November 2021, https://open.spotify.com/episode/4sw1lmC36jwMYTrVZJl6U7?si=f1459052e4b14fe7.

3. Emily Rodriguez, interview by Kelsey Vander Vliet Ranyard, August 27, 2021. All quotations by Emily in this chapter result from this interview.

4. Ashley Mitchell, interview by Kelsey Vander Vliet Ranyard, July 14, 2021. All quotations by Ashley in this chapter result from this interview.

5. Shonda Larson, interview by Kelsey Vander Vliet Ranyard, August 24, 2021. All quotations by Shonda in this chapter result from this interview.

NOTES

6. Erika Gonzales, interview by Kelsey Vander Vliet Ranyard, July 27, 2021. All quotations by Erika in this chapter result from this interview.

CHAPTER 9

1. Mellisa Lathion, interview by Kelsey Vander Vliet Ranyard, October 7, 2021. All quotations by Mellisa this chapter result from this interview.

2. Sarah Schmidth, interview by Kelsey Vander Vliet Ranyard, November 13, 2022. All quotations by Sarah in this chapter result from this interview.

3. Erika Gonzales, interview by Kelsey Vander Vliet Ranyard, July 27, 2021. All quotations by Erika G. in this chapter result from this interview.

4. Rickie Solinger, Wake Up Little Susie (New York: Routledge, 2000).

5. Emily Rodriguez, interview by Kelsey Vander Vliet Ranyard, August 27, 2021. All quotations by Emily in this chapter result from this interview.

6. Ashley Mitchell, interview by Kelsey Vander Vliet Ranyard, July 14, 2021. All quotations by Ashley in this chapter result from this interview.

7. Erica Shaw, interview by Kelsey Vander Vliet Ranyard, November 18, 2022. All quotations by Erica S. in this chapter result from this interview.

CHAPTER 10

1. Alexandra Coelho, Maja de Brito, and António Barbosa, "Caregiver Anticipatory Grief," Current Opinion in Supportive and Palliative Care 12, no. 1 (March 2018): 52 57, doi:https://doi.org/10.1097/spc.0000000000000321.

2. Sarah Schmidth, interview by Kelsey Vander Vliet Ranyard, November 13, 2022. All quotations by Sarah in this chapter result from this interview.

3. Muthoni Gaciku Kittredge, interview by Kelsey Vander Vliet Ranyard, September 27, 2021. All quotations by Muthoni in this chapter result from this interview.

4. Carolyn Knight and Alex Gitterman, "Ambiguous Loss and Its Disenfranchisement: The Need for Social Work Intervention," Families in Society: The Journal of Contemporary Social Services 100, no. 2 (November 2018): 165, doi:https://doi.org/10.1177/1044389418799937.

5. Denise Côté Arsenault and Kara Donato, "Emotional Cushioning in Pregnancy after Perinatal Loss," Journal of Reproductive and Infant Psychology 29, no. 1 (February 2011): 81, doi:https://doi.org/10.1080/02646838.2010.513115.

6. Ashley Mitchell, interview by Kelsey Vander Vliet Ranyard, July 14, 2021. All quotations by Ashley in this chapter result from this interview.

7. Amy Erickson, interview by Kelsey Vander Vliet Ranyard, November 3, 2022. All quotations by Amy in this chapter result from this interview.

8. Bridget F. Hutchens and Joan Kearney, "Risk Factors for Postpartum Depression: An Umbrella Review," Journal of Midwifery & Women's Health 65, no. 1 (January 22, 2020), doi:https://doi.org/10.1111/jmwh.13067.

9. S. Ayers et al., "The Aetiology of Post-Traumatic Stress Following Childbirth: A Meta-Analysis and Theoretical Framework," Psychological Medicine 46, no. 6 (2016): 1121–34, doi:https://doi.org/10.1017/S0033291715002706.

10. Liliana Dell'Osso et al., "Lifetime Mood Symptoms and Adult Separation Anxiety in Patients with Complicated Grief And/or Post-Traumatic Stress Disorder: A Preliminary Report," Psychiatry Research 198, no. 3 (August 2012): 436–40, doi:https://doi.org/10.1016/j.psychres.2011.12.020.

11. Carolyn Knight and Alex Gitterman, "Ambiguous Loss and Its Disenfranchisement: The Need for Social Work Intervention," Families in Society: The Journal of Contemporary Social Services 100, no. 2 (January 2018): pp. 164-173, https://doi.org/10.1177/1044389418799937, 170.

CHAPTER 11

1. "Six Words: 'Black Babies Cost Less to Adopt,'" *National Public Radio*, June 27, 2013, https://www.npr.org/2013/06/27/195967886/six-words-black-babies-cost-less-to-adopt.

2. A. S., "Discount Babies," *The Economist*, May 14, 2010, https://www.economist.com/free-excIt hange/2010/05/14/discount-babies.

3. Rickie Solinger, *Wake Up Little Susie* (New York: Routledge, 2000). 24-25.

4. Muthoni Gaciku Kittredge, interview by Kelsey Vander Vliet Ranyard, September 27, 2021. All quotations by Muthoni in this chapter result from this interview.

5. Kari Sandven and Michael D. Resnick, "Informal Adoption among Black Adolescent Mothers.," American Journal of Orthopsychiatry 60, no. 2 (1990): 210–24, doi:https://doi.org/10.1037/h0079158.

6. Brian Paul Gill, "Adoption Agencies and the Search for the Ideal Family, 1918-1965," in Adoption in America (Ann Arbor: The University of Michigan Press, 2002), 160–80.

7. Rickie Solinger, *Wake Up Little Susie* (New York: Routledge, 2000).

8. Brian Paul Gill, "Adoption Agencies and the Search for the Ideal Family, 1918-1965," in *Adoption in America* (Ann Arbor: The University of Michigan Press, 2002), 160–80.

9. Allana Jackson-Wade, interview by Kelsey Vander Vliet Ranyard, December 7, 2022. All quotations by Allana in this chapter result from this interview.

10. Erika Gonzales, interview by Kelsey Vander Vliet Ranyard, July 27, 2021. All quotations by Erika G. in this chapter result from this interview.

11. Amy Seek, interview by Kelsey Vander Vliet Ranyard, November 12, 2022. All quotations by Amy S. in this chapter result from this interview.

12. Erica Shaw, interview by Kelsey Vander Vliet Ranyard, November 18, 2022. All quotations by Erica S. in this chapter result from this interview.

Chapter 12

1. Jessie Mattos, interview by Kelsey Vander Vliet Ranyard, January 18, 2023.
2. Allana Jackson-Wade, interview by Kelsey Vander Vliet Ranyard, December 6, 2022.
3. Gordon Neufeld, PhD, "Session One: Becoming Attached," Recorded Class Lecture (The Art & Science of Transplanting Children Course, 2011).
4. Erin Mason, interview by Kelsey Vander Vliet Ranyard, August 11, 2021. All quotations by Erin in this chapter result from this interview.
5. Ashley Mitchell, interview by Kelsey Vander Vliet Ranyard, July 14, 2021. All quotations by Ashley in this chapter result from this interview.

Chapter 13

1. March, Karen. "Birth Mother Grief and the Challenge of Adoption Reunion Contact." *American Journal of Orthopsychiatry* 84, no. 4 (2014): 409. https://doi.org/10.1037/ort0000013. 409.
2. March, Karen. "Birth Mother Grief and the Challenge of Adoption Reunion Contact." *American Journal of Orthopsychiatry* 84, no. 4 (2014): 409. https://doi.org/10.1037/ort0000013. 416.
3. Amy Erickson, interview by Kelsey Vander Vliet Ranyard, November 3, 2022. All quotations by Amy E. in this chapter result from this interview.
4. March, Karen. "Birth Mother Grief and the Challenge of Adoption Reunion Contact." *American Journal of Orthopsychiatry* 84, no. 4 (2014): 409. https://doi.org/10.1037/ort0000013.
5. Katie Monroe, interview by Kelsey Vander Vliet Ranyard, August 17, 2021.
6. Amy Seek, interview by Kelsey Vander Vliet Ranyard, November 12, 2022.
7. Kaedra Blue, interview by Kelsey Vander Vliet Ranyard, November 28, 2022. All quotations by Kaedra in this chapter result from this interview.
8. March, Karen, "Birth Mother Grief and the Challenge of Adoption Reunion Contact.," *American Journal of Orthopsychiatry* 84, no. 4 (2014): pp. 409-419, https://doi.org/10.1037/ort0000013, 416.
9. March, Karen, "Birth Mother Grief and the Challenge of Adoption Reunion Contact.," *American Journal of Orthopsychiatry* 84, no. 4 (2014): pp. 409-419, https://doi.org/10.1037/ort0000013, 416.
10. Candace Cahill, interview by Kelsey Vander Vliet Ranyard, August 14, 2021. All quotations by Candace in this chapter result from this interview.
11. Adeline Wyman Battalen et al., "Birth Mothers Now Birth Grandmothers: Intergenerational Relationships in Open Adoptions," *Adoption Quarterly* 22, no. 1 (October 25, 2018): 65, doi:https://doi.org/10.1080/10926755.2018.1488327.
12. Janelle Ison, interview by Kelsey Vander Vliet Ranyard, January 26, 2023.
13. Sarah Schmidth, interview by Kelsey Vander Vliet Ranyard, November 13, 2022.
14. Mellisa Lathion, interview by Kelsey Vander Vliet Ranyard, October 7, 2021.

NOTES

CHAPTER 14

1. Angela Tucker, "Navigating Openness," Workshop (Heritage Camps for Adoptive Families, August 16, 2022).
2. Ellen Herman, "Adoption History: Adoption History in Brief," *Dark wing.uoregon.edu*, February 24, 2012, https://darkwing.uoregon.edu/~adoption/topics/adoptionhistbrief.htm.
3. Barbara Yngvesson, "Refiguring Kinship in the Space of Adoption," *Anthropological Quarterly* 80, no. 2 (2007): 565, doi:10.1353/anq.2007.0036.
4. Lori Holden, "'Real' in Adoption and How It Splits Our Babies," *Lavender Luz*, April 22, 2013, https://lavenderluz.com/real-in-adoption-splits-our-babies/.
5. I deliberately do not separate these two words with a slash in an effort to convey wholeness and integration.
6. Sara Easterly, "Moses and Me: A Biblical and Personal Case for Honoring Birth Mothers," *Godspace*, November 17, 2018, https://godspacelight.com/2018/11/17/moses-and-me-a-biblical-and-personal-case-for-honoring-birth-mothers/.

CHAPTER 15

1. Rebecca, interview by Lori Holden, January 4, 2022. All quotations in this chapter from Rebecca result from this interview.
2. Beth, interview by Lori Holden, *Personal*, September 13, 2022.
3. Mallory, interview by Lori Holden, July 22, 2022.
4. Chris Mara, "Urban Dictionary: Adoptoraptor," *Urban Dictionary*, December 24, 2011, https://www.urbandictionary.com/define.php?term=Adoptoraptor.
5. Karla, interview by Lori Holden, September 8, 2022.
6. Leslie, interview by Lori Holden, July 22, 2022.

CHAPTER 16

1. Mallory, interview by Lori Holden, July 22, 2022. All quotations in this chapter from Mallory result from this interview.
2. Rebecca, interview by Lori Holden, January 4, 2022.
3. Leslie, interview by Lori Holden, July 22, 2022. All quotations in this chapter from Leslie result from this interview.
4. Scott D. Ryan et al., "Open Adoptions in Child Welfare: Social Worker and Foster/Adoptive Parent Attitudes," *Journal of Public Child Welfare* 5, no. 4 (August 31, 2011): 445–66, doi:10.1080/15548732.2011.599772.
5. Suzanne Bachner and Maggie Gallant, Attunement in Adoptive Parenting, interview by Lori Holden, *Adoption: The Long View Podcast*, episode 302. Adopting.com, March 4, 2022, https://www.adopting.com/adoption-podcasts/adoption-the-long-view/attunement-in-adoptive-parenting.

CHAPTER 17

1. Amelie Rosengren, "Omnia Vincit Amor: Love in Ancient Rome," *Latinitium*, February 14, 2018, https://latinitium.com/omnia-vincit-amor-love-in-ancient-rome/.
2. Karla, interview by Lori Holden, September 8, 2022. All quotations in this chapter from Karla result from this interview.
3. Beth, interview by Lori Holden, September 13, 2022. All quotations in this chapter from Beth result from this interview.
4. Lisa, interview by Lori Holden, May 19, 2023. All quotations in this chapter from Lisa result from this interview.
5. Sujata, interview by Lori Holden, May 19, 2023. All quotations in this chapter from Sujata result from this interview.
6. Prentis Hemphill, "Boundaries Are the Distance at Which I Can Love You and Me Simultaneously.," *Instagram*, April 5, 2021, https://www.instagram.com/p/CNSzFO1A21C/.
7. Acton Institute, "Lord Acton Quote Archive," *Acton Institute*, 2022, https://www.acton.org/research/lord-acton-quote-archive.
8. Leah Campbell, Cultivating Openness in Your Adoption, interview by Lori Holden, *Adoption: The Long View Podcast*, August 7, 2020, https://www.adopting.com/adoption-podcasts/adoption-the-long-view/interview-with-leah-campbell.
9. Paul Sunderland, "Relinquishment and Adoption: Understanding the Impact of an Early Psychological Wound," *YouTube.com* (International Conference on Addiction and Associated Disorders, May 2019), https://youtu.be/PX2Vm18TYwg. All quotations in this chapter from Paul Sunderland come from this source.
10. Margaret A. Keyes et al., "Risk of Suicide Attempt in Adopted and Nonadopted Offspring," *Pediatrics* 132, no. 4 (September 9, 2013), https://publications.aap.org/pediatrics/article-abstract/132/4/639/64833/Risk-of-Suicide-Attempt-in-Adopted-and-Nonadopted.
11. Amanda Woolston et al., Adoption and Suicide Prevention: Adult Adoptees Speak Out, interview by Maureen McCauley, October 26, 2021, https://www.youtube.com/watch?v=4gWAGLNZpaA. All quotations in this chapter from Amanda come from this source.
12. Kevin Barhydt et al., Adoption and Suicide Prevention: Adult Adoptees Speak Out, interview by Maureen McCauley, October 26, 2021, https://www.youtube.com/watch?v=4gWAGLNZpaA.
13. Lynelle Long et al., Adoption and Suicide Prevention: Adult Adoptees Speak Out, interview by Maureen McCauley, October 26, 2021, https://www.youtube.com/watch?v=4gWAGLNZpaA. All quotations in this chapter from Lynelle come from this source.
14. Maureen McCauley et al., Adoption and Suicide Prevention: Adult Adoptees Speak Out, interview by Maureen McCauley, October 26, 2021, https://www.youtube.com/watch?v=4gWAGLNZpaA.

15. Elizabeth, interview by Lori Holden, May 19, 2023. All quotations in this chapter from Elizabeth result from this interview.

CHAPTER 18

1. Cynthia, interview by Lori Holden, July 26, 2022. All quotations in this chapter from Cynthia result from this interview.

2. For more on this topic, read the book *The Child Catchers* by Kathryn Joyce or the article "The New Question Haunting Adoption" in *The Atlantic* (https://www.theatlantic.com/politics/archive/2021/10/adopt-baby-cost-process-hard/620258/)

3. Lorelai, interview by Lori Holden, January 8, 2023. All quotations in this chapter from Lorelai result from this interview.

4. Joanna Ivey, The Right (and Wrong) Way to Tell Your Child Their Adoption Story, interview by Lori Holden, *Adoption: The Long View Podcast*, June 3, 2022, https://www.adopting.com/adoption-podcasts/adoption-the-long-view/the-right-and-wrong-way-to-tell-your-child-their-adoption-story.

5. Joanna Ivey, The Right (and Wrong) Way to Tell Your Child Their Adoption Story, interview by Lori Holden, *Adoption: The Long View Podcast*, June 3, 2022, https://www.adopting.com/adoption-podcasts/adoption-the-long-view/the-right-and-wrong-way-to-tell-your-child-their-adoption-story.

CHAPTER 19

1. Melanie Notkin, "The Invisible Infertility," *Www.psychologytoday.com* (Psychology Today, August 14, 2011), https://www.psychologytoday.com/us/blog/savvy-auntie/201108/the-invisible-infertility#:~:text=In%20it%20I%20talked%20about.

2. "Industry Market Research, Reports, and Statistics," *Ibisworld.com* (IBISWorld, October 2, 2022), https://www.ibisworld.com/united-states/market-research-reports/adoption-child-welfare-services-industry/.

3. David Crary, "As Number of Adoptions Drops, Many US Agencies Face Strains," *AP NEWS*, April 30, 2017, https://apnews.com/article/d5e9cb8ae51c4c32adb7d989234ec760.

4. "Industry Market Research, Reports, and Statistics," *Ibisworld.com* (IBISWorld, October 2, 2022), https://www.ibisworld.com/united-states/market-research-reports/adoption-child-welfare-services-industry/.

5. David Crary, "As Number of Adoptions Drops, Many US Agencies Face Strains," *AP NEWS*, April 30, 2017, https://apnews.com/article/d5e9cb8ae51c4c32adb7d989234ec760.

6. Dawn Davenport and Tracy Whitney, "Adoption in the US - How Many? How Much? How Long Do They Take?," *Creating a Family*, April 30, 2018, https://creatingafamily.org/adoption-category/adoption-blog/adoption-cost-length-time/.

Notes

7. Eun Koh, PhD et al., "Adoption by the Numbers," *Adoptioncouncil.org* (National Council for Adoption, May 2022), https://bit.ly/NCFA-adoption-numbers.

8. Gretchen Sisson, PhD " 'Choosing Life': Birth Mothers on Abortion and Reproductive Choice," *Women's Health Issues* 25, no. 4 (July 2015): 349–54, doi:10.1016/j.whi.2015.05.007.

9. Gretchen Sisson, PhD " "Scotus Is Talking a Lot about Adoption, so Here's What the Data Show," *Twitter Thread*, December 1, 2021, https://twitter.com/gesisson/status/1466082617665548296.

10. Among people who do not parent, whether by choice or not, there is no consensus about what to call themselves. Childless? Childfree? Childfree Not By Choice? Other options? Each of these terms have acceptors and detractors, as do "birth mother" vs "first mother" in adoption. This phenomenon of non-consensus over identity terms is not surprising, as the labels we use address the core of who we see ourselves to be. For consistency, this text uses Childfree Not By Choice, with apologies to those who would prefer something else.

11. Linda Rooney, "No Kidding in NZ: Pronatalism and Those 'as a Parent' Comments," *No Kidding in NZ*, August 23, 2021, https://nokiddinginnz.blogspot.com/2021/08/pronatalism-and-those-as-parent-comments.html.

12. Jess, interview by Lori Holden, May 19, 2022. All quotations from Jess in this chapter result from this interview.

13. "How Common Is Infertility?," https://www.nichd.nih.gov/, February 8, 2018, https://www.nichd.nih.gov/health/topics/infertility/conditioninfo/common#:~:text=About%209%25%20of%20men%20and

14. Greg, interview by Lori Holden, May 19, 2022. All quotations from Greg in this chapter result from this interview.

15. Gordon Neufeld, PhD, Separation, Trauma, and Healing in Adoption with Dr. Gordon Neufeld, interview by Sara Easterly, Kelsey Vander Vliet Ranyard, and Lori Holden, *Adoption Unfiltered Video Series*, May 31, 2022, https://youtu.be/WeHLnrhPkaQ.

Chapter 20

1. "Completing a Home Study," *AdoptUSkids.org*, 2019, https://www.adoptuskids.org/adoption-and-foster-care/how-to-adopt-and-foster/getting-approved/home-study.

2. "Home Study Requirements for Prospective Parents in Domestic AdoptionChild Welfare Information Gateway," *Www.childwelfare.gov*, 2021, https://www.childwelfare.gov/topics/systemwide/laws-policies/statutes/homestudyreqs-adoption/.

3. Centers for Disease Control and Prevention, "Fast Facts: Preventing Adverse Childhood Experiences," *Www.cdc.gov*, September 3, 2020, https://www.cdc.gov/violenceprevention/aces/fastfact.html.

Notes

4. Brad Reedy, PhD, "Self Care Is Not Selfish (Q&A)," *Www.youtube.com*, September 9, 2022, 1:31 to 2:06, https://www.youtube.com/watch?v=zrojqQjIMOk. This builds on the work of Daniel J. Siegel, M.D.

5. Brad Reedy, PhD, "The Shadow and Feeling Overwhelmed (Q&A)," *Www.youtube.com* (Evoke Therapy Programs, September 6, 2022), https://www.youtube.com/watch?v=wnQGfy08hVU.

6. Jen Winkelmann, interview by Lori Holden, July 29, 2022. All quotations in this chapter from Jen Winkelmann result from this interview.

7. Resources for learning about attachment include Inward Bound's Blueprints Program, Trust-Based Relational Intervention (TRBI®), Nurturing Parenting, Evoke Therapy Programs, the Neufeld Institute, and many others. Books include *Journey of the Heroic Parent* by Brad Reedy, PhD, and *Parenting from the Inside Out* by Daniel J. Siegel, MD, and Mary Hartzell.

8. Gordon Neufeld, PhD, "Session Eight: Putting the Developmental Approach into Practice," Recorded Class Lecture (Neufeld Institute Power to Parent III: Common Challenges Course, 2017).

Part IV

1. Stephen L. Salter, PsyD, "The Culture of Positivity and the Mistreatment of Trauma," April 17, 2013, https://networktherapy.com/library/articles/Culture-of-Positivity-and-the-Mistreatment-of-Trauma/.

2. Francis Weller, MFT, *The Wild Edge of Sorrow: Rituals of Renewal and the Sacred Work of Grief* (Berkeley: North Atlantic Books, 2015), 22.

Chapter 21

1. Lanise Antoine Shelley, interview by Sara Easterly, July 27, 2022.

2. Fred Rogers, *The World according to Mister Rogers: Important Things to Remember* (New York: Hachette Books, 2003), 55.

3. Richard Wagamese, *Embers: One Ojibway's Meditations* (Maderia Park, BC, Canada: Douglas & McIntyre, 2016), 21.

4. Sara Easterly, "Enjoying Picture Books with Children" (Neufeld Institute, 2014).

5. Gordon Neufeld, PhD, Separation, Trauma, and Healing in Adoption with Dr. Gordon Neufeld, interview by Sara Easterly, Kelsey Vander Vliet Ranyard, and Lori Holden, *Adoption Unfiltered Video Podcast*, May 31, 2022, https://youtu.be/WeHLnrhPkaQ.

6. Alice Miller, *Thou Shalt Not Be Aware: Society's Betrayal of the Child.* (New York: Meridian Books, 1986).

7. Tammy Perlmutter, interview by Sara Easterly, November 18, 2022. All quotations in this chapter from Tammy Perlmutter result from this interview.

8. Astrid Castro, interview by Sara Easterly, August 15, 2022. All quotations in this chapter from Astrid Castro result from this interview.

9. Tony Hynes, Problematic Behaviors of Birth Parents with Tony Hynes, interview by Sara Easterly, Kelsey Vander Vliet Ranyard, and Lori Holden, *Adoption Unfiltered Video Podcast*, May 17, 2022, https://youtu.be/ENzs7fdEClM. All quotations in this chapter from Tony Hynes result from this interview.

10. Lily McLaughlin, interview by Sara Easterly, November 21, 2022. All quotations in this chapter from Lily McLaughlin result from this interview.

11. Deborah MacNamara, PhD, *Rest, Play, Grow: Making Sense of Preschoolers (or Anyone Who Acts like One)* (Vancouver, BC, Canada: Aona Books, 2016), 232.

12. Deborah MacNamara, PhD, *Rest, Play, Grow: Making Sense of Preschoolers (or Anyone Who Acts like One)* (Vancouver, BC, Canada: Aona Books, 2016), 242.

13. Deborah MacNamara, PhD, *Tantrums, Tears, and Frustrations in Kids*, Website, Deborah MacNamara, 2019, https://macnamara.ca/downloads/.

14. Cynthia Landesberg, interview by Sara Easterly, *Personal*, July 20, 2022. All quotations in this chapter from Cynthia Landesberg result from this interview.

15. Amanda Medina, interview by Sara Easterly, June 22, 2021. All quotations in this chapter from Amanda Medina result from this interview.

16. Peter Levitt, *Fingerpainting on the Moon: Writing and Creativity as a Path to Freedom* (New York: Harmony Books, 2003), 2.

17. Joyce Maguire Pavao, EdD, LCSW, LMFT, Child-Centered Adoption: A Conversation with Dr. Joyce Maguire Pavao, interview by Steven Hassan, *The Influence Continuum with Dr. Steven Hassan*, July 4, 2022, https://podcasts.apple.com/us/podcast/child-centered-adoption-a-conversation-with-dr/id1603773245?i=1000568718557.

18. Holly, interview by Sara Easterly, August 10, 2022. All quotations in this chapter from Holly result from this interview.

19. Shelise Gieseke, interview by Sara Easterly, July 27, 2022.

20. Donna Turner, interview by Sara Easterly, August 7, 2022.

21. Diego Vitelli, LMFT, interview by Sara Easterly, July 20, 2022. All quotations in this chapter from Diego Vitelli result from this interview.

22. Joyce Maguire Pavao, EdD, LCSW, LMFT, Child-Centered Adoption: A Conversation with Dr. Joyce Maguire Pavao, interview by Steven Hassan, *The Influence Continuum with Dr. Steven Hassan*, July 4, 2022, https://podcasts.apple.com/us/podcast/child-centered-adoption-a-conversation-with-dr/id1603773245?i=1000568718557.

23. David Bohl, MA, CASC, MAC, interview by Sara Easterly, July 29, 2021.

24. Kayla Zheng, interview by Sara Easterly, August 6, 2022.

25. Sara Easterly and Linda Easterly, *Searching for Mom: A Memoir* (Seattle: Heart Voices, 2019), 53.

Notes

CHAPTER 22

1. Gordon Neufeld, PhD, Separation, Trauma, and Healing in Adoption with Dr. Gordon Neufeld, interview by Sara Easterly, Kelsey Vander Vliet Ranyard, and Lori Holden, *Adoption Unfiltered Video Podcast*, May 31, 2022, https://youtu.be/WeHLnrhPkaQ.
2. Francis Weller, *The Wild Edge of Sorrow: Rituals of Renewal and the Sacred Work of Grief* (Berkeley: North Atlantic Books, 2015), 20.
3. Amanda Medina, interview by Sara Easterly, June 22, 2021. All quotations in this chapter from Amanda Medina result from this interview.
4. Damon Davis, interview by Sara Easterly, June 26, 2021. All quotations in this chapter from Damon Davis result from this interview.
5. Daniel J. Levitin, *This Is Your Brain on Music: The Science of a Human Obsession* (New York: Dutton (Penguin Group), 2006), 11–12.
6. Rich Uhrlaub, MEd, interview by Sara Easterly, July 28, 2021. All quotations in this chapter from Rich Uhrlaub result from this interview.
7. Julian Washio-Collette, interview by Sara Easterly, July 30, 2022.
8. Kathy Mackechney, LCSW, interview by Sara Easterly, July 5, 2021. All quotations in this chapter from Kathy Mackechney result from this interview.
9. Donna Turner, interview by Sara Easterly, August 7, 2022.
10. Lily McLaughlin, interview by Sara Easterly, November 21, 2022.
11. Mar Meislin, interview by Sara Easterly, July 29, 2022. All quotations in this chapter from Mar Meislin result from this interview.
12. Carmen Hinckley, interview by Sara Easterly, January 17, 2023.
13. David Bohl, MA, CASC, MAC, interview by Sara Easterly, July 29, 2021.
14. Holly, interview by Sara Easterly, August 10, 2022.
15. Lanise Antoine Shelley, interview by Sara Easterly, July 27, 2022.
16. Diego Vitelli, LMFT, interview by Sara Easterly, July 20, 2022.

CHAPTER 23

1. Astrid Castro, interview by Sara Easterly, August 15, 2022. All quotations in this chapter from Astrid Castro result from this interview.
2. Joanna Ivey, The Right (and Wrong) Way to Tell Your Child Their Adoption Story, interview by Lori Holden, *Adoption: The Long View Podcast*, June 3, 2022, https://www.adopting.com/adoption-podcasts/adoption-the-long-view/the-right-and-wrong-way-to-tell-your-child-their-adoption-story.
3. Diego Vitelli, LMFT, interview by Sara Easterly, July 20, 2022. All quotations in this chapter from Diego Vitelli result from this interview.
4. Marci Purcell, interview by Sara Easterly, November 21, 2022.

Bibliography

A. S. "Discount Babies." *The Economist*, May 14, 2010. https://www.economist.com/free-exchange/2010/05/14/discount-babies.

Acevedo, Nicole. "A Painful Truth: Guatemalan Adoptees Learn They Were Fraudulently Given Away." *NBC News*, December 8, 2019. https://www.nbcnews.com/news/latino/painful-truth-guatemalan-adoptees-learn-they-were-fraudulently-given-away-n1095066.

Acton Institute. "Lord Acton Quote Archive." *Acton Institute*, 2022. https://www.acton.org/research/lord-acton-quote-archive.

AdoptUSkids.org. "Completing a Home Study," 2019. https://www.adoptuskids.org/adoption-and-foster-care/how-to-adopt-and-foster/getting-approved/home-study.

Ayers, S. R. Bond, S. Bertullies, and K. Wijma. "The Aetiology of Post-Traumatic Stress Following Childbirth: A Meta-Analysis and Theoretical Framework." *Psychological Medicine* 46, no. 6 (2016): 1121–34. doi:https://doi.org/10.1017/S0033291715002706.

Bachner, Suzanne, and Maggie Gallant. Attunement in Adoptive Parenting. Interview by Lori Holden. *Adoption: The Long View Podcast*, March 4, 2022. https://www.adopting.com/adoption-podcasts/adoption-the-long-view/attunement-in-adoptive-parenting.

Battalen, Adeline, Christina M. Wyman, Ruth McRoy Sellers, and Harold D. Grotevant. "Birth Mothers Now Birth Grandmothers: Intergenerational Relationships in Open Adoptions." *Adoption Quarterly* 22, no. 1 (October 25, 2018): 65. doi:https://doi.org/10.1080/10926755.2018.1488327.

Beach, Hannah, and Tamara Neufeld Strijack. *Reclaiming Our Students: Why Children Are More Anxious, Aggressive, and Shut Down than Ever—and What We Can Do about It*. Page Two Books, 2020.

Berebitsky, Julie. "Rescue a Child and Save the Nation: The Social Construction of Adoption in the Delineator, 1907-1911." In *Adoption in America: Historical Perspectives*, 124–39. Ann Arbor: The University of Michigan Press, 2002.

Beth. Interview by Lori Holden. *Personal*, September 13, 2022.

Blue, Kaedra. Interview by Kelsey Vander Vliet Ranyard, November 28, 2022.

Bibliography

Bohl, MA, CASC, MAC, David. Interview by Sara Easterly, July 29, 2021.

Bohl, MA, David B., and Jamie Marich, PhD, *Relinquishment and Addiction: What Trauma Has to Do with It*. Milwaukee: HenschelHAUS Publishing, 2021.

Bohl, David B. *Parallel Universes: The Story of Rebirth*. Milwaukee: Henschel-HAUS Publishing, 2018.

Cahill, Candace. Interview by Kelsey Vander Vliet Ranyard, August 14, 2021.

Campbell, Leah. Cultivating Openness in Your Adoption. Interview by Lori Holden. *Adoption: The Long View Podcast*, August 7, 2020. https://www.adopting.com/adoption-podcasts/adoption-the-long-view/interview-with-leah-campbell.

Castro, Astrid. Interview by Sara Easterly, August 15, 2022.

Centers for Disease Control and Prevention. "Fast Facts: Preventing Adverse Childhood Experiences." *Www.cdc.gov*, September 3, 2020. https://www.cdc.gov/violenceprevention/aces/fastfact.html.

Chau, Adam, and Kevin Ost-Vollmers, eds. *Parenting as Adoptees*. CQT Media And Publishing, 2012.

www.childwelfare.gov. "Home Study Requirements for Prospective Parents in Domestic Adoption - Child Welfare Information Gateway," 2021. https://www.childwelfare.gov/topics/systemwide/laws-policies/statutes/homestudyreqs-adoption/.

Coelho, Alexandra, Maja de Brito, and António Barbosa. "Caregiver Anticipatory Grief." *Current Opinion in Supportive and Palliative Care* 12, no. 1 (March 2018): 52–57. doi:https://doi.org/10.1097/spc.0000000000000321.

Collins Sullivan, Meghan. "For Romania's Orphans, Adoption Is Still a Rarity." *National Public Radio*, August 19, 2012. https://www.npr.org/2012/08/19/158924764/for-romanias-orphans-adoption-is-still-a-rarity.

Côté Arsenault, Denise, and Kara Donato. "Emotional Cushioning in Pregnancy after Perinatal Loss." *Journal of Reproductive and Infant Psychology* 29, no. 1 (February 2011): 81. doi:https://doi.org/10.1080/02646838.2010.513115.

Crary, David. "As Number of Adoptions Drops, Many US Agencies Face Strains." *AP NEWS*, April 30, 2017. https://apnews.com/article/d5e9cb8ae51c4c32adb7d989234ec760.

Cynthia. Interview by Lori Holden, July 26, 2022.

Davenport, Dawn, and Tracy Whitney. "Adoption in the US - How Many? How Much? How Long Do They Take?" *Creating a Family*, April 30, 2018. https://creatingafamily.org/adoption-category/adoption-blog/adoption-cost-length-time/.

Davis, Damon. *Who Am I Really?* Self-published, 2019.

Davis, Damon. Interview by Sara Easterly, June 26, 2021.

Dell'Osso, Liliana, Claudia Carmassi, Laura Musetti, Chiara Socci, M. Katherine Shear, Ciro Conversano, Icro Maremmani, and Giulio Perugi.

BIBLIOGRAPHY

"Lifetime Mood Symptoms and Adult Separation Anxiety in Patients with Complicated Grief And/or Post-Traumatic Stress Disorder: A Preliminary Report." *Psychiatry Research* 198, no. 3 (August 2012): 436–40. doi:https://doi.org/10.1016/j.psychres.2011.12.020.

Easterly, Sara. "Enjoying Picture Books with Children." Neufeld Institute, 2014.

Easterly, Sara. "Moses and Me: A Biblical and Personal Case for Honoring Birth Mothers." *Godspace*, November 17, 2018. https://godspacelight.com/2018/11/17/moses-and-me-a-biblical-and-personal-case-for-honoring-birth-mothers/.

Easterly, Sara, and Linda Easterly. *Searching for Mom: A Memoir*. Seattle: Heart Voices, 2019.

Elizabeth. Interview by Lori Holden, May 19, 2023.

Erickson, Amy. Interview by Kelsey Vander Vliet Ranyard, November 3, 2022.

Fessler, Ann. *The Girls Who Went Away: The Hidden History of Women Who Surrendered Children for Adoption in the Decades before Roe v. Wade*. New York: Penguin Group, 2006.

Gaciku Kittredge, Muthoni. Interview by Kelsey Vander Vliet Ranyard, September 27, 2021.

Geographies of Kinship. Mu Films, 2019.

Gieseke, Shelise. Interview by Sara Easterly, July 27, 2022.

Gill, Brian Paul. "Adoption Agencies and the Search for the Ideal Family, 1918-1965." In *Adoption in America*, 160–80. Ann Arbor: The University of Michigan Press, 2002.

Gonzales, Erika. Interview by Kelsey Vander Vliet Ranyard, July 27, 2021.

Greg. Interview by Lori Holden, May 19, 2022.

Harness, Susan Devan. *Bitterroot: A Salish Memoir of Transracial Adoption*. Lincoln: University of Nebraska Press, 2108.

Harness, Susan Devan. Interview by Sara Easterly, July 16, 2021.

Harris, MD, Nadine Burke. "How Childhood Trauma Affects Health across a Lifetime." Presented at the TEDMED 2014: Unlocking Imagination, 2014. https://tedmed.com/talks/show?id=293066.

Heim, Erin M. *Adoption in Galatians and Romans*. BRILL, 2017.

Hemphill, Prentis. "Boundaries Are the Distance at Which I Can Love You and Me Simultaneously." *Instagram*, April 5, 2021. https://www.instagram.com/p/CNSzFO1A21C/.

Herman, Ellen. "Adoption History: Adoption History in Brief." *Darkwing.uoregon.edu*, February 24, 2012. https://darkwing.uoregon.edu/~adoption/topics/adoptionhistbrief.htm.

Heywood, Joanna. "The Children Sent to a DR Congo 'Holiday Camp' Never to Come Back." *BBC News*, August 14, 2019. https://www.bbc.com/news/world-europe-48948774.

Hinckley, Carmen. Interview by Sara Easterly, January 17, 2023.

Bibliography

Holden, Lori. "'Real' in Adoption and How It Splits Our Babies." *Lavender Luz*, April 22, 2013. https://lavenderluz.com/real-in-adoption-splits-our-babies/.

Holden, Lori. "Open Adoption Grid: Adding a Dimension to the Open Adoption Spectrum." *LavenderLuz.com*, January 12, 2013. https://lavenderluz.com/open-adoption-grid/.

Holly. Interview by Sara Easterly, August 10, 2022.

Hutchens, Bridget F., and Joan Kearney. "Risk Factors for Postpartum Depression: An Umbrella Review." *Journal of Midwifery & Women's Health* 65, no. 1 (January 22, 2020). doi:https://doi.org/10.1111/jmwh.13067.

Hynes, Tony. Adoption in Interracial & LGBTQ+ Families. Interview by Lori Holden. *Adoption: The Long View Podcast*, September 2, 2022. https://www.adopting.com/adoption-podcasts/adoption-the-long-view/adoption-in-interracial-lgbtq-families.

Hynes, Tony. Problematic Behaviors of Birth Parents with Tony Hynes. Interview by Sara Easterly, Kelsey Vander Vliet Ranyard, and Lori Holden. *Adoption Unfiltered Video Podcast*, May 17, 2022. https://youtu.be/ENzs7fdEClM.

Hynes, Tony. *The Son with Two Moms*. Self-published, 2014.

Ibisworld.com. "Industry Market Research, Reports, and Statistics." IBISWorld, October 2, 2022. https://www.ibisworld.com/united-states/market-research-reports/adoption-child-welfare-services-industry/.

Ison, Janelle. Interview by Kelsey Vander Vliet Ranyard, January 26, 2023.

Ivey, Joanna. The Right (and Wrong) Way to Tell Your Child Their Adoption Story. Interview by Lori Holden. *Adoption: The Long View Podcast*, June 3, 2022. https://www.adopting.com/adoption-podcasts/adoption-the-long-view/the-right-and-wrong-way-to-tell-your-child-their-adoption-story.

Jackson-Wade, Allana. Interview by Kelsey Vander Vliet Ranyard, December 6, 2022.

Janov, PhD, Arthur. "Life before Birth: How Experience in the Womb Can Affect Our Lives Forever." *Journal of Prenatal and Perinatal Psychology and Health* 23, no. 3 (March 2009). https://birthpsychology.com/wp-content/uploads/journal/published_paper/volume-23/issue-3/4O02a7Ng.pdf.

Jess. Interview by Lori Holden, May 19, 2022.

Jones, PhD, Jo, and Paul Placek, PhD, "Adoption: By the Numbers." Edited by Chuck Johnson and Megan Lestino. National Council for Adoption, 2017.

Joyce, Kathryn. "How Ethiopia's Adoption Industry Dupes Families and Bullies Activists." *The Atlantic*, December 21, 2011. https://www.theatlantic.com/international/archive/2011/12/how-ethiopias-adoption-industry-dupes-families-and-bullies-activists/250296/.

Joyce, Kathryn. *The Child Catchers: Rescue, Trafficking, and the New Gospel of Adoption*. New York: Publicaffairs, 2013.

Karla. Interview by Lori Holden, September 8, 2022.

Bibliography

Keyes, Margaret A., Stephen M. Malone, Anu Sharma, William G. Iacono, and Matt McGue. "Risk of Suicide Attempt in Adopted and Nonadopted Offspring." *Pediatrics* 132, no. 4 (September 9, 2013). https://publications.aap.org/pediatrics/article-abstract/132/4/639/64833/Risk-of-Suicide-Attempt-in-Adopted-and-Nonadopted.

Kim, JaeRan, and Angela Tucker. "The Inclusive Family Support Model: Facilitating Openness for Post Adoptive Families." *Child & Family Social Work* 25, no. 1 (July 26, 2019). doi:https://doi.org/10.1111/cfs.12675.

Knight, Carolyn, and Alex Gitterman. "Ambiguous Loss and Its Disenfranchisement: The Need for Social Work Intervention." *Families in Society: The Journal of Contemporary Social Services* 100, no. 2 (November 2018): 165. doi:https://doi.org/10.1177/1044389418799937.

Koh, PhD, Eun, Ryan Hanlon, PhD, Laura Daughtery, PhD, and Abigail Lindner. "Adoption by the Numbers." *Adoptioncouncil.org*. National Council for Adoption, May 2022. https://bit.ly/NCFA-adoption-numbers.

Landesberg, Cynthia. "Adoption Is Not a Fairy-Tale Answer to Abortion." *The Washington Post*, June 20, 2022. https://www.washingtonpost.com/opinions/2022/06/20/adoption-not-fairy-tale-alternative-to-abortion/.

Landesberg, Cynthia. "Passover: An Adoptee's Story." *Adoption Squared*, April 7, 2022. https://www.adoptionsquared.com/post/passover-an-adoptee-s-story.

Landesberg, Cynthia. Interview by Sara Easterly. *Personal*, July 20, 2022.

Larson, Shonda. Interview by Kelsey Vander Vliet Ranyard, August 24, 2021.

Lathion, Mellisa. Interview by Kelsey Vander Vliet Ranyard, October 7, 2021.

Leland, John. "For Adoptive Parents, Questions without Answers." *The New York Times*, September 16, 2011. https://www.nytimes.com/2011/09/18/nyregion/chinas-adoption-scandal-sends-chills-through-families-in-united-states.html.

Leslie. Interview by Lori Holden, July 22, 2022.

Levitin, Daniel J. *This Is Your Brain on Music: The Science of a Human Obsession*. New York: Dutton (Penguin Group), 2006.

Levitt, Peter. *Fingerpainting on the Moon: Writing and Creativity as a Path to Freedom*. New York: Harmony Books, 2003.

Lisa. Interview by Lori Holden, May 19, 2023.

Londoño, Ernesto. "Stolen at Birth, Chilean Adoptees Uncover Their Past." *The New York Times*, December 17, 2017. https://www.nytimes.com/2021/12/17/world/americas/chile-adoption-pinochet.html.

Lorelai. Interview by Lori Holden, January 8, 2023.

Long, Lynelle, Jessenia Parmer, Amanda Woolston, and Kevin Barhydt. Adoption and Suicide Prevention: Adult Adoptees Speak Out. Interview by Maureen McCauley, October 26, 2021. https://www.youtube.com/watch?v=4gWAGLNZpaA.

Mackechney, LCSW, Kathy. Interview by Sara Easterly, July 5, 2021.

Bibliography

MacNamara, PhD, Deborah. *Rest, Play, Grow: Making Sense of Preschoolers (or Anyone Who Acts like One)*. Vancouver, BC, Canada: Aona Books, 2016.

MacNamara, PhD, Deborah. *Tantrums, Tears, and Frustrations in Kids*. Website, Deborah MacNamara, 2019. https://macnamara.ca/downloads/.

Mallory. Interview by Lori Holden, July 22, 2022.

Maloney, Anastasia. "Haiti Orphanages Hotspot of Child Trafficking, Abuse, Says Charity." *Reuters*, June 22, 2017. https://www.reuters.com/article/us-haiti-children-trafficking/haiti-orphanages-hotspot-of-child-trafficking-abuse-says-charity-idUSKBN19D2PO.

March, Karen. "Birth Mother Grief and the Challenge of Adoption Reunion Contact." *American Journal of Orthopsychiatry* 84, no. 4 (2014): 409–19. doi:https://doi.org/10.1037/ort0000013.

Maslow, Abraham. *Hierarchy of Needs*. Visual representation of Maslow's hierarchy, 1943.

Mason, Erin. Interview by Kelsey Vander Vliet Ranyard, August 11, 2021.

Maté, MD, Gabor. *When the Body Says No: The Cost of Hidden Stress*. Toronto: Vintage Canada, 2004.

Mattos, Jessie. Interview by Kelsey Vander Vliet Ranyard, January 18, 2023.

McCloud, Raquel. Interview by Kelsey Vander Vliet Ranyard, December 9, 2022.

McCool, Alice. "'I Want My Kids Back': How Overseas Adoptions Splinter Uganda's Families." *The Guardian*, May 29, 2020. https://www.theguardian.com/global-development/2020/may/29/i-want-my-kids-back-how-overseas-adoptions-splinter-ugandas-families.

McLaughlin, Lily P. *Love Letters by LilyPearl*. Self-published, 2022.

McLaughlin, Lily P. Interview by Sara Easterly, November 21, 2022.

Mead, MD, MA, Veronique P. *Adverse Babyhood Experiences (ABEs)*. The Chronic Illness & Trauma Connection Series, Book 4. Chronic Illness Trauma Studies, 2018.

Mead, MD, MA, Veronique P. "Adverse Babyhood Experiences (ABEs) Increase Risk for Infant and Maternal Morbidity and Mortality, and Chronic Illness." *Journal of Prenatal and Perinatal Psychology and Health* 34, no. 4 (2020).

Mead, MD, MA, Veronique P. *The Science of How Trauma & Adverse Life Experiences Interact with Genes to Shape Health, Why It's Not in Your Head, and How Healing Trauma Offers Hope for Reducing Symptoms of Chronic Illness*. The Chronic Illness & Trauma Connection Series, Book 1: An Overview. Chronic Illness Trauma Studies, 2020.

Medina, Amanda. Interview by Sara Easterly, June 22, 2021.

Meislin, Mar. Interview by Sara Easterly, July 29, 2022.

Miller, Alice. *Thou Shalt Not Be Aware: Society's Betrayal of the Child*. New York: Meridian Books, 1986.

Mitchell, Ashley. Interview by Kelsey Vander Vliet Ranyard, July 14, 2021.

Bibliography

Mosia, Hilary. "The Baby-Selling Scheme: Poor Pregnant Marshall Islands Women Lured to the US." *The Guardian,* January 7, 2021. https://www.theguardian.com/world/2021/jan/08/the-baby-selling-scheme-poor-pregnant-marshall-islands-women-lured-to-the-us.

Naftzger, LICSW, Katie. Interview by Sara Easterly, July 8, 2021.

Naftzger, Katie. *Parenting in the Eye of the Storm: The Adoptive Parent's Guide to Navigating the Teen Years.* Philadelphia: Jessica Kingsley Publishers, 2017.

National Public Radio. "More South Korean Adoptees Who Were Sent Overseas Demand Probes into Their Cases," December 9, 2022. https://www.npr.org/2022/12/09/1141912093/south-korea-adoptees-fraud-investigation-western-families.

National Public Radio. "Six Words: 'Black Babies Cost Less to Adopt,'" June 27, 2013. https://www.npr.org/2013/06/27/195967886/six-words-black-babies-cost-less-to-adopt.

Neufeld Institute. "Dr. Gordon Neufeld." Accessed October 5, 2022. https://neufeldinstitute.org/about-us/dr-gordon-neufeld/.

Neufeld, PhD, Gordon. *Hold on to Your Kids.* 2004. Reprint, Toronto: Vintage Canada, 2013.

Neufeld, PhD, Gordon. "Neufeld's Traffic Circle Model of Frustration." *Neufeld Institute,* September 22, 2022. https://www.youtube.com/watch?v=cLYaQ4WX4xw.

Neufeld, PhD, Gordon. Separation, Trauma, and Healing in Adoption with Dr. Gordon Neufeld. Interview by Sara Easterly, Kelsey Vander Vliet Ranyard, and Lori Holden. *Adoption Unfiltered Video Podcast,* May 31, 2022. https://youtu.be/WeHLnrhPkaQ.

Neufeld, PhD, Gordon. "Session Eight: Putting the Developmental Approach into Practice." Recorded Class Lecture. Presented at the Neufeld Institute Power to Parent III: Common Challenges Course, 2017.

Neufeld, PhD, Gordon. "Session Five: Making Sense of Alarm Problems." Recorded Class Lecture. Presented at the Neufeld Intensive II: The Separation Complex Course, 2016.

Neufeld, PhD, Gordon. "Session Four: Making Sense of Alarm." Recorded Class Lecture. Presented at the Neufeld Intensive II: The Separation Complex Course, 2016.

Neufeld, PhD, Gordon. "Session One: Becoming Attached." Recorded Class Lecture. Presented at the The Art & Science of Transplanting Children Course, 2011.

Neufeld, PhD, Gordon. "Session Three: Problems Rooted in Separation-Triggered Pursuit." Recorded Class Lecture. Presented at the Neufeld Intensive II: The Separation Complex Course, 2016.

Neufeld, PhD, Gordon. "Session Twelve: Problems Rooted in Defensive Detachment." Recorded Class Lecture. Presented at the Neufeld Intensive II: The Separation Complex Course, 2016.

https://www.nichd.nih.gov/. "How Common Is Infertility?" February 8, 2018. https://www.nichd.nih.gov/health/topics/infertility/conditioninfo/common#:~:text=About%209%25%20of%20men%20and.

Notkin, Melanie. "The Invisible Infertility." *Www.psychologytoday.com*. Psychology Today, August 14, 2011. https://www.psychologytoday.com/us/blog/savvy-auntie/201108/the-invisible-infertility#:~:text=In%20it%20I%20talked%20about.

Pace Christie, Judy, and Lisa Wingate. *Before and After: The Incredible Real-Life Stories of Orphans Who Survived the Tennessee Children's Home Society*. New York: Ballantine Books, 2019.

Pavao, EdD, LCSW, LMFT, Joyce Maguire. "About." *Pavao Consulting*. Accessed October 5, 2022. http://www.pavaoconsulting.com/about.

Pavao, EdD, LCSW, LMFT, Joyce Maguire. Child-Centered Adoption: A Conversation with Dr. Joyce Maguire Pavao. Interview by Steven Hassan. *The Influence Continuum with Dr. Steven Hassan*, July 4, 2022. https://podcasts.apple.com/us/podcast/child-centered-adoption-a-conversation-with-dr/id1603773245?i=1000568718557.

Pavao, EdD, LCSW, LMFT, Joyce Maguire. "Thoughts of an Adoptee By-The-Sea." *Pavao Consulting*, July 1996. http://site-4sgcknkk.dotezcdn.com/uploads/4A253959B094F655.pdf?v=0.

Pavao, EdD, LCSW, LMFT, Joyce, and Maureen McCauley. "Joyce Maguire Pavao Speaks out against CHIFF." *Light of Day Stories*, April 2, 2014. https://lightofdaystories.com/category/joyce-maguire-pavao/.

Pavao, Joyce Maguire. *The Family of Adoption*. 1998. Reprint, Boston: Beacon Press, 2005.

Perlmutter, Tammy. Interview by Sara Easterly, November 18, 2022.

Perry, MD, PhD, Bruce D., and Oprah Winfrey. *What Happened to You?: Conversations on Trauma, Resilience and Healing*. New York: Flatiron Books, 2021.

Peterson, Dawn. *Indians in the Family: Adoption and Politics of the Antebellum Expansion*. Cambridge, Mass: Harvard University Press, 2017.

Pheby, James. "Campaigners Say U.K. 'Forced Adoption' Scandal Far from Over." *The Japan Times*, July 17, 2022. https://www.japantimes.co.jp/news/2022/07/17/world/crime-legal-world/uk-forced-adoption-scandal/.

Purcell, Marci. Interview by Sara Easterly, November 21, 2022.

Rebecca. Interview by Lori Holden, January 4, 2022.

Reedy, PhD, Brad. "Self Care Is Not Selfish (Q&A)." *Www.youtube.com*, September 9, 2022. https://www.youtube.com/watch?v=zrojqQjIMOk.

Reedy, PhD, Brad. "The Shadow and Feeling Overwhelmed (Q&A)." *Www.youtube.com*. Evoke Therapy Programs, September 6, 2022. https://www.youtube.com/watch?v=wnQGfy08hVU.

Rodriguez, Emily. Interview by Kelsey Vander Vliet Ranyard, August 27, 2021.

Rogers, Fred. *The World according to Mister Rogers: Important Things to Remember*. New York: Hachette Books, 2003.

Rooney, Linda. "No Kidding in NZ: Pronatalism and Those 'as a Parent' Comments." *No Kidding in NZ*, August 23, 2021. https://nokiddinginnz.blogspot.com/2021/08/pronatalism-and-those-as-parent-comments.html.

Root, Tik. "The Baby Brokers: Inside America's Murky Private-Adoption Industry." *TIME Magazine*, June 3, 2021. https://time.com/6051811/private-adoption-america/.

Rosengren, Amelie. "Omnia Vincit Amor: Love in Ancient Rome." *Latinitium*, February 14, 2018. https://latinitium.com/omnia-vincit-amor-love-in-ancient-rome/.

Ryan, Scott D., Gardenia Harris, Donna Brown, Doris M. Houston, Susan Livingston Smith, and Jeanne A. Howard. "Open Adoptions in Child Welfare: Social Worker and Foster/Adoptive Parent Attitudes." *Journal of Public Child Welfare* 5, no. 4 (August 31, 2011): 445–66. doi:https://doi.org/10.1080/15548732.2011.599772.

Salter, PsyD, Stephen L. "The Culture of Positivity and the Mistreatment of Trauma," April 17, 2013. https://networktherapy.com/library/articles/Culture-of-Positivity-and-the-Mistreatment-of-Trauma/.

Sandven, Kari, and Michael D. Resnick. "Informal Adoption among Black Adolescent Mothers." *American Journal of Orthopsychiatry* 60, no. 2 (1990): 210–24. doi:https://doi.org/10.1037/h0079158.

Schmidth, Sarah. Interview by Kelsey Vander Vliet Ranyard, November 13, 2022.

Scott, Marion. "Forced Adoption Scandal: How Many Women Were given These Tablets? We Have No Idea." *The Sunday Post*, August 1, 2021. https://www.sundaypost.com/fp/forced-adoption-scandal/.

Seek, Amy. Interview by Kelsey Vander Vliet Ranyard, November 12, 2022.

Shaw, Erica. Interview by Kelsey Vander Vliet Ranyard, November 18, 2022.

Shelley, Lanise Antoine. Interview by Sara Easterly, July 27, 2022.

Singley, Carol J. "Building a Nation, Building a Family: Adoption in Nineteenth-Century American Children's Literature." In *Adoption in America: Historical Perspectives*, 51–81. Ann Arbor: The University of Michigan Press, 2002.

Sisson, PhD, Gretchen. "'Scotus Is Talking a Lot about Adoption, so Here's What the Data Show." *Twitter Thread*, December 1, 2021. https://twitter.com/gesisson/status/1466082617665548296.

Sisson, PhD, Gretchen. "'Choosing Life': Birth Mothers on Abortion and Reproductive Choice." *Women's Health Issues* 25, no. 4 (July 2015): 349–54. doi:https://doi.org/10.1016/j.whi.2015.05.007.

Solinger, Rickie. *Wake Up Little Susie*. New York: Routledge, 2000.

Stephens, Alice, and Sara Easterly. Review of *Adopting for God*, by Soojin Chung. *Englewood Review of Books*, May 19, 2022. https://englewoodreview.org/soojin-chung-adopting-for-god-feature-review/.

Stolen Childhoods. Audio Documentary. SoundCloud: KFAI's MinneCulture, 2017.

Bibliography

Sujata. Interview by Lori Holden, May 19, 2023.

Sunderland, Paul. "Relinquishment and Adoption: Understanding the Impact of an Early Psychological Wound." *YouTube.com*. International Conference on Addiction and Associated Disorders, May 2019. https://youtu.be/PX2Vm18TYwg.

Sunderland, Paul. "Relinquishment and Adoption: Understanding the Impact of an Early Psychological Wound - ICAAD." *International Conference on Addiction and Associated Disorders*. ICAAD.com, August 1, 2019. https://web.archive.org/web/20201111191418/https://www.icaad.com/blog/relinquishment-and-adoption-understanding-the-impact-of-an-early-psychological-wound.

Tremblay, Kimberly A., and Elizabeth Soliday. "Effect of Planning, Wantedness, and Attachment on Prenatal Anxiety." *Journal of Prenatal and Perinatal Psychology and Health* 27, no. 2 (December 2012): 97–119.

Tucker, Angela. "Navigating Openness." Workshop. Presented at the Heritage Camps for Adoptive Families, August 16, 2022.

Turner, Donna. Interview by Sara Easterly, August 7, 2022.

Uhrlaub, MEd, Rich. Interview by Sara Easterly, July 28, 2021.

van der Kolk, MD, Bessel. *The Body Keeps the Score: Mind, Brain and Body in the Transformation of Trauma*. London: Penguin Books, 2014.

Vander Vliet Ranyard, Kelsey, and Celeste Liversidge. "How to Choose an Adoption Professional." Podcast. *Thinking about Adoption*, November 2021. https://open.spotify.com/episode/4sw1lmC36jwMYTrVZJl6U7?si=f1459052e4b14fe7.

Verny, MD, Thomas R. "What Cells Remember: Toward a Unified Field Theory of Memory." *Journal of Prenatal and Perinatal Psychology and Health* 29, no. 1 (September 2014).

Verrier, Nancy Newton. *Coming Home to Self: The Adopted Child Grows Up*. Baltimore: Gateway Press, Inc., 2003.

Verrier, Nancy Newton. "The Primal Wound." Presented at the Indiana Adoption Network/National Association of Adoptees and Parents Adoption Happy Hour, June 5, 2020. https://www.youtube.com/watch?v=bsEgDHkLhzg.

Verrier, Nancy Newton. *The Primal Wound: Understanding the Adopted Child*. Baltimore: Gateway Press, Inc., 1993.

Vitelli, LMFT, Diego. Interview by Sara Easterly, July 20, 2022.

Wagamese, Richard. *Embers: One Ojibway's Meditations*. Maderia Park, BC, Canada: Douglas & McIntyre, 2016.

Walker, MA, Pete. *Complex PTSD: From Surviving to Thriving*. New York: Azure Coyote, 2013.

Washio-Collette, Julian. "Gift." *Anne Heffron's Blog*, November 29, 2021. https://www.anneheffron.com/blog/2021/11/29/gift-guest-blog-post-by-julian-washio-collette.

Washio-Collette, Julian. Interview by Sara Easterly, July 30, 2022.

Bibliography

Weller, MFT, Francis. *The Wild Edge of Sorrow: Rituals of Renewal and the Sacred Work of Grief.* Berkeley: North Atlantic Books, 2015.

Wiechhand, Rebecca, and Kathleen Strottman. "2014 Adoption Attitudes & Awareness Survey." The Congressional Coalition on Adoption Institute, April 15, 2014.

Wilson-Buterbaugh, Karen. *The Baby Scoop Era: Unwed Mothers, Infant Adoption and Forced Surrender.* Karen Wilson-Buterbaugh, 2017.

Wingfield, MA, Carol A. "The Role of Shame in Infant Development." *Journal of Prenatal and Perinatal Psychology and Health* 26, no. 2 (December 2011): 121–26.

Winkelmann, Jen. Interview by Lori Holden, July 29, 2022.

Yngvesson, Barbara. "Refiguring Kinship in the Space of Adoption." *Anthropological Quarterly* 80, no. 2 (2007): 565. doi:https://doi.org/10.1353/anq.2007.0036.

Yoon, Gihyun, Joseph Westermeyer, Marion Warwick, and Michael A. Kuskowski. "Substance Use Disorders and Adoption: Findings from a National Sample." Edited by Antonio Verdejo García. *PloS One* 7, no. 11 (November 2012). https://www.ncbi.nlm.nih.gov/pmc/articles/PMC3499473/.

Zheng, Kayla. Interview by Sara Easterly, August 6, 2022.

Index

abandonment, 7, 21, 39, 43, 47, 51, 52, 59, 74, 75, 86, 88, 90, 93, 100, 183, 190, 193, 197, 231
abortion, 91, 98, 101, 204
acceptance: of an adoptee's full story, 230; external, 104, 119, 125, 127, 133; of a full range of emotions, 162-163, 185-186, 192, 208, 224-225, 230, 251; internal, 68-69, 123, 126, 128-129, 147, 149, 150, 151, 152, 153, 174, 207-208, 222, 245, 248. *See also* adaptation
adaptation, 55, 65, 66-69, 71, 73, 76, 128, 187, 236, 240, 242, 245
addiction, 28, 47, 70, 75-76, 91, 189
adolescence, 41, 50, 73, 96, 183, 187-188, 191, 232, 236
The Adoptee Mentoring Society, 234, 265
Adoptees Connect, 28, 265
Adoptee Voices writing groups, 5, 18, 26, 31, 242, 265
adoption-competent therapy, 201, 202, 233-234. *See also* adoption-fluent therapy

adoption-fluent therapy, xiv, 36, 113, 190, 215-218, 233-234, 242-243, 254-255. *See also* adoption-competent therapy
Adoption Knowledge Affiliates (AKA), 31, 193, 234, 265
Adoption Mosaic, 9, 27, 32, 40, 193, 234, 252, 265
Adoption Network Cleveland, 193, 234, 265
adoption professionals, xiv, xv, 2-3, 13-14, 107-114, 116, 117, 119, 122, 127, 131-132, 156, 177, 253-257
Adoption Search Resource Connection (ASRC), 31, 265
The Adoptive and Foster Family Coalition of New York (AFFCNY), 234, 265
adrenaline-based problems, 55-56, 61
agitation-based problems, 55-56
alarm, alarming, 21, 41, 52, 54-65, 69, 73, 74, 83, 95, 189, 224-225, 238, 242. *See also* anxiety
anger, angry, 10, 34, 35, 37, 52, 70-72, 76, 162, 173, 192, 198, 199, 214, 224, 229, 244, 247. *See also* attack, attacking

Index

anxiety, anxiety-based problems, 29, 36, 44, 48, 54-65, 70, 71, 91, 96, 121, 126, 127, 153, 182, 224. *See also* alarm, alarming

Armstrong, Patrick Samuel Yung, 89

attachment, attachments, attaching: to caregivers and others, 21, 37, 46, 48, 49, 50, 56, 183, 217, 233-234; diagnoses, problems with, 49, 233-234; fantasy attachments, fantasies, 45, 46-47, 149, 166, 178, 229; first attachments, 21, 22-23, 33, 35, 37, 38, 42, 45, 58, 59, 67, 86, 88, 164, 172, 182, 226, 237; hunger, 48; instincts, 20-22, 49, 51, 53; needs, 36, 42, 53, 201, 225, 227, 236-238; science and study of, 5, 12, 19, 25, 36, 41, 42, 66-67, 75, 211-218, 231, 242, 243, 256; village, 3-4, 232-234; wounds, 8, 18, 23, 27, 35, 36, 37-42, 47, 49, 53, 57, 71, 83, 87, 90, 92, 101, 138, 149, 152, 182, 187, 188, 189, 213, 214, 215, 222, 227, 235, 237, 242, 243, 246. *See also* connection; separation trauma

attachment-safe discipline. *See* discipline

attack, attacking, 66, 69-74, 224, 225, 227-228

attention, scattered, 56. *See also* agitation-based problems

baby fever, 167-169
Baby Scoop Era, 22-23, 29, 31, 99, 118, 132, 215

Bachner, Suzanne, 178
Barhydt, Kevin, 190
Beach, Hannah, 70
belonging, 11, 30, 44, 60, 80, 81-82, 83-84, 95, 97, 124, 143, 174, 212, 227, 236, 239-240, 247
birth control, 79
birth father, 11, 14-15, 22, 94, 103, 110, 118, 139, 140, 190
blank slate, 57, 181
Blue, Kaedra, 151, 153
Bohl, David, 28, 35, 38, 40, 58, 75, 76, 234, 245, 264
both/and, BothAnd, 72, 162-163, 175-176, 177, 186, 188, 225. *See also* emotions, conflicting/mixed
boundaries, 34, 125, 135, 140-141, 142, 148, 186-187, 233, 247
Bowlby, John, 19
brain: activity, 57; associations, 242; development, 56, 64, 153, 182; emotional brain, 66, 73, 67, 240, 242; plasticity, 42, 65; science, 19, 25, 75. *See also* neuroscience
brokers, 107-109

Cahill, Candace, 151-152, 264
Campbell, Joseph, 239
Campbell, Leah, 186-187
Carp, E. Wayne, 263
Carroll, Rebecca, 89, 264
Castro, Astrid, 9, 27, 40, 86-87, 89, 225, 237, 252, 253-254, 255
Catholic church, 30-31, 94-95, 98-99, 244. *See also* religion and adoption

INDEX

Celia Center, Inc., 75, 234, 265
Center for Adoption Support and Education (C.A.S.E.), 33, 234, 265
Child Rescue Campaign, 78
child trafficking. *See* trafficking
Christianity, 90-102, 115-119, 196, 243-244. *See also* religion and adoption
Chung, Nicole, 89, 264
classism, 78-80, 88, 91, 101, 134
clinginess, 56. *See also* anxiety, anxiety-based problems
closed adoption, 14-15, 27, 29, 94, 133, 148-150, 160-163, 177, 225-226, 250
closeness. *See* connection
Coalition for Truth and Transparency in Adoption (CTTA), 31, 265
code-switching, 81
coercion, 15, 23, 79, 101, 123, 254
colonialism, 78, 84-85, 101
colorblind ideology, 27, 82, 184, 199
community of support: for adoptees, 27, 73, 190, 233-234, 246-248; for adoptive parents, 178, 192-193, 232-233; for birth parents, 113, 122, 125, 127, 128, 129, 133; cultural/racial, 88, 132-133; infertility-related, 209; religious/spiritual, 95, 97-98, 101, 119, 184
comparison, 42, 62-63. *See also* sibling relationships.
complex-PTSD/complex trauma, 29, 36, 263. *See also* post-traumatic stress disorder (PTSD)

Concerned United Birthparents (CUB), 128, 265
Congressional Coalition on Adoption Institute (CCAI), 6
connection: as the antidote to separation, 225-228, 231, 238, 247; disruption of, 35; to first families, ancestors, culture, 38, 51, 88, 163, 179, 226, 237; in relationships, feelings of, 46, 58, 124, 163, 172, 176, 178, 186, 188, 190, 193, 200, 212, 214, 226, 251; in relationships, lacking feelings of, 49-50; to self, 217; threats to/fears around, 60, 189. *See also* attachment; separation
constellation, xiv, 2-4, 7-8, 11, 75, 100, 101, 102, 124, 130, 135, 145
contact *versus* openness, 14-15, 158-161, 163, 180
control: over emotions, 72; in parenting, 51, 179, 200, 214, 224, 227; feeling a lack of, 60-61, 63, 64, 67-68, 75, 161, 166, 214; in relationships, 49, 56, 61, 117. *See also* alarm; frustration
corruption, 91, 99-101, 196-198, 250
cortisol, 36, 57, 64, 182
counseling. *See* adoption-competent therapy; adoption-fluent therapy

Davis, Damon, 28, 241, 246, 247, 264
Davis Maxon, Allison, 264

defenses, 12, 69, 180, 223, 228, 238; softening, 221-223, 236. *See also* defensive detachment

defensive detachment, 21, 43, 49-53, 69, 74, 120, 151, 224-225

depend, dependence, depending, 41, 49, 52, 57, 59, 65, 188, 225, 238, 247-248

depression, 29, 36, 57, 74, 91, 96, 127

digestive issues, 56, 63. *See also* anxiety, anxiety-based problems

DiMartile, Torie, 89

Dinwoodie, April, 89

discipline: attachment-safe, 227-228; separation-based (and the problems of), 41, 52, 59, 227

divided/split loyalty, 39-40, 60, 94-95, 148, 152, 154, 162, 164, 172, 177-178, 251

DNA/DNA testing, 14, 64, 87, 172, 176, 249. *See also* genes, genetics

Dusky, Lorraine, 264

Easterly, Sara, 5, 31-32, 311; *Searching for Mom: A Memoir*, 5, 18, 31, 90, 237, 264, 311. *See also* Adoptee Voices writing groups

EMDR (Eye Movement Desensitization and Reprocessing), 242

emotions: of adoptees in response to separation, 21-22, 43-53, 54-65, 66-76, 92, 185, 189, 236; of adoptive parents, 167, 170, 176, 179, 187, 214, 232, 234, 251; of birth parents, 105, 120-122, 123-126, 140, 149-150; conflicting/mixed, 69, 72, 86, 152, 153, 245; emotional rest, 46, 50, 58, 59, 64, 119, 236, 239; expressing/feeling, 190, 208, 221-224, 240-242, 246; making space for, 162-163, 185, 192, 208, 224-225, 230, 251; normalizing, 231; numbness to or not feeling, 190; preverbal, 3, 36. *See also* alarm, alarming; frustration; separation-triggered pursuit

emotional cushioning, 126

Erickson, Amy, 127, 149

estrangement, 34, 192

ethical storytelling, 9

ethics in adoption, 23, 102, 245, 250-251, 252, 255, 257

Evans, Aselefech, 89, 264

Eye Movement Desensitization and Reprocessing (EMDR), 242

facing separation. *See* separation

false self, 42, 45, 46, 48, 50

family preservation, 79, 91, 265

fantasies. *See* attachment fantasy

fawn response, 43, 46. *See also* separation-triggered pursuit

fees, adoption, 79, 131, 254

Fessler, Ann, 22, 263

fog, adoption, 8-9, 69, 73, 120, 161, 202

foster care, xiv, 20, 26, 29, 31, 32, 46, 51, 58, 63, 86, 92, 157, 204, 224, 234

frustration, 21, 39, 52, 66-76, 83, 185, 200, 215, 224, 225, 227, 232, 234, 235, 238, 242
Frustration Traffic Circle, 66-68, 70-72, 73, 185, 240-241, 265
futility, 17, 65, 68-69, 74, 76, 208, 236

Gaciku Kittredge, Muthoni, 122-123, 132, 133
Gagel, Katie, 89
genes, genetics, 44, 54, 60-61, 64, 163, 166, 172, 181, 188. *See also* mirroring: genetic
Gibney, Shannon, 89, 264
Gieseke, Shelise, 32, 41, 44, 45, 62, 70-71, 81-82, 83, 84, 88, 89, 233
Glaser, Gabrielle, 263
Gonzales, Erika, 114, 117, 134-135
gratefulness/gratitude, expectations of, 39-40, 86, 91, 92
grief/grieving, 129, 207, 219-220, 240-242, 245; adoptees, 13, 38, 41, 48, 58, 72, 74, 75, 76, 183, 185, 201, 221-224; adoptive parents, 135, 155, 165-171, 175, 199, 213, 214, 235, 244, 251; anticipatory, 121-122; birth parents, 103, 109, 110-113, 118-119, 120-129, 133, 138, 149, 150, 153; counseling, 28, 208; disenfranchised, 38, 123-126; infertility-related, 165-169; second-hand, 74, 169-170
Grow Beyond Words therapist directory, 234, 265

Guida-Richards, Melissa, 89, 264
guilt, 10, 220: adoptees, 40; adoptive parents, 169-170, 197, 235-236; birth parents, 11, 152, 219

Harlow, Harry, 19
Harness, Susan Devan, 32, 81, 83, 85, 87, 88, 89, 245, 264
Harris, Nadine Burke, 64
healing, 4, 5, 12, 18, 27, 29, 65, 71, 76, 87, 103, 104, 113, 119, 122, 127, 129, 164, 172, 192, 208, 219-248; specifically for adoptive parents, 175, 176, 179-180, 212-214, 216, 217; in community, 125, 128, 129, 190, 209, 242, 246-248; through feeling sadness, 76, 190, 208, 219, 221-224, 240-242; spiritual/religious, 31, 94, 119, 243-245; spontaneous nature of, 65. *See also* adoption-competent therapy; adoption-fluent therapy; emotions: expressing/feeling health: emotional/mental health, xiii, 25, 30, 32, 35, 48, 58-63, 64-65, 76, 80, 95-97, 111, 113, 114, 120-129, 131, 140, 178, 237; family health, 23; physical health, 1, 63-64, 111; spiritual health, 90-102
Heffron, Anne, 264
Heim, Erin M., 90
Heller, Laurence, 263
Henness, Jade, 89
high-risk behavior, 56. *See also* adrenaline-based problems

Hinckley, Carmen, 27, 87, 245
Hoffman, Kevin, 89, 264
Holden, Lori, 5-6, 311; *Adoption, The Long View* podcast, 6, 199, 252; *The Open-Hearted Way to Open Adoption: Helping Your Child Grow Up Whole*, 6, 264, 311
Holly, 29, 36, 39, 50, 73, 76, 80, 87, 231, 232, 246
Holt, Harry and Bertha, 99
human trafficking. *See* trafficking
Hynes, Tony, 15, 32-33, 38, 40, 72, 83, 89, 226, 228-229, 264
hypervigilance, 55, 189. *See also* alarm, alarming; anxiety
hypothalamic-pituitary-adrenal (HPA) stress response. *See* stress response

IFS (Internal Family Systems), 242
Inclusive Family Support Model, 160-161, 265
Indian Child Welfare Act, 32
infertility and fertility, 92, 165-169, 203, 205-206, 209, 215
insecurity, insecure: adoptees, 59, 94, 136; adoptive parents: 7, 37, 136, 155, 168, 172-180, 186, 251; birth parents: 127, 130, 143; housing, 123, 134
instincts of separation. *See* separation: emotional responses to
InterCountry Adoptee Voices, 30, 190, 265
intercountry/international adoption, 7, 23, 26-27, 29-30, 32, 85, 98, 105, 167, 182-184; exploitation, unethical practices: 79, 99; openness in intercountry adoptions: 87, 157, 250
Internal Family Systems, 242
Internet's role in adoption, 107-108, 113-114, 141
interracial adoption, 7, 15, 26, 27, 28, 30, 32, 33, 41, 67, 77-78, 80-89, 184, 193, 233, 264
isolation, 25, 36, 40-41, 53, 61-62, 83, 84, 85, 123, 166, 190, 247, 250; racial, 30, 80, 82, 83, 84, 85, 229
Ison, Janelle, 152
Ivey, Joanna, 199, 252

Jackson-Wade, Allana, 133, 140
Janov, Arthur, 57, 64
Joyce, Kathryn, 79, 90, 196
Judaism, 28, 30-31, 90, 93-95, 196, 201, 244

Kain, Kathy L., 263
Kaplan Roszia, Sharon, 264
Keithley, Marcie, 264
Kim, JaeRan, 89, 160

Landesberg, Cynthia, 28, 93, 97, 98, 196, 198-202, 229
LaPierre, Aline, 263
Larson, Shonda, 113, 114
Lathion, Mellisa, 117, 118, 119, 153
LDS (The Church of Jesus Christ of Latter-day Saints), 29. *See also* religion and adoption

learning: about culture, language, race, 87-88, 133, 233; difficulty, 56, 232. *See also* agitation-based problems
Lee, Jia Sun, 89
legal: advice, fraudulent, 109; certifications, lack of, 108; representation, 107, 111, 255; termination of rights, 148. *See also* post-adoption contact agreement (PACA)
Levine, Peter A., 263
Levitin, Daniel J., 242
Levitt, Peter, 230
Lifetime Healing Foundation, 128, 265
Long, Lynelle, 89, 190
Lorenz, Konrad, 19
lucky adoptee, 38-40, 181, 201, 243. *See also* narratives, adoption

Mackechney, Kathy, 29, 243, 246
Mason, Erin, 142
Maté, Gabor, 4, 19, 61, 263, 265
math of openness. *See* openness: math of
Mattos, Jessie, 140
maturation, 9, 18, 42, 45, 53, 72, 76, 148, 175, 187, 191, 192, 221-238, 245
McCauley, Maureen, 191
McCloud, Raquel, 143
McLaughlin, Lily P., 30, 51, 85, 227, 232, 244
McNamara, Deborah, 227-228
Mead, Veronique, 57, 58, 65
Medina, Amanda, 27, 45, 49, 55, 71, 89, 229, 230, 241, 248
meditation, 201, 244-245

Meislin, Mar, 30, 31, 38, 75, 94-95, 98-99, 244, 247
Menakem, Resmaa, 263
Mennonite church, 27, 93, 97-98. *See also* religion and adoption
Miller, Alice, 223
mirroring: cultural and racial, 81, 88; genetic, 44, 163, 188. *See also* genes/genetics
Mitchell, Ashley, 111, 119, 126, 143-144
Monroe, Katie, 150
Montes de Oca, Carlyn, 264
Mooney, Harrison, 89, 264
Moses, 90, 93-94, 163
Mother Teresa's Orphanage, 29

Naftzger, Katie, 29-30, 43, 55, 59, 64, 74, 86, 263
name, names: and adoptee complexities, 26; adoption in God's, 99; for birth/first family members, 152, 183; -calling, 83, 168
narratives, adoption, 4, 7, 39, 85-87, 94, 103, 117, 178, 197, 199-201, 202, 253, 257. *See also* gratefulness/gratitude, expectations of; lucky adoptee; saviorism
natalism. *See* pronatalism
National Association of Adoptees and Parents (NAAP), 193, 234, 265
National Council For Adoption, 2, 203, 204
nervous system, 58, 63-64, 218
Neufeld, Gordon, 19, 20, 21-22, 35, 43, 49, 55, 57, 59, 60, 64,

66-70, 73, 142, 208, 217, 223, 236, 240
Neufeld Institute, 5, 32, 265, 311
neuroscience, 65, 242. *See also* brain science

obsessions, 56. *See also* anxiety, anxiety-based problems
On Your Feet Foundation, 128, 265
open adoption, 6, 14, 264; adoptees, 40, 42, 47, 51, 58, 63, 228, 250; adoptive parents, 157-161, 163, 170, 173, 175, 184-187, 226; birth parents, 104, 109-112, 114, 123-124, 126, 134, 137-145, 148-153, 261; court-ordered, 33; grid, 159, 161; post-visit meltdowns, 184-186
openness, 137, 154, 156, 157, 177, 178, 188, 212, 257, 265; how to elevate, 161-163; in adoptive parenting, 180, 193, 216, 218, 228-230, 251; math of, 163-164; in post-adoption contact, 255; and race, 256; in relationships, 136, 139-140, 144, 145, 169, 172; and religion, 95; and transparency, 15, 105; *versus* contact, 158-161
orphanage, 30, 32, 169
orphan crisis, 99
Oyler, Stephanie, 89

PACA (post-adoption contact agreement), 111, 255
panic attacks, 56. *See also* anxiety, anxiety-based problems

patriarchy, 22-23, 97, 99, 101, 116
Pavao, Joyce Maguire, xiii-xv, 19, 65, 80, 230, 233, 263
peer support groups, 3, 242
people-pleasing, 18, 37, 46, 48, 96
perfectionism, 17, 37, 47-48, 92, 96, 214, 235
Perlmutter, Tammy, 32, 46, 51, 60, 61, 62, 63, 74, 224
Perry, Bruce, 56, 63, 263
Phillips, Zara, 264
phobias, 56. *See also* anxiety, anxiety-based problems
post-adoption contact agreement (PACA), 111, 255
postpartum depression (PPD), 127
post-placement support, 105, 122, 145, 265; and grief, 128; and race, 133; scarcity of, 106-114
post-traumatic stress disorder (PTSD), 126-127, 189. *See also* complex-PTSD/complex trauma
post-visit meltdowns, 184-186
power dynamics/power imbalance, 175, 218, 251, 253; adoption professionals, 114; between nations, 79; in open adoption, 103, 103-136, 141, 142, 155-156, 186-187; powerlessness, 39, 166, 169, 214
PPD (postpartum depression), 127
pre-adoption education, 139-140, 144, 177, 199, 216-217, 255-256

Index

pregnancy: loss, 165, 205, 213; unplanned, 40, 57, 91, 101, 106, 116-117, 120, 123, 127
privilege, 86-87, 130-131, 135-136, 155-156, 252-253. *See also* power dynamics/ power imbalance
professionals. *See* adoption professionals
pro-life, 91, 98, 101
pronatalism, 203-210
PTSD (post-traumatic stress disorder), 126-127, 189. *See also* complex-PTSD/complex trauma
Purcell, Marci, 31, 86, 256
purity culture, 116-117
pursuit. *See* separation-triggered pursuit

Quiroz, Pamela Anne, 263

racism, 23, 62, 77-89, 91, 97, 101, 133, 233; anti-racism and education, 27, 256
recklessness, 56. *See also* agitation-based problems
Reedy, Brad, 213, 263
reform, 4, 18, 27, 31-32, 100-102, 156, 157, 251-257
regulation: emotional, 217-218; legal, 107-109, 114, 250
rejection: feelings and fears of, 42, 52, 55, 75, 90, 127; secondary rejection, 150
religion and adoption, 27, 79, 90-102, 115-119, 195-202, 243
relinquish, relinquished, relinquishment: adoptee experience, 7, 36, 39, 54, 58, 60, 75, 90, 183, 189, 190, 231, 242, 245, 246; birth parent experience, 13, 103-104, 105, 111, 112-114, 115-119, 120-129, 132, 138, 142, 143, 146-148, 149, 150, 152, 153; *versus* parenting, 204; religious pressures to, 98, 115-119; terminology, 15; twice relinquished, 29, 49. *See also* religion and adoption
rescue narrative. *See* saviorism.
resilience, 55, 65, 245
resisting closeness. *See* defensive detachment
rest, emotional. *See* emotions: emotional rest
restlessness, 56. *See also* agitation-based problems; emotions: emotional rest
reunion, 27, 51, 74, 87, 99, 103, 134, 146, 148-150, 151-152
Rockingham, Bonita, 27, 77, 93, 97, 101, 102
Rodriguez, Emily, 111, 118, 119
Rogers, Mister (Fred), 222
Roorda, Rhonda, 89
Rosenberg, Stanley, 263

sadness. *See* grief
Salter, Stephen L., 219
saviorism, 48, 77-79, 80, 91, 100
Schmidth, Sarah, 117, 121-122, 126, 153
secrets, secrecy, 1, 14, 25, 31, 45-46, 50, 60, 93, 133, 150, 177, 249
security, secure, 44, 50, 53, 64, 148, 178, 179, 180, 188,

213, 215. *See also* insecurity, insecure
Seek, Amy, 135, 150-151, 176, 264
self-attack, 66, 73, 74. *See also* suicide/suicidal ideation
self-reflection, 214, 217, 251-252
separation, 36, 41, 49, 51, 53, 56, 67, 83-84, 147, 217, 233, 236, 242, 246, 249; in adolescence, 187-188; anticipation of/facing, 20, 35, 55, 58, 60, 63, 71, 73, 95, 120, 142, 225, 243; antidote for, 247; anxiety, 121, 127; avoidance, 55, 58; emotional responses to, 20-22, 35-76, 213, 224, 231, 238; from first attachments (adoptees), 18, 21, 33, 35, 37, 38, 42, 50, 52, 58, 59, 93, 149, 182; from relinquished children (birth parents), 121, 123, 127, 138, 142, 149; nighttime separation, 222, 228; reducing separation, 225-228, 231; trauma or wounding, 1, 17, 18, 20, 35, 49, 53, 91, 101, 138, 152, 169, 182, 215, 235, 237, 250, 257; unbearable, 49, 50, 52, 73, 84. *See also* attachment; connection
separation-based discipline. *See* discipline
separation-triggered pursuit, 21, 43-48, 53, 69, 74, 83, 225
shame, 52, 131, 177, 224, 227, 250, 251; for adoptees, 40, 41, 48, 51, 54, 59-60, 62, 63, 71, 91, 92, 94, 233; for adoptive parents, 169, 173, 200, 201, 251; for birth parents, 117, 119, 123, 127, 148; from infertility, 155, 166; and secrecy, 1, 25, 249; and sex, 22, 23, 116
Shaw, Erica, 119, 135-136
Shelley, Lanise Antoine, 30, 39, 41, 47, 48, 81, 84, 85, 88, 89, 221-222, 246
shyness, in reverse, 49, 51
sibling relationships, 27, 28, 29, 30, 31, 41, 42, 44, 49, 62-63, 71, 80, 146, 153
Siegel, Daniel J., 263
Sisson, Gretchen, 204
Small, Cameron Lee, 89
social media, 92, 113, 141, 174
Soliday, Elizabeth, 57
Solinger, Rickie, 118, 264
somatic therapy, 242
split loyalty. *See* divided/split loyalty
Stephens, Alice, 100
stress hormones, 57, 63-64. *See also* cortisol
stress response, 61, 63-64
Strijack, Tamara, 70
substance use disorder (SUD). *See* addiction
suicide/suicidal ideation, 29, 41, 66, 70, 73-74, 78, 91, 96, 189-191, 237. *See also* self-attack
Sunderland, Paul, 7, 189
Support Texas Adoptee Rights (STAR), 31
Swan, Ferera, 89

Tann, Georgia, 78

terminology, adoption-related, 15
Terrell, Stephen J., 263
therapy: for adoptees, 36, 60, 65, 96, 190, 231, 234, 235, 237, 242-243, 244, 254, 265; for adoptive parents, 218, 233; for birth parents, 112-114, 122-123, 127, 254, 265; family therapy, xiv, 19, 191, 201, 202, 216, 233-234, 254, 265; related to infertility, 208. *See also* adoption-competent therapy; adoption-fluent therapy; Grow Beyond Words therapist directory
trafficking, 23, 196-198
transparency. *See* openness
transracial adoption. *See* interracial adoption
trauma. *See* complex-PTSD/complex trauma; separation: trauma or wounding; post-traumatic stress disorder (PTSD)
Tremblay, Kimberly A., 57
Tucker, Angela, 89, 160, 264
Turner, Donna, 29, 36, 46, 55, 61-62, 64, 73, 74, 233, 243

Uhrlaub, Rich, 31, 36, 94, 242, 244, 247, 248

van der Kolk, Bessel, 56, 263
Vander Vliet Ranyard, Kelsey, 5-6, 311; *Love, Your Birth Mom* documentary, 311; *Twisted Sisterhood* podcast, 6, 311
Verny, Thomas R., 64
Verrier, Nancy Newton, 20, 21, 60, 263
Vitelli, Diego, 28, 37, 39, 40, 42, 82, 98, 233, 235, 236, 237, 248, 254, 255

Wagamese, Richard, 222
Walker, Pete, 263
Washio-Collette, Julian, 29, 49, 71-72, 242
Weller, Francis, 220, 241
white supremacy, 85, 88, 97, 233
Wilson-Buterbaugh, Karen, 22
Winfrey, Oprah, 56, 263
Winkelmann, Jen, 215-216, 217, 218
Wizard of Oz, 239
Woolston, Amanda, 190, 191
worrying, incessant, 56. *See also* anxiety, anxiety-based problems

Zheng, Kayla, 30, 39, 40, 72, 73, 80, 82, 83, 88, 94, 96, 237

About the Authors

Sara Easterly, an adoptee, is an award-winning author of essays and books, including her memoir, *Searching for Mom*. She is the founder of Adoptee Voices and a trained facilitator with the Neufeld Institute. Sara lives outside of Seattle with her husband, two daughters, and a menagerie of rescued fur-babies. Visit her at saraeasterly.com.

Kelsey Vander Vliet Ranyard, a birth parent, works on domestic adoption policy matters for a nonprofit. She is the co-host of the first-birth mom podcast, *Twisted Sisterhood*, as well as co-producer of the documentary, *Love, Your Birth Mom*. Kelsey lives in Northern California with her husband and daughter.

Lori Holden, an adoptive parent, is the author of *The Open-Hearted Way to Open Adoption*. She lives in Denver, Colorado, with her husband. Their daughter and son are living their best lives as young adults who frequently stop by for home cooking or laundry facilities. Visit Lori at LavenderLuz.com.

More at AdoptionUnfiltered.com.